Macroeconomics as Systems Theory

"Wagner brings the complexity revolution to macroeconomics, which has side-stepped it until now. We have not known how to do complexity macroeconomics, but with this important book Wagner has shown us the way. Key is the synthesis of process and structure. Fresh entrepreneurial dreams jostle together in a common institutional framework that constrains and shapes the resulting turbulent flow of economic life. Wagner's theory enables us to use complexity tools to work out the macroeconomic consequences of this microeconomic jostling. A macroeconomics revolution is nigh."

—**Roger Koppl**, *Professor Finance, Syracuse University*

"Wagner's approach to macroeconomics represents a major step away from mainstream macroeconomics. He depicts the macroeconomy as a complex interaction among individuals, all of whom have their own plans. This stands in contrast with the aggregate nature of macroeconomic analysis, whether one is thinking of macroeconomic aggregates in a Keynesian framework or incorporating microfoundations in a representative agent framework. Wagner's macroeconomy is a spontaneous order in which institutions can evolve to facilitate mutually beneficial interactions among individuals. This thought-provoking book will change the way readers think about macroeconomics."

—**Randall G. Holcombe**, *DeVoe Moore Professor of Economics, Florida State University*

"This book is an important contribution to the debate on the nature and scope of macroeconomic analysis. Wagner warns us against questionable attempts to aggregate, measure and draw doubtful recipes for policy-making. Instead, he sticks to his subjectivist guns, bridges the gap between micro- and macroeconomics, and offers new insights into the role of institutions. Wagner deserves praise for this impressive scholarly achievement. While developing a literature that began with the Scottish Enlightenment, his pages provide path-breaking ideas that will capture the attention of the professional economist and fascinate those who believe it is high time we start thinking out of the orthodox box."

—**Enrico Colombatto**, *Professor of Economics, University of Turin*

Richard E. Wagner

Macroeconomics as Systems Theory

Transcending the Micro-Macro Dichotomy

Richard E. Wagner
Department of Economics
George Mason University
Fairfax, VA, USA

ISBN 978-3-030-44467-9   ISBN 978-3-030-44465-5   (eBook)
https://doi.org/10.1007/978-3-030-44465-5

This Palgrave Macmillan imprint is published by the registered company Springer Nature
Switzerland AG
The registered company address is: Gewerbestrasse 11, 6330 Cham, Switzerland

PREFACE

This book examines macroeconomic theory from within a nonconventional analytical window provided by theories pertaining to complex systems, in contrast to conventional theories grounded on aggregation. The resulting difference in analytical perspective is huge. In 1919, the Swedish economist Erik Lindahl, in an essay that was later included in his 1939 collection of *Studies in the Theory of Capital and Income*, set forth what I think is the first explicit distinction between micro and macro levels of economic analysis. Lindahl assigned to micro theory the domain of *individual choice* and assigned to macro theory the domain of *societal interaction* among choosers. Lindahl's disjunction between micro and macro leads directly to the recognition that economies are complex systems of human interaction whose properties cannot be discerned simply through aggregation over the individuals who constitute a society. Lindahl's essay remained in Swedish until it was published in English in 1939. In the interim, John Maynard Keynes's (1936) *General Theory of Employment, Interest, and Money* was published and almost immediately achieved professional dominance; ever since macroeconomics has centered on aggregation and not on human interaction along with the phenomena that emerge through interaction.

In contrast, this book recurs to Lindahl's distinction between choice and interaction. Hence, macro phenomena are complex phenomena that often are not direct products of someone's choice because they emerge through interaction among choosers. Such phenomena are often characterized by such notions as invisible hands and spontaneous orders. It should be noted, however, that "spontaneous order" is not synonymous with an absence of prevision and planning. To the contrary, societies are rife with planning. Every person and entity in society makes and pursues plans. A society is a complex *ecology of plans*. That ecology, however, is not plausibly reducible to a single plan because the actual achievement of such reduction lies beyond anyone's capacity. This situation means simply that macro outcomes emerge within an ecology of plans that contains myriad agents who are pursuing their plans inside an environment where other people are doing the same thing, and often in a manner where plans conflict with one another.

To describe a phenomenon as having emerged spontaneously as against having been chosen is not automatically to describe those outcomes as socially beneficial in some fashion. For instance, recessions and depressions can be emergent outcomes just as can periods of sustained material progress. The standard macro approach posits the presence of some external agent, a form of *deus ex machina*, who acts with a single-minded devotion to promoting socially beneficial over socially harmful outcomes. In contrast, the ecological orientation I pursue here abandons the presumption that political agents are a special breed of humanity that is wise in ways that ordinary people are not. To the contrary, political agents operate with the same range of desires and limitations on their capacities as everyone else in society.

Lindahl's formulation points toward an ecological treatment of macro theory where the relation between micro and macro is a relation between the parts of something and the entirety of that thing. Within an ecological scheme of thought, the institutional arrangements that people generate through interaction are a central feature of any effort at macro theorizing, for institutions, along with organizations and societal norms, are macro and not micro phenomena. Yet contemporary macro theorizing gives but minimal attention to institutions, usually by referring to such things as price rigidity or incomplete contracting. The absence of any serious concern with the relation between institutional arrangements and macro theory reflects the choice-theoretic character of contemporary macro theorizing where institutions are merely data. By contrast, institutions are emergent products of human interaction within the interactionist orientation explored here.

This book treats macroeconomic theory as a theory of society organized through the pursuit of economizing action when a significant feature of such action is the generation of such meso-level phenomena as commercial and civil organizations, conventions and standards, arrangements regarding money and credit, legal conventions, and political organizations. Conventional macro theory presents a national economy as a collection of such aggregate variables as output, employment, investment, and a price level, and seeks to develop theoretical relationships among those variables. In contrast, the social-theoretic approach to macro or social theory this book sets forth treats the standard macro variables as having been shaped through social institutions, conventions, and processes that in turn are generated through interaction among economizing persons. The relation between micro and macro levels of analysis is a relationship between the parts of something and the entirety of that thing. Micro denotes the individual entities whose actions and interactions generate the phenomena we designate as macro. The object denoted as macro is thus of a higher order of complexity than the object denoted as micro. This book sketches this vision of a social-theoretic orientation toward the societal entirety of human interaction.

Fairfax, USA   Richard E. Wagner

ACKNOWLEDGMENTS

Three anonymous readers from Palgrave Macmillan offered much helpful advice and appreciated succor prior to my preparation of the final version of this book. During the spring 2018 and 2019 semesters at George Mason University, students in my advanced graduate class on market process theory worked through earlier versions of the manuscript, offering valuable constructive criticism along the way. Those students are too numerous to mention here by name, and it would be invidious of me to single out some of them for particular mention. All the same, I do want to express my gratitude to them for their fine help and support. Besides those anonymous students, I would like to express explicit gratitude to Abigail Devereaux who preceded those two classes and who worked with me as I was exploring whether to undertake this endeavor. Once I decided to do so, moreover, she joined me as a colleague in some complementary lines of research while she was completing her dissertation and is now pursuing her academic career at Wichita State University.

CONTENTS

LIST OF FIGURES

CHAPTER 1

Macroeconomics as Systems Theory: Setting the Stage

Macroeconomics entails theorizing about the entirety of an economic system, in contrast to microeconomics which entails theorizing about various parts of that system. This distinction suggests the image of someone standing in a hot-air balloon as it ascends from a town square. As the ascension continues, a wider field of vision appears; however, the clarity of individual objects on the ground weakens. An economic system in its entirety is obviously an object of great interest because its qualities and properties affect the lives of everyone who inhabits that social system. While it is easy to understand why economists would seek to theorize about economic systems in their entirety, a significant challenge accompanies that theoretical effort because no one can see that system in its entirety (Veetil and Wagner 2015). Theorists cannot see the object about which they theorize, and yet they theorize about it all the same. This situation is not unusual. It is common. No physicist has seen gravity, and yet physicists theorize about it and its properties. Those theoretical efforts are guided by a desire to explain such observable phenomena as the rising and falling of tides in relation to the moon's proximity. Economists face a similar situation. They, too, observe such phenomena as variability in wealth across time and place, and seek to theorize about the underlying processes that might generate those observations.

To be sure, economics, or social theory more generally, pertains to different types of objects than does physics, or the natural sciences generally. Humans are part of the natural world, so human actions are subject to natural processes. For instance, humans will die without receiving water or food at regular intervals. They will also die if exposed to extreme temperatures for prolonged periods. And even if experienced temperatures are not that extreme, humans become distinctly uncomfortable when exposed to temperatures above 80 degrees Fahrenheit or below 60 degrees, and so seek to change their environment through heating or cooling. Humans are biological creatures, so are subject to biological as well as physical laws. Indeed, it is possible to develop an economic theory around the imaginary actions of a Robinson Crusoe alone on his island. Such theories could be described as laws of a natural economy in recognition of Crusoe's struggle for survival within the natural world.

But we find Crusoe alone only in our imaginations. That aloneness, moreover, creates severe analytical problems because Crusoe cannot duplicate himself. If you start with Crusoe, you can never get to society. Yet all of our observations of humans, both historical and archeological, pertain to humans living in the groups that we designate variously as tribes or societies. This situation of humans existing in groups creates analytical challenges and opportunities that extend beyond any effort to reduce humans to adherence to physical and biological laws. Sure, as part of the natural world humans are subject to the laws of natural science. Their living together in societies, however, creates a further menu of analytical questions, and with that menu speaking to what Norbert Elias (1939 [1982]) describes as *The Civilizing Process*, which pertains to the varied settings within which infants mature into adults. This menu of questions takes us to the brink of the chasm that separates theorizing about micro or individual phenomena from theorizing about macro or social phenomena. Macroeconomics construed as systems theory pertains to some concept of society as a whole, in contrast to theorizing about the individual entities that constitute that society. Indeed, macroeconomics construed as systems theory has much in common with what Joseph Schumpeter (1954: 12–22) described as economic sociology as one of the five branches of economics, the others being theory, history, statistics, and political economy.

Any scheme of thought will start with intuitive hunches that are organized through the analytical tools and techniques that an author possesses. As the Preface notes, so far as I am aware Erik Lindahl advanced the first explicit distinction between microeconomics and macroeconomics. He did this in 1919 in a paper in Swedish that wasn't published in English until Lindahl (1919 [1939]). For Lindahl, what he described as microeconomics pertained to individual *action*, while macroeconomics was the domain of *interaction* among individuals within society. Micro thus pertains to the parts of an economic system while macro pertains to the entirety of that system. Lindahl wrote at the time when the development of national income accounting was just getting underway, and with Dianne Coyle (2015) providing a lucid account of that development. Moreover, the analytical schema of systems theory awaited development when Lindahl articulated his micro–macro distinction. In the absence of analytical tools for thinking about systems of interacting agents, it is easy to understand how macro variables came to be treated as aggregations over the activities of the economizing entities within a society.

But aggregation over individual entities is not the only way a macro theory can be articulated. An alternative approach is through systems theory, where the micro–macro relationship is exemplified beautifully by Thomas Schelling (1978) who set forth an analytical template for exploring how system-level properties can emerge out of micro-level interaction, including situations where rational individual action can generate systemic outcomes that can be disagreeable to a good number of the participants. Starting with Ludwig Bertalanffy (1968), the idea of systems theory as pertaining to the systematic study of parts-to-whole relationships took a sizeable step forward, and with Ervin Laszlo (1996) and Donella Meadows (2008) providing succinct statements of the challenges of thinking in terms of systems of interacting agents. Any system can be described as containing elements along with connections among those elements. The performance of the system depends on both the properties of the elements and the pattern of connection among the elements. There are two distinct formats through which someone can theorize about systems of interacting elements. One format arises when those elements are mechanical or robotic. The other format pertains to systems where the elements are creative or volitional. This difference between types of system makes all the difference in the world for theorizing about economies in their entirety.

Contemporary economic theory typically treats economies as mechanical, as illustrated by repeated references to "economic mechanisms" and similar notions. In contrast, this book is grounded on the presumption that economic systems contain agents who are creative and can exercise volition. When macro theory is approached within the framework of systems theory, it becomes an adventure in theorizing about invisible hands (Clower 1994; Aydinonat 2008) and spontaneously generated social order (Howitt and Clower 2000).

The Network Architecture of Economic Systems

All systems, whether populated by mechanical or creative entities, have an architecture based on some pattern of connection among the entities that constitute the system. Graph theory provides a convenient analytical framework for working with systems of interacting agents, with Richard Trudeau (1993) making a lucid presentation of graph theory and with Jason Potts (2000) developing system-theoretic ideas lucidly in a microeconomic context. Within a graph-theoretic framework, the entities are commonly denoted as nodes and the connections denoted as edges. Figures 1.1 and 1.2 contrast two forms of network architecture that will be used often in this book. Both networks contain 15 nodes. Those networks differ in their patterns of connection among the participants, and with a central presumption of network theory being that patterns of connection have significant analytical work to do. Where Fig. 1.1 denotes a monocentric or homophonic network, Fig. 1.2 denotes a polycentric or polyphonic network.

Both terms pertain to the same formal distinction but have been developed within different contexts. The pair monocentric–polycentric has been invoked in social settings, originally by Michael Polanyi's (1951) treatment of liberty within society and then elaborated often by Vincent Ostrom, especially as found in Ostrom (1999). The pair homophonic–polyphonic pertains to literature and music, which Mikhail Bakhtin (1981, 1984) expresses lucidly in distinguishing between settings where

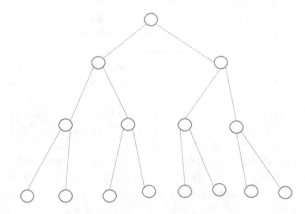

Fig. 1.1 A monocentric or homophonic network

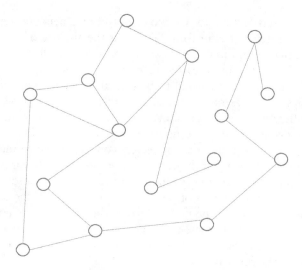

Fig. 1.2 A polycentric or polyphonic network

all figures in a story speak through the author and settings where the figures speak among themselves. Existing macroeconomic theory operates almost wholly within a monocentric or homophonic voice. In contrast, this book explores how macroeconomics might be reoriented in a polycentric or polyphonic direction.

Figure 1.1 illustrates a monocentric or homophonic network. Figure 1.1 resembles the tables of organization that sometimes appear in textbooks on management and organization. Monocentric networks are governed by relationships of superior-to-subordinate; someone who occupies a higher node in that network holds superior rank to those who occupy lower nodes. Any such sketch is an abstraction from a reality that is more complex than the sketch depicts. Figure 1.1 invites the image of higher nodes issuing orders to lower nodes, and with those lower nodes responding to those orders and subsequently being evaluated by those higher nodes. The relationship superior-subordinate flows in two directions, as all relationships do, with orders flowing downward and actions flowing upward. As usual with such abstractions, both truth and fiction inhabit Fig. 1.1. This book is not about organization theory, so no effort will be made to develop more complex depictions of the actual operation of organizations that have nominally monocentric character.

Figure 1.2 sets forth a polycentric or polyphonic network. One thing that is immediately apparent from Fig. 1.2 is the absence of any obvious concept of higher and lower or superior and inferior. All nodes are created equal, as it were, or at least as they seem superficially to be. In both panels, all nodes are constructed to be the same size to avoid cluttering the graphics as well as to avoid dealing with possible analytical implications of differing size and significance of nodes. With respect to the pattern of connection among the nodes in Fig. 1.2, two points are worth mentioning. First, the graph is completely connected, which means that starting from any node you can travel to every other node without leaving the graph. There are no orphans as it were, or no Robinson Crusoes to recur to a common idiom of economic theory. Second, the density of connection varies among the nodes. Two of the 15 nodes are connected to only one node. Most of the nodes are connected to two other nodes. One node is connected to three other nodes, and with one node being connected to five other nodes.

A significant economic-theoretic question regarding the application of concepts from graph theory concerns the scalability of graphs. If the network depicted by Fig. 1.1 were to expand from 15 to 30 nodes, would a similar pattern of connectivity remain or would there be a tendency for some nodes to become increasingly popular relative to the other nodes? In the former case, a network is described as being scalable. With scalable networks, an expansion in the size of the network does not change network architecture to any significant extent. Sure, there will be differences among nodes in the number of their connections, but the distribution of connections among nodes will not change significantly with expansions in the size of the network. Connections, in other words, are formed randomly as new nodes enter the graph.

The alternative to a scalable network is a scale-free network. The distribution of connections is not generated randomly as new nodes enter the graph. To the contrary, new nodes might reflect preference for attaching to densely connected nodes. To the extent this is so, an expansion in the size of the graph will confer some advantage on densely connected nodes. This possibility might resemble a rich get richer setting, but we should also remember that graph theory is an abstraction that might not capture everything of relevance. For instance, an expansion in the number of connections via preferential attachment increases the managerial problems that the participants who operate inside that node must resolve. There are well-known limits on the ability of organizations to manage their affairs, some of which is subsumed under the concept of diseconomies of scale. If this situation obtains, there will be limits to preferential attachment that is obscured by simply assuming that new attachments follow some nonrandom process in mechanistic fashion.

A related consideration excluded from Fig. 1.1, but which will be explored in later chapters, concerns the properties of interaction between market-based entities that form under the principles and institutions of private property and political-based entities that form under the principles and institutions of public property. It is conventional to treat the two types of entity as indistinguishable, as distinct from their being merely similar. In the latter case, a system of political economy that contains both market-based and political-based entities will exhibit different properties along the lines that Wagner (2016) sets forth in describing democratically established political enterprises as *peculiar* forms of business enterprise. They are enterprises, to be sure, in that they provide services that are both valued by some people and paid for by other people, only the valuers and the payers do not comprise identical sets. Looking ahead, Chapter 8 will explain that standard questions regarding whether the recession of 2008 is a product of excessive or insufficient regulation is a category mistake that arises from inadequacies in our theories of macroeconomics and political economy. More generally, the system-theoretic framework this book employs will explain how systems can exert causal force on society even though systems are inanimate, and with Fredrick Pryor (2008) exploring this theme.

DSGE: Construing Economies as Mechanistic Systems

Léon Walras (1874) set in motion the economic-theoretic tradition of treating economies as mechanistic systems. Walras conceptualized an economy as an equilibrated set of relationships. To be sure, Walras took his construction as being more of an analytical extremum or stalking horse than as a depiction of the ways of the world. All the same, Walras's formulation inspired a parade of refinements over the following century that resulted in formal proofs of necessary conditions that if they held an economy would be in a state of equilibrium, and with Roy Weintraub (1993) exploring the development of general equilibrium theory. To be sure, no theorist has claimed that those necessary conditions describe economic reality. Most theorists have proceeded differently by arguing that a failure for those conditions to hold would potentially though not necessarily offer scope for political action to improve the performance of an economic system.

The Walrasian scheme of thought has morphed into what is now known as dynamic stochastic general equilibrium (DSGE). Similar to Walras, the economic system is still construed as a set of equilibrated relationships among economizing entities. Only now, those relationships are subject to exogenous shocks that disturb previous relationships which in turn call for readjustments. Thus, an economy is subject to the turbulence of continual change, only that change is exogenous, meaning it comes from outside the system, as against being an internal feature of an economic system. Absent exogenous shocks, the system is static both at the system-level and with respect to the nodes that constitute that system. While economic theory speaks of individuals as making choices, the theory does not genuinely incorporate choice into its analytics. People act as they are programmed to act by the utility functions they are presumed to possess and by the market-clearing prices they face. Within this analytical scheme, people are reduced to robotic status, as Ross Emmett (2006) sets forth in contrasting Frank Knight's approach to individual action with that of George Stigler and Gary Becker (1977).

Mechanistic systems can be relatively simple or exceedingly complex, but in either case it is interaction among the parts of the system that govern the system's performance. A building's heating system is relatively simple; the system of coding that sends missiles into space is so complex that no person has written the entire code. All such systems entail expectations of what would constitute desired performance. Should actual performance fall short of expectations, the problem of mechanism design and repair arises, which speaks to diagnosing and repairing the source of poor performance. Economists mostly operate within the parameters appropriate for mechanical systems. DSGE theories, moreover, reduce what might have been a complex, creative system to simple mechanism. If an economy exists in a state of equilibrium, an economy that contains millions or even billions of agents can be analytically reduced to a single, representative agent.

This situation illustrates the Janus-headed character of our theoretical constructions. As a positive matter, theoretical constructions allow us to dig more deeply into our materials of interest to uncover phenomena that might have been hidden from view at more superficial levels of examination. But there is also a negative side to any theoretical construction, which is the hardening of analytical focus that it fosters. This pertains to what is often called the problem of tractability. Some theories might allow easier or sharper answers to questions than other theories. While this situation offers good reason for pursuing such theories, that pursuit often impedes the development of alternative theories. One theory may well enable sharper answers to one set of questions than another theory, which supports opting for sharper answers. But a different theory might pose a menu of different questions that would never have been posed within the other theory, and that alternative menu might be able to address significant questions if only that theory had been pursued. Theorizing about economic systems in their entirety can over some conceptual domains be helped by the closed form of equilibrium theorizing while over other conceptual domains an open-ended approach to theorizing about economic systems might yield useful insight.

OEE: Construing Economies as Creative and Volitional Systems

We can agree that a macro theory pertains to the whole of the economic activities within a society, in contrast to micro theories which pertain to parts of that whole. But how might we conceptualize that object when we can't even see it? This calls for what Joseph Schumpeter (1954) called a "pre-analytical cognitive vision" that a theorist subsequently sets forth. At this point we come to one of those many forks in the theoretical road. The most commonly traveled branch of that fork stipulates the existence of a set of equilibrated relationships among the members of a society. Such theorists don't take this stipulation as a literal truth about society, but rather use it as an analytical point of departure for trying to render sensible their observations about aggregate economic variables. While the formality of equilibrium theory since Walras (1874) has revolved around the presumption that the parts of an economic system comprise a coherent pattern, the equilibrium vision sets aside concern with and interest in the processes through which that coherence might come about.

To pursue the generation of such coherence, this book seeks to incorporate some social-theoretic ideas about open-endedness, emergence, evolution, and complexity into a macro theory, two early efforts at which were Wagner (Wagner 2012a, b) and a recent effort of which is Devereaux and Wagner (2020) in contrasting DSGE with OEE macro frameworks, and with OEE referring to open-ended and evolutionary. Some of these alternative ideas pertain to new ways of conceptualizing the social organization of economic activity. Others of them pertain to new ways of conceptualizing the operation of political processes. Taken together, both sets of ideas transform the distinct realms of discourse represented by micro and macro theory into a singular orientation for economic theory where micro and macro refer to different theoretical levels of analysis that nonetheless refer to the same analytical object—a society of economizing persons.

Within this OEE vision, the macro whole emerges and changes through interaction among the entities that constitute the whole. The order of theoretical development runs from individual actions and interactions to the emergence of macro patterns. By contrast, the DSGE vision starts by postulating a macro pattern and then moves to stipulation of what individual actions would support that macro pattern. For a macro economy to be in a state of equilibrium, it must be the case that no unexploited gains from trade exist among micro entities. This micro condition requires in turn deep-level congruity in desired actions among the members of a society. If the system is presumed to be in equilibrium, the individual members of that system must likewise be in personal equilibrium given the options they face.

We must remember that economic theory constitutes a coherent organon, or at least its practitioners aspire to that status. To be sure, that status has never been fully attained within the history of economic theory, for competing and contrasting visions have always been in play. But central tendencies have always existed within economic theory, and with Mary Morgan (2012) surveying the history of economics in terms of the models that economists have created. In this respect, it has long been conventional for economists to posit the analytical construction of a utility maximizing individual. No one has ever seen such a creature. The point of the construction, however, is not to capture some existential quality of humanity but is simply to create an intellectual framework that allows a theorist to organize the observations that a chosen theoretical framework says are relevant for theoretical explanation. It is not that people have utility functions that they maximize. It is only that use of that model enables the theorist to bring order to the theory-constructed observations that he or she thinks are significant. This familiar model requires that people can list the options they face, rank them against their scale of values, and estimate the objective likelihood of each option. For a given list of options and prices, individual choice is thus stochastically determinate. For individual choice to be determinate, the entire system must be in a state of equilibrium, for otherwise individuals will be unable to maximize their assigned utility functions. Hence, the theoretical construction of a utility-maximizing individual maps onto the analytical construction of a society as being in stochastic general equilibrium. Neither of these constructions has ever been directly observed, but they have enabled theorists to weave numerous theoretical tales.

What is at stake in choosing between DSGE and OEE analytical frameworks? Both frameworks can accommodate disturbances to a theorized state of full coordination among economic actors and their activities. For DSGE, all such disturbances must be exogenous shocks to an equilibrated system. By contrast, disturbances are an operating feature of the OEE framework where people are continually engaged in such activities as creating new businesses, inventing new techniques, and perhaps just acting on desires to try something new. Disturbance comes from inside the social system in the OEE framework, in contrast to the exogenous character of disturbance in the DSGE framework. Disturbance, moreover, can be beneficial to some people and harmful to others, but it is a feature of progressive societies in any case.

ORDER WITHOUT EQUILIBRIUM: WHAT OBJECT FOR A MACRO-LEVEL THEORY?

A society as distinct from individual members of that society is the object at which a macro theory aims. Equilibrium theories typically posit that societies exist in states of equilibrium that are disturbed by exogenous shocks. These theories thus posit two primary properties of societies as analytical objects: (1) societies have orderliness or regularity and (2) societies entail turbulence of varying intensity. These two features comprise the primary stylized facts for a macro theory. To be sure, orderliness is an intelligible concept without invoking equilibrium, as Fleetwood ([1996] 2015) explains with respect to F. A. Hayek. Indeed, orderliness without equilibrium is the central point of departure for the OEE approach to macro theory. The social world is intelligible to the inhabitants of a society, which means that they can navigate their way inside society. But the social world is also turbulent, which means that people often will find themselves having to adapt to unexpected situations they confront, as well as sometimes inserting actions into the society that compel adaptations by other people.

To assume that a social system is orderly does not *ipso facto* require that it must be assumed to reside in a state of equilibrium where there exist no changes that are in the process of happening. This is so because the presumption of equilibrium pertains to a state of existence that stands outside time and so in no way refers to any process that operates through time (O'Driscoll and Rizzo 1985; Wagner 2010). Equilibrium theories are told in the passive voice where things just happen, but no one makes them happen as a reflection of their pursuit of plans. There is no room for pursuing plans within an equilibrium theory because the pursuit of plans requires action through time, and yet equilibrium theory is constructed as if time has ended. To recur to an image Wagner (2007) sets forth, equilibrium theories treat societies as parades whose organizational qualities are established by a parade marshal. In contrast, non-equilibrium theories treat societies as crowds of pedestrians leaving a stadium after an event. Both parades and crowds are orderly in that a participant inside either societal configuration understands how to act successfully within those different configurations. Turbulence is internal to a crowd whereas it is external to a parade.

Equilibrium theories seek to explain the changes in a set of snapshots taken at distinct intervals by relating those changes to changes in some set of data, typically changes in technologies, prices, and incomes. In contrast, non-equilibrium theorizing seeks to explain processes of development that occur inside some interval of time, as these processes are set in motion by people forming and pursuing plans. Spending is primitive data within an equilibrium theory because plans are not integral to the theoretical construction. Within the non-equilibrium, process-oriented theorizing pursued here, it is plans that comprise the primitive data out of which social configurations emerge. For instance, technology doesn't just change, for it changes in consequence of people forming and pursuing plans. The social world that we all inhabit and experience, doesn't just happen or isn't just there as data. To the contrary, it is an emergent product of people forming and pursuing their various plans of action. Prices, for that matter, are not data, for they likewise are products of interaction among plans and the requirements for resource inputs those plans entail.

Macroeconomics, the theory of the entirety of economic activity within a society, has mostly construed its observations as aggregations over the economic activities of the individuals who constitute the society. Such a macro theory thus takes the variables of the NIPA accounts as comprising the relevant variables for macro theory. This leads to the conceptualization that macroeconomics is the study of the relationships among such broad economic aggregates as output, investment, consumption, and an index of prices. Within the DSGE framework, the NIPA accounts supply the aggregate magnitudes that are relevant for macro theorizing, meaning that these magnitudes capture the reality that is the object of macro theory. Macro theorists subsequently face the challenge of formulating models that explain observed patterns of relationships among those aggregate variables. Without NIPA and similarly constructed aggregate variables, there would be no macro variables for theorists to explain.

Yet societies would continue to exist, just as they did before the advent of national income accounting. And those societies would still be characterized as containing orderliness amid turbulence. In contrast to the DSGE vision, the OEE vision treats macroeconomics as the study of the constitution or the generation of societal patterns of economic activity. To some extent the NIPA accounts obviously pertain to societal patterns, but more is involved in the description and analysis of those patterns than the NIPA accounts allow. This alternative focus on societal patterns recurs to Erik Lindahl's (1919 [1939]) distinction between micro as pertaining to individual choice and macro as pertaining to interactions among individuals. Interaction will typically generate phenomena that are *not* products of individual action. Someone who observes several independent Robinson Crusoes on their different islands will not observe quarrels, trade, prices, or organizations. These things are activities that emerge only through *interaction* among people. This simple recognition, moreover, reminds us that any examination of societal patterns and properties will place in its analytical foreground the organizations and institutional arrangements that emerge through interaction, and with the resource allocations about which the NIPA accounts speak being relegated to the analytical background. The theoretical move from micro to macro is a move from the parts of something to the whole of that thing, and so is an upward movement in the scale of complexity. In contrast, DSGE theories entail similar phenomenal simplicity to micro theories. It is as if a macro theory were just a micro theory spoken of more loudly: where individual markets clear or don't, the same can be said of the market considered as an aggregate of markets.

Standard macro theorizing treats spending as the prime primitive variable, as reflected in the intimate connection between macro theory and the NIPA accounts. In contrast, the conceptual framework this book pursues treats entrepreneurial plans and not spending as providing the primitive variables for a macro-level theory. Spending, which can be observed, is derived from plans, which are unobservable save for how they manifest in spending. To make plans the primitive variable entails shifting the analytical focus away from resource allocation onto the institutional arrangements within which people within a society relate to one another. As a later chapter will examine, a key feature of those institutional arrangements concerns the relationship between private ordering and public ordering. Changes in this private–public mix can have significant macroeconomic implications.

An emergent reformulation of macro theory would abandon what Mitchel Resnick (1994) described as "the centralized mindset," which describes the strong tendency of theorists to attribute orderly patterns to some ordering agent. In contrast, Resnick explained that in many cases those orderly patterns emerge through interaction among people as against being imposed by some ordering agent. The fundamental order of movement within a society, in other words, would be from the bottom to the top and not from the top to the bottom; it would be polyphonic and not homophonic, to recur to Mikhail Bakhtin's (1981, 1984) analysis of dialogue in literature. One outcome of this emergent formulation would seem to be unification of micro and macro, as intermediated by meso-level organizations (Dopfer et al. 2004; Potts and Morrison 2007), in contrast to the present micro—macro disjunction. An emergent or ecological reformulation of micro-level theory would maintain the principle of rational individual conduct, only it would work with creative and not robotic individuals, thereby rendering individual action indeterminate to some extent. This is not to render individual action chaotic, for it is certainly not that. Rather it is to say that individual action entails margins of creativity and is not wholly static. This situation means in turn that creative action continually injects change into society, and with that change not being reasonably described as exogenous shocks but rather as outcomes of some intelligible social process. Rather than treating spending as captured by the NIPA accounts as the primitive data with which macro theories deal, the ecological formulation advanced in this book treats individual plans and their execution as causing spending, both its volume and its timing.

Figure 1.3 illustrates a bi-planar societal architecture entailing a micro-level of human action and interaction along with a macro level that describes the results of such actions and interactions. Alternatively, Fig. 1.3 could have been presented in tri-planar fashion by distinguishing between micro- and meso-levels. This alternative representation would show individuals on the micro-level forming into various enterprises and organizations, including governmental, on the meso level, and with activities on those two levels projecting onto the macro level. Either sketch would illustrate the same point, but the bi-planar sketch is simpler to sketch and to follow. The lower part of Fig. 1.3 illustrates patterns of interaction among micro and meso entities. Some of those entities are

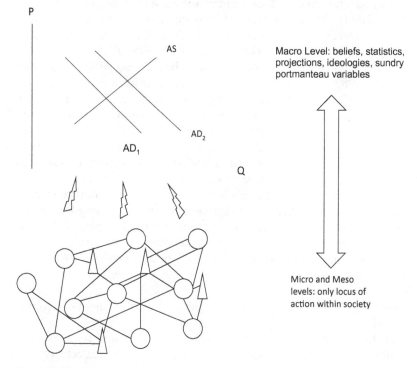

Fig. 1.3 Emergence of aggregate variables within an ecology of plans

depicted as circles while others are depicted as triangles. The circles pertain to privately organized entities while the triangles pertain to politically organized entities. This distinction between types of entity will take on significance when matters of political economy are examined starting with Chapter 6. For now, that distinction is simply a means of holding a place for later recognition that political entities operate inside a society's system of political economy, as against standing outside that system as might befit the centralized mindset. The upper part of Fig. 1.3 illustrates the emergence of macro-level variables through interaction among entities at the micro- and meso-levels of society.

While all action occurs at the micro-level, the macro-level variables are not inert. To the contrary, they inject causal force into society, only the path by which such causal force enters society is complex and not simple (Pryor 2008). While it is reasonable to speak of the micro foundations of macro theory, it is also reasonable to speak of the macro foundations of micro theory, of which Georg Simmel's (1900) *Philosophy of Money* illustrates wonderfully and cogently and which is also pertinent to John Foster's (1987) effort to place macroeconomics into an evolutionary setting. Simmel opened his book by asserting that not a word in that book is about economics. To be sure, Simmel's assertation raises a question about the object of economics, which shall be examined momentarily. Simmel's book was directed at the changing beliefs within society as to the appropriateness of different social boundaries between buying services for money and supplying those services in kind. For instance, one could support an elderly parent in one's home or pay a nursing home to provide that care. Simmel's interest was in exploring the ever-changing boundaries regarding what kinds of activities conventional public opinion supports as suitable for organization through market transactions. From Simmel's formulation and from Fig. 1.3, it is a relatively short step to see that macro theory of the OEE type merges readily into the territory Schumpeter (1954) characterized as economic sociology, though much in this respect also depends on how the subject matter of economic theory is defined.

In this respect, another of those forks in the analytical road concerns whether economic theory pertains to that subset of human activity concerned with the material conditions of life or whether it pertains to all conscious economizing action where people are construed as seeking to attain states of existence that they value more highly than what they presently experience, and with Lionel Robbins (1932) being the canonical presentation of this disjunction. Those states almost invariably have material qualities, but they are not limited to material qualities. For instance, a person might choose to establish a business despite the prospects of failure not because that person estimated that doing this would increase his or her net worth but because that person didn't want to work under the direct supervision of someone else. A system of economic organization based on private property allows space for people to pursue their dreams and aspirations, no matter how idiosyncratic, provided only that they finance those dreams at their own expense. Where DSGE models incline toward treating macro theory as concerned with the material conditions of life, the OEE scheme of analysis opens readily and easily into a universal treatment of all societal activity organized around economizing action.

Equilibrium as Personal Mental Map: Observers vs. Participants

The central claim of systems theory is that the performance properties of any system depend on both the elements that carry action and the pattern of connection among those elements. For human population systems, moreover, those performance properties also depend on the creative and moral imaginations of the participants. Systems can thus change either as participants develop new repertoires of action or form new patterns of connection. From the perspective of developing a macro-level theory where change emerges from within the system, it is necessary to conceptualize that system in some non-equilibrium fashion. To do this requires, in turn, a conceptualization of the acting agents as creative and not robotic.

To accomplish this, it is necessary to distinguish between two distinct orientations: that of an *observer* and that of a *participant*. An observer stands apart from an action and theorizes about it. A participant carries the action and imagines how it might play out. Equilibrium theories advance explanations from the perspective of observers of actions. Non-equilibrium theories seek to make reality intelligible from the perspective of people who create and pursue plans. This dichotomy maps onto two distinct images of probability in relation to action. It is also worth noting that in their summary presentation of the work of the Bloomington School of institutional analysis, Aligica and Boettke (2009) include interviews with both Elinor and Vincent Ostrom. In her interview, Elinor Ostrom distinguishes the Ostrom's work from that of most social theorists by explaining that where most theorists seek to separate themselves from their objects of interest, the Ostroms sought to penetrate their objects of interest so they could theorize from inside the object.

The expected utility framework that accompanies the DSGE model adopts the perspective of the observer. Someone observes a set of people who walk between their homes and their jobs. The observer embraces the challenge of giving a parsimonious explanation of what he or she observes. After a century of working with models of constrained optimization, it is perhaps easy to understand and appreciate the compelling power that most economists assign to expected utility theory. Indeed, it is hard to see whatever alternative form of *ex post* explanation could satisfy an economist who sought to explain the residues of past action that have been reduced to data. The *expected* part of expected utility theory appears to speak to beliefs about future possibilities (Shackle 1961, 1972), and yet data necessarily refer to past actions and not to future actions. Since past action is completed, for the data pertain to earlier trips between home and work, the mode of explanation must be deterministic. Adopting the posture of an observer forces the theorist to embrace a deterministic analytical framework.

The explanatory situation is different for a theorist who seeks to render the world intelligible from the perspective of the people whose actions subsequently will generate the data that later are recorded. From the *ex post* perspective of an observer, expected utility theory is a parsimonious framework for ordering observations though it is also worth noting that choice settings are often undecidable (Chaitin et al. 2011). But that *ex post* ordering is irrelevant to the choices of actions that participants make going forward into the future. Participants unavoidably face the *ex ante* situation of choosing a plan of action in advance of realizing the consequences of that action. An observer faces an *ex post* challenge, but for a participant the challenge has *ex ante* character. The conjunction of equilibrium theory and rationality in expectation has eliminated the distinction between *ex ante* and *ex post* orientations toward economic phenomena. This elimination entails an egregious category mistake whereby the category of past action is merged with the category of future action, effectively destroying any uncertainty associated with the consequences of acting today to achieve future outcomes. This elimination, however, is an artifact of pursuing economic theory exclusively within the passive voice motif wherein equilibrium theory creates the illusion that tomorrow is just like today, save for an error term with zero mean. That error term, moreover, pertains to an entire ecology of actions, and not to individual actions. But it is individual actions where *ex ante* is alive that is the locus of action that leads to the emergence of subsequent macro-level experience.

It is with respect to *ex ante* considerations where theories of personal probability come into play, as illustrated by Savage (1954), Shackle (1961, 1974), and McCann (1994). An actor forms a plan at T_1 based on some anticipation of an outcome or imagined range of outcomes at T_2. Both the formation of a plan and the projection of possible outcomes entail acts of imagination for which recourse to data might have some informative value but without having determinative value. When faced with this setting, people may well differ in the intensity of the animal spirits that reside within them. Some people will allow other people to hire their services in exchange for an advance payment on the value the hiring agent anticipates will be yielded by those efforts. For such people to receive payment in advance of realization of the value their efforts yield, there must be other people who are willing to do the hiring and to live on any residual between the contracted payments they must make and the income sale of the product generates (Knight 1921).

Individual action in forming and executing plans can be placed within the framework of personal probability theory. An actor decides upon a plan of action and sets it in motion. From the actor's perspective, that action is *ipso facto* reasonable or rational, because the alternative would entail claiming that people seek deliberately to fail at what they set about doing. There are many reasons why individual plans might not work out as their initiators hoped they would, but no one would propose to explain the failures of plans as an intentional act. Plans are based on beliefs about future possibilities, as well as about the actions of other people, most of them probably unknown to the actor, that either interfere with or complement the actor's plan. A world in which many enterprises fail is an ordinary outcome of interaction among economizing agents.

Personal probability, however, does not conform to the axioms of the frequency approach to probability that pertains to such settings as playing roulette or craps. For frequentist probability, there is a listable space of possible outcomes and associated probabilities of occurrence. Expected values are computable and the probability of the sum of possible outcomes is one. For personal probability, however, the sum of possible outcomes is indefinite. It is not apparent what accuracy in expectation might mean in this situation. People act on their beliefs or presumptions about the future conditions they will face based on the actions they take today, and the accuracy of those beliefs will be revealed only when the future arrives.

Behavioral economists typically claim that people suffer from several biases that undermine Pareto efficiency, as if anyone could observe Pareto efficiency as against inferring it from a particular model, and with Angner (2012) providing a clear survey of behavioral economics. One of those biases is a form of optimism where people overestimate their chance of success at some endeavor. A set of graduates asked to declare whether they will have above- or below-average success at what they pursue will overwhelmingly assert above-average prospects. Does this pattern of belief reflect some state of imperfection, as many behavioral economists claim? Alternatively, it could reflect a working property of a social system where people are free to choose their aspirations and associated activities, as distinct from having them imposed on them by some agency. Among other things, such considerations suggest that an output gap has limited merit as a means of describing systemic outcomes, because the composition of any such gap also matters. In one setting people may be fully employed doing jobs they dislike and have even been drafted to perform. In another setting they may be pursuing with variable success activities they have chosen, and which give them great joy. The standard macro concept of an output gap has but incomplete value as an indicator regarding the performance of an economic system. The ability of that system to accommodate people in pursuing their dreams and plans is surely also a relevant systemic indicator that touches upon the analytical domain of economic theory.

REGARDING THE MICRO–MACRO DIALECTICS OF ECONOMIC THEORY

All societies exhibit regularities, as do the individuals who comprise those societies. Those regularities comprise what can be described as stylized facts, and which can serve as objects of explanation for macro theories. In this respect, most macro theorists emphasize a narrow range of stylized facts regarding relationships among such aggregate variables as real and nominal wages, interest rates, and the like. Left aside from standard recitations of stylized facts are surely two facts of overwhelming significance that should surely reside at the core of any macro-level theory.

One such fact is the observation that all societies seem to "work" in the sense of people feeding and housing themselves, reproducing themselves, and so on. Sure, the conditions under which people do this vary hugely across time and place. All the same, it is surely a significant stylized fact that all societies exhibit generally though not fully coordinated character without the presence of coordinating agent or officer. It was in recognition of this coordinated character that inspired the initial examination of social-level coordination by the Spanish Jesuits associated with the University of Salamanca (Grice-Hutchinson 1978), and where the classical economists extended that recognition of self-organization. The other fact is that societies invariably entail turbulence, both within their borders and among societies. There is almost no such thing as a flat-line equilibrium detectable in history. It's even doubtful whether flat-line features can be truly detected in highly traditional societies. And they certainly are not detectable in modern societies. Turbulence along with coordination are stylized facts that pertain to all modern societies, and the challenge to economic theory is to explain both of these as ordinary working properties of systems of interaction among economizing agents.

Western thought since the ancient Greeks has embraced logical claims on behalf of the law of the excluded middle. The law of the excluded middle claims that a statement cannot be both true and false. This is a matter of logic that often is a sensible claim to make, but not always. The law of the excluded middle implies that a society will be either fully or incompletely coordinated. Full coordination was the default presumption of the classical economists. Keynes sought to replace that presumption with one of incomplete coordination, with full coordination being a special or limiting case of a more general situation. This style of thought follows from embrace of the law of the excluded middle, for an economy cannot be both coordinated and uncoordinated. This logical statement, however, pertains only to models grounded on states of rest or equilibrium. It does not pertain to models grounded on processes of motion or development, where the process is driven forward through continual wrestling with a dialectical tension.

The contrary principle of yin-and-yang pertains to a class of observations where what we observe reflects some tension between opposites. Sailing a boat illustrates this dialectical tension. One can sail into a headwind, only one must do so by continually maneuvering the sail to reconcile the tension between the opposing forces acting on the sail, causing the boat to zig and zag toward its destination. Likewise, the generation of coordination within social systems of economic interaction entails resolution between forces of maintenance and forces of creativity. There will be owners of existing plans who seek to propel their plans forward through time. There will also be creators of new plans who seek to give life to their plans, and with those plans sometimes upsetting in various ways previously existing plans. What results is an ongoing process of some plans being created while others are abandoned, and with there being no reason other than analytical convenience to assume that magnitudes of the two types of plan-based disturbance add to zero.

The dialectical principle of yin-and-yang commends recognition that societies are continually in motion, neither static nor chaotic but a variable mixture of both. Micro- and meso-level interactions generate macro-level phenomena, while macro-level phenomena, including perceptions, feedback onto micro-level action. The macro and micro- levels of an economic system are incorporated into a single explanatory framework, as the orthodox interest in micro-foundations commends, but without that interest being neutered by the presumption that economic observations pertain to states of equilibrium. The ecology of plans that operates inside a society (Wagner 2012a) is not a sentient creature but it does exhibit systemic coherence similar to what Vernon Smith (2008) sets forth.

Two Probability Concepts
Necessary for Macro Theory

A system-theoretic approach to macro theory requires use of two distinct concepts of probability, one objective and the other subjective or personal. These different concepts pertain to the two distinct levels of analysis that Fig. 1.3 portrays. Standard macro theories portray only the upper level and does so in stand-alone fashion. To be sure, many macro theorists have embraced calls to ground their theories on micro-level foundations. Those foundations, however, are illusory with respect to a social theory that entails creative action inside an ecology of plans. Reduction of a society to a representative agent may be suitable for a parade but not for a sea of humanity moving in various directions (Kirman 1992).

Figure 1.3 illustrates a unified treatment of micro- and macro-levels of analysis when a society is conceptualized as an ecology of interacting plans. The lower part of Fig. 1.3 characterizes a society as a network of interacting enterprises. Some of those enterprises are denoted by circles; the remainder are denoted by triangles. These different denotations of the enterprises within a society will take on significance in later chapters because they distinguish between market-based and politically based enterprises, which in turn has much analytical work to do in the alternative conceptualization of macro theory this book pursues. For now, though, that distinction can be suppressed. The lower part of Fig. 1.3 illustrates networks of transactions among the entities that comprise an economic system. The enterprises contained within the lower part of Fig. 1.3 are all pursuing plans that must reflect some personal state of belief regarding possible histories for that plan. The sponsors of those plans can plausibly differ in numerous ways, one useful dimension of which is their degree of optimism or confidence about their plans along the lines that Roger Koppl (2014) sets forth. While the future at which a plan aims might truly be unknowable, it is nonetheless imaginable. There is no necessity that all sponsors of plans form the same mental image of their imagined possibilities. Those sponsors inject their plans into history all the same, awaiting the societal valuations of those plans as history unfolds. This is the world of personal probability where people act on their beliefs, always hoping for the best but knowing that not all plans succeed.

The upper level of Fig. 1.3 summarizes the results of past action. It pertains to previously initiated action and not to planned action currently being set in motion. Only by assuming that all entrepreneurial action is undertaken by a representative agent will the portrait in the upper level correspond temporally speaking to the portrait in the lower level of Fig. 1.3. A theorist could attempt to explain the data portrayed in the upper level. To do this would require a presumption that all action reflects an identical view of the possible outcomes of any action, which is what reduction of a society to a representative agent accomplishes. It is a mistake to think the two parts of Fig. 1.3 speak to contemporaneous actions. To the contrary, action must precede the collection of data. This situation means that a macro theory must work with two probability concepts. It is a subjectivist or personalistic notion of probability that is relevant for entrepreneurial action and for understanding why some people work for wages while other people choose to live off the residual between what their enterprises earn and what they must pay people to work for those enterprises.

The micro-level of society is an arena where plans are injected into society, as well as being the arena where the success or failure of those plans are determined. The macro-level summarizes the consequences of interactions among those plans, with some returning capital gains to their sponsors while other sponsors suffer capital losses. Those gains and losses can in turn be rendered intelligible in terms of objective concepts of probability through a form of retrodiction where present observations are extended backward. Such retrodiction would claim that failed enterprises over-estimated the demands for their products or services, and with the sponsors of successful enterprises being in the opposite position. In any case, a social economic process yields *ex post* evaluations of the *ex ante* plans that entrepreneurs inserted into society.

A Macro Economy as an Ecology of Plans

Wagner (2012a) sets forth a framework for treating a macro economy as an ecology of plans wherein macro-level phenomena supervene on micro-level interaction, as Fig. 1.3 illustrates. Within this scheme of thought, no action occurs on the macro level, for the macro-level denotes a congeries of statistics, projections, beliefs, and ideologies. Action can occur only on the micro- and meso- levels. Among other things, this scheme of analysis reveals that there is no such thing as action on the entirety of a social system. Social systems change through individual actions and interactions, but it is meaningless to speak of acting on the society or economy in its entirety. Just as no one can truly apprehend the societal entirety other than in a purely formal manner (Hayek 1937), so is it impossible to speak meaningfully and substantively of acting to transform a social system as an entirety, as distinct from acting to change parts or precincts within the system. With respect to Fig. 1.3, action can only occur on the ground or micro-level. How far and to what extent such action projects onto the macro-level depends on how that action is received within the micro nexus.

Transformation there can be, and such transformation is continually underway. But all transformation begins at individual nodes within the ecology of plans and spreads into the ecology, depending on various factors to be considered momentarily. In Fig. 1.3, the circles denote private entities and the triangles denote political entities. Political action can transform a social system, but so can private action as the development of automobiles or cell phones illustrates. Whatever the source of transformative energy, it is injected at the micro-level of enterprise action, and with any macro-level properties being emergent properties of interaction among entities.

To illustrate the point, suppose a political entity, a legislature, enacts a prohibition on some product that presently is widely used within the society. The enactment of legislation will enter the society by instructing policing agencies to detect people who use the product and instructing legal officers to prosecute those the police detect. The extent to which this legislation brings about societal transformation, as well as what kind of transformation it brings about, depends both on the responses taken by the relevant political entities and on the responses taken by the affected private entities. A process of societal transformation will have been set in motion, but it is not a transformation that corresponds to the comparative static image of social planning as typically portrayed in expositions of the applied theory of public policy.

To prohibit something that many people like to do will generally not be accepted passively by those who produce or consume the proscribed items. Yes, the effort at proscription will create discernable transformation at the societal level. But, no, that transformation will not conform to any before-and-after or with-and-without description where the proscribed items simply vanish. A legislatively articulated prohibition of alcohol or recreational drugs will not by itself stop people from doing what they like doing. Prohibition will increase the cost of doing business, leading to some decrease in supply and reduction in consumption. But it will also induce multiple changes in commercial organization and operation as people seek out alternative channels for fulfilling their desires without being detected and jailed.

Most generically, this means that the ordinary commercial model of a seller having a publicly announced place of business and buyers choosing or not to frequent that place will no longer be commercially viable in the presence of police officers now rewarded by arresting people frequenting those places. New forms of doing business will be created as entrepreneurs seek new ways for meeting consumer demands. Along various channels, procedures and methods for securing pre-approval of customers will be developed, driving commerce underground. Prohibition likewise can offer second sources of income for political officials and police officers. To be sure, some members within the relevant class of persons will be more susceptible to securing second sources of income than others, and we may further expect to find the creation of further patterns of connection that seek to ascertain just who those people might be. Furthermore, the openness that characterizes commercial transactions will be transformed into generalized suspiciousness because prohibition creates a need for sellers to distinguish between genuine customers and spies who seek to arrest buyers and sellers. Yes, political initiative can promote societal transformation, but the character of any resulting transformation will be a complex matter that depends on the pattern of responses within the ecology of plans that constitute a society.

It is surely informative to compare drug prohibition with traffic regulation in this respect. Drug prohibition encounters much resistance from people who see nothing wrong with such usage, and who view prohibitors as infringing on the peaceful conduct of their lives. Prohibition would force drug consumers to choose patterns of consumption they value less highly because dominant members of society want to force them to consume differently. Political action in this case is pretty much straightforwardly redistributive, in that mostly it seeks to impose costs on some for the benefit of others. It is surely different with traffic control. Many might agree that speed limits often are too low, and yet there is surely wide recognition that traffic rules are not significantly redistributive and, instead, are instruments of general benefit in enabling people to operate relatively safely on congested roadways.

Plans vs. Spending Within a Macro Ecology

The lower part of Fig. 1.3 distinguishes between private and political entities within the ecology of plans that comprise a society, but it portrays connections in homogeneous fashion. This portrayal corresponds to the common analytical framework of macro theory where the prime variable of analytical interest is spending. When it comes to spending, political spending is identical with private spending. Within this analytical presupposition, a decrease in private spending can be offset by an increase in political spending, thus keeping aggregate spending unchanged, at least as a textbook exercise.

The situation changes once spending is recognized as deriving from enterprise plans, and with the types of connections among enterprises reflecting the differing imperatives that animate enterprises organized within a framework of private property as compared with those organized within a framework of public property. The theory of economic calculation (Roberts 1971; Boettke 2001) can be spun as a comparative analysis of two pure social forms: liberalism or private property and collectivism or public property. The principle of economic rationality holds that people will choose higher yielding over lower yielding uses of their assets. This could be done in a natural setting such as would characterize a Robinson Crusoe alone on his island. In a social setting, however, rationality is a complex relationship among people and their activities and is not a simple relationship between Crusoe and nature. The theory of markets explains how prices summarize much significant information that is useful in forming judgments about possible lines of economic activity. Prices can never be sufficient statistics for rational action, except in a stationary state where history has ended, and life repeats itself endlessly. Otherwise, which is to say always, prices are valuable economizers on the effort devoted to deliberation, but effective economizing action still requires judgment.

For instance, the owner of a park will face a variety of economizing choices in putting together an enterprise. The owner's capital will have to be allocated among land, buildings, equipment, and personnel. Each of these categories, moreover, entails many options. Land can vary in area, terrain, and location. Choices will have to be made about the types of equipment to install and the apportionment of the land among different uses. At the stage of enterprise planning, these various elements will be collapsed into projections of revenue and expense. While there is no guarantee that such projections will be accurate, the position of the enterprise owner as a residual claimant gives that owner incentive to be accurate because he or she will bear the losses from inaccurate judgments. Information about prices facilitates the making of commercial judgments, though such information is never a substitute for such judgment, as George Shackle (1972) explains with particular lucidity in describing the indispensable place of imagination and judgment in economic action.

Alternatively, suppose the social order is collectivist and not liberal. There is no private property and no market for ownership in enterprises. There might be production for use but there is no production for exchange. The problem of putting resources to use in generating output that people value is still present, only market prices are of no help in forming judgments. Such instruments as surveys and polls are still available. Using these instruments is equivalent, more or less, to reading tea leaves. As with real tea leaves, much depends on the discernment of the reader and on the importance of different judgments the reader of those tea leaves makes. Playgrounds will still be established and will be equipped in some fashion. Any expansion or contraction in the sizes of playgrounds, or changes in their equipment, will not occur through changes in market-generated valuations of those enterprises, and yet changes will occur even within collectively organized societies. All societies work in this respect, though liberal societies more fully than collectivist societies.

Actual societies are neither liberal nor collective, but rather feature entangled strands of both features (Wagner 2007, 2016). The question at issue is how knowledge might be assembled within those precincts organized through political activity and interactions. If political precincts are independent of market precincts, a form of additive political economy results where economic calculation operates in market precincts while calculation is absent in political precincts. Within a framework of entangled political economy, however, there is commingling among the precincts and not separation. This situation casts a different light on the problem of calculation and the use of knowledge within societies.

Friedrich Hayek (1937, 1945) posed the problem of economic coordination as one of explaining how an orderly pattern of economic activity can arise when no person or agency has access to anything but a tiny part of the knowledge that would be necessary actually to construct that pattern. In those papers, Hayek took an orderly pattern to mean systemic equilibrium as expressed by the Walrasian framework. Later, he came to recognize that orderly patterns did not require a presumption of systemic equilibrium. With respect to Bertalanffy's (1968) distinction between creative and robotic systems, general equilibrium theory treats economic systems as robotic. Originally, Hayek embraced this point of analytical departure in thinking of arriving at the Walrasian end-state as his analytical objective. Later, he came to realize that his conceptualization rotated around recognition that societies were evolving and creative, even kaleidic. Wagner (2010) illustrates the distinction by comparing a parade and a crowd of pedestrians leaving a stadium after a game. Both social configurations are orderly, in that participants understand their environment and can operate effectively within it. The parade is reasonably reducible to an entity with point mass as a center of gravity. The crowd of pedestrians heading for their various destinations cannot be so reduced. Yet the crowd presents orderly though continually changing patterns as the participants head toward their planned destinations. It is the orderliness of the pedestrian crowd and not that of the parade that was the societal configuration that Hayek (1935) thought required explanation, even though he stated the problem he sensed in terms of Walrasian equilibrium.

If Hayek's underlying analytic motif were stated in equilibrium terms, it would be one of generated and not stipulated equilibrium, as the papers collected in Joshua Epstein (2006) and David Colander (2006) illustrate.

It's also central to Bruno Latour's (2005) claim that social theories are inadequate if they explain social phenomena in terms of other social phenomena because doing this leaves social phenomena unexplained. The relevant challenge for a social theory is to explain how social phenomena emerge out of interaction among non-social phenomena. Hayek's analytical call was to explain the emergence of orderly economic patterns of market prices out of preceding conditions that were disorderly or at least incompletely ordered. Within this analytical endeavor, prices are emergent phenomena and not phenomena that exist prior to market transactions. To explain coordination thus requires something beyond market prices. The emergence of observed patterns of economic activity cannot be explained by using prices exclusively as data. To the contrary, such patterns emerge through economic interaction among market participants, and with the quality of coordination depending on the processes through which coordination emerges.

In contrast, the prevalent theoretical procedure is to postulate the existence of equilibrium without trying to explain how equilibrium might emerge from some non-equilibrium point of departure. Indeed, when economists have looked into Hayek's formulation, as illustrated by Grossman and Stiglitz (1976, 1980), they typically conclude that markets fail to generate sufficient knowledge to secure efficient coordination. This conclusion is reached by using a version of search theory. Within this framework, the efficiency character of market pricing depends on the amount of search people undertake in their capacities as output demanders and input suppliers. In this analytical schema, one person's search provides benefits for other people who are also able to gain from any resulting improvements in the state of coordination. Coordination is thus a public good, with market failure resulting because of people free ride on the knowledge-creating efforts of other people.

This contemporary reinterpretation of the problem Hayek posed has pushed Hayek's problem out of sight, though it must be recognized that Hayek's original formulation could be read as embracing the Walrasian end-state as an analytical destination. For Grossman, Stiglitz, and other contributors to this literature, Hayek's problem is construed as claiming that market participants will engage in sufficient search activity to create and maintain a Pareto efficient state of market equilibrium. Yet, one person's effort to search for price information enables other people to free ride on those search activities. As is customary with models of free riding, an inefficient supply of knowledge will be acquired, leading to a Pareto inefficient equilibrium.

But that hypothesis has not been truly refuted because it has not been truly addressed. The contemporary literature treats coordination as a *state* of existence. In contrast, Hayek treats coordination as a *process* that continues without end. To explain a process entails a different analytical challenge than to explain a state. A state pertains to some set of observations at some instant. One state might pertain to t_1, another state might pertain to t_2, and comparative statics seeks to reconcile both states with the different data that pertains to those states. A process pertains to interaction among participants over some interval of time. The object of explanation is the interval $|t_1-t_2|$, with Hayek's claim being that the movement from t_1 to t_2 arises within processes where market participants experiment, explore, and otherwise acquire knowledge that they put to use, and with observed systemic properties emerging through societal interaction. Claims of Pareto efficiency are undefined in Hayek's emergent dynamic framework because Pareto efficiency pertains only to allegations of unexploited gains from trade at some instant. Within a continuing process of change, Pareto efficiency has no meaning.

It's observationally clear that market processes entail the creation and use of knowledge. Even if we conceptualize equilibrium at some instant, t_1, we must employ some market process to generate some latter instant, t_2. Leaving aside wholly speculative questions pertaining to Pareto efficiency, it's obvious that the movement from t_1 to t_2 entails the creation and use of knowledge. Rather than postulating data and positing that that data pertains to a state of equilibrium, Hayek argues simply that the acquisition and use of what is commonly taken as data is actually an economic problem to be characterized and explained. Contemporary literature postulates some equilibrated societal situation and pronounces it as being inefficient within the terms of that postulation. That literature makes no effort to explain how that situation might have come about. Yet prices do not exist prior to transactions, regardless of how loudly economists offer pronouncements about *given* market prices. To the contrary, prices emerge through market transactions, and change through those transactions. If economic coordination is truly to be explained, that explanation cannot start from some stipulated set of equilibrium prices because the establishment of prices, and changes in those prices are parts of the ongoing coordinative process.

It is, moreover, theoretically unsatisfactory to embrace a model of stipulated prices by claiming that most people take most prices as data most
of the time. This observation is clearly an empirical regularity, but macro
regularities of this type cannot serve as substitutes for theoretical explanation. Suppose in Schelling-like (1978) fashion, a grid is populated with
100 agents. These agents comprise a society, which is instantiated as a
set of movement rules that keep the agents within some proximity to
one another. More explicitly, no agent allows more than three squares
to intervene from the nearest neighbor. Furthermore, no agent seeks to
move onto a square occupied by another agent. Starting from some initial
distribution of people over the relevant grid, suppose five of the agents
move in some particular direction. The other agents will adapt to maintain
the required spacing. The five innovating agents will then move again, and
with that process continuing indefinitely. At any instant, this society would
seem to be in stasis, as the claim that the society is in static equilibrium
could not be rejected at the five percent level of significance. Yet by the
very construction of the model, the society is in perpetual motion, and is
led by the five outlying innovators along the lines of Malcolm Gladwell's
(2008) analysis of outliers as prime carriers of successful change, as well
as Joseph Schumpeter's (1934) recognition that entrepreneurship is the
locus of leadership within capitalist societies.

References

Aligica, P.D., and P.J. Boettke. 2009. *Challenging Institutional Analysis and
Development: The Bloomington School*. London: Routledge.
Angner, E. 2012. *A Course in Behavioral Economics*. Houndmills, UK: Palgrave
Macmillan.
Aydinonat, N.E. 2008. *The Invisible Hand in Economics*. London: Routledge.
Bakhtin, M. 1981. *The Dialogic Imagination*, ed. Michael Holquist. Austin: Uni-
versity of Texas Press.
Bakhtin, M. 1984. *Problems of Dostoevsky's Poetics*, ed. Caryl Emerson. Minneapo-
lis: University of Minnesota Press.
Bertalanffy, L. 1968. *General System Theory*. New York: George Braziller.
Boettke, P.J. 2001. *Calculation and Coordination*. London: Routledge.
Chaitin, G., F.A. Doria, and N.C.A. de Costa. 2011. *Gödl's Way: Exploration
into an Undecidable World*. Boca Raton, FL: CRC Press.
Clower, R.W. 1994. The Fingers of the Invisible Hand. *Brock University Review*
3: 3–13.

Colander, D. (ed.). 2006. *Post Walrasian Macroeconomics*. Cambridge: Cambridge University Press.

Coyle, D. 2015. *GDP: A Brief but Affectionate History*. Princeton, NJ: Princeton University Press.

Devereaux, A., and R.E. Wagner. 2020. Contrasting Visions for Macroeconomic Theory: DSGE and OEE. *American Economist* 65: 28–50.

Dopfer, K., J. Foster, and J. Potts. 2004. Micro-Meso-Macro. *Journal of Evolutionary Economics* 14: 263–279.

Elias, N. 1982 [1939]. *The Civilizing Process*. New York: Pantheon Books.

Emmett, R.N. 2006. De Gustibus est Disputandum: Frank H. Knight's response to George Stigler and Gary Becker's 'De Gustibus non est Disputandum'. *Journal of Economic Methodology* 13: 97–111.

Epstein, J.M. (ed.). 2006. *Generative Social Science: Studies in Agent-Based Computational Modeling*. Princeton, NJ: Princeton University Press.

Fleetwood, S. [1996] 2015. Order Without Equilibrium: A Critical Realist Interpretation of Hayek's Notion of Spontaneous Order. *Cambridge Journal of Economics* 20: 729–747.

Foster, J. 1987. *Evolutionary Macroeconomics*. London: Routledge.

Gladwell, M. 2008. *Outliers: The Story of Success*. New York: Little, Brown.

Grice-Hutchinson, M. 1978. *Early Economic Thought in Spain, 1177–1749*. London: Allen & Unwin.

Grossman, S.J., and J.E. Stiglitz. 1976. Information and Competitive Price Systems. *American Economic Review* 66: 246–253.

Grossman, S.J., and J.E. Stiglitz. 1980. On the Impossibility of Informationally Efficient Markets. *American Economic Review* 70: 393–408.

Hayek, F.A. 1935. *Prices and Production*, 2nd ed. London: Routledge and Kegan Paul.

Hayek, F.A. 1937. Economics and Knowledge. *Economica* 4: 33–54.

Hayek, F.A. 1945. The Use of Knowledge in Society. *American Economic Review* 35: 519–530.

Howitt, P., and R. Clower. 2000. The Emergence of Economic Organization. *Journal of Economic Behavior & Organization* 41: 55–84.

Kirman, A. 1992. Whom or What Does the Representative Individual Represent? *Journal of Economic Perspectives* 6: 117–136.

Koppl, R. 2014. *From Crisis to Confidence: Macroeconomics After the Crash*. London: Institute of Economic Affairs.

Knight, F.H. 1921. *Risk, Uncertainty, and Profit*. Boston: Houghton-Mifflin.

Laszlo, E. 1996. *The Systems View of the World*. Cresskill, NJ: Hampton Press.

Latour, B. 2005. *Reassembling the Social: An Introduction to Actor-Network Theory*. Oxford: Oxford University Press.

Lindahl, E. (1919 [1939]). *Studies in the Theory of Capital and Income*. London: Allen & Unwin.

McCann, C.R. 1994. *Probability Foundations of Economic Theory*. London: Routledge.

Meadows, D.H. 2008. *Thinking in Systems*. White River, VT: Chelsea Green.

Morgan, M. 2012. *The World in the Model: How Economists Work and Think*. Cambridge: Cambridge University Press.

O'Driscoll, G.P., and M.J. Rizzo. 1985. *The Economics of Time and Ignorance*. Oxford: Basil Blackwell.

Ostrom, V. 1999. Polycentricity. In *Polycentricity and Local Public Economies*, ed. Michael D. McGinnis, 52–74, 119–138. Ann Arbor: University of Michigan Press.

Polanyi, M. 1951. *The Logic of Liberty*. Chicago: University of Chicago Press.

Potts, J. 2000. *The New Evolutionary Microeconomics: Complexity, Competence, and Adaptive Behavior*. Cheltenham, UK: Edward Elgar.

Potts, J., and K. Morrison. 2007. Meso Comes to Markets. *Journal of Economic Behavior & Organization* 63: 307–312.

Pryor, F.L. 2008. System as a Causal Force. *Journal of Economic Behavior & Organization* 67: 545–559.

Resnick, M. 1994. *Turtles, Termites, and Traffic Jams*. Cambridge, MA: MIT Press.

Robbins, L. 1932. *An Essay on the Nature and Significance of Economic Science*. London: Macmillan.

Roberts, P.C. 1971. *Alienation and the Soviet Economy*. Albuquerque: University of New Mexico Press.

Savage, L. 1954. *The Foundations of Statistics*. London: Wiley.

Schelling, T.C. 1978. *Micromotives and Macrobehavior*. New York: Norton.

Schumpeter, J.A. 1934. *The Theory of Economic Development*, 2nd ed. New York: Oxford University Press.

Schumpeter, J.A. 1954. *History of Economic Analysis*. New York: Oxford University Press.

Shackle, G.L.S. 1961. *Decision, Order, and Time in Human Affairs*. Cambridge: Cambridge University Press.

Shackle, G.L.S. 1972. *Epistemics and Economics*. Cambridge: Cambridge University Press.

Shackle, G.L.S. 1974. *Keynesian Kaleidics*. Edinburgh: Edinburgh University Press.

Simmel, G. 1900 [1990]. *The Philosophy of Money*, 2nd ed. London: Routledge.

Smith, V.L. 2008. *Rationality in Economics*. Cambridge: Cambridge University Press.

Stigler, G.J., and G.S. Becker. 1977. Die Gustibus non est Disputandum. *American Economic Review* 67: 76–90.

Trudeau, R.J. 1993. *Introduction to Graph Theory*. New York: Dover Publications.

Veetil, V.P., and R.E. Wagner. 2015. Treating Macro Theory as Systems Theory: How Might It Matter? *Advances in Austrian Economics* 19: 119–143.

Wagner, R.E. 2007. *Fiscal Sociology and the Theory of Public Finance*. Cheltenham, UK: Edward Elgar.

Wagner, R.E. 2010. *Mind, Society, and Human Action: Time and Knowledge in a Theory of Social Economy*. London: Routledge.

Wagner, R.E. 2012a. A Macro Economy as an Ecology of Plans. *Journal of Economic Behavior & Organization* 82: 433–444.

Wagner, R.E. 2012b. Viennese Kaleidics: Why It's Liberty More Than Policy That Calms Turbulence. *Review of Austrian Economics* 25: 283–297.

Wagner, R.E. 2016. *Politics as a Peculiar Business: Insights from a Theory of Entangled Political Economy*. Cheltenham, UK: Edward Elgar.

Walras, L. 1874 [1954]. *Elements of Pure Economics*. Homewood, IL: Richard D. Irwin.

Weintraub, E.R. 1993. *General Equilibrium Analysis: Studies in Appraisal*. Ann Arbor: University of Michigan Press.

CHAPTER 2

Models of Social Order: Mechanical vs. Creative

All theorists agree that a macro-level theory should pertain to properties of the entirety of an economic system, in contrast to micro-level theories which pertain either to individual entities within the system or to subsets of those entities, with the latter being described as entailing a meso-level of analysis by Dopfer et al. (2004) and by Potts and Morrison (2007). The divergence between Keynes's (1936) treatment of macro as pertaining to aggregate spending and Lindahl's (1919 [1939]) treatment of macro as pertaining to interaction among economizing entities was a fateful choice when it emerged through professional usage during the decade following publication of Keynes's *General Theory*. Nonetheless, and in fairness to Keynes and in the service of accuracy to Lindahl, it should be noted that Lindahl's analytical execution of his distinction between micro as action and macro as interaction could not be executed effectively with the analytical tools and concepts that were in use in the early twentieth century. There was little option for Lindahl but to run his analysis within a presumption of systemic equilibrium, which in turn enabled complex patterns of interaction among economizing entities to be reduced to the actions of a representative agent. All the same, the distinction between agent action and interaction among agents points in divergent analytical directions, due to the distinction between phenomena suitable for aggregation and phenomena that arise through emergence.

To illustrate the distinction between aggregation and emergence, compare two ways of measuring the speed at which two sets of four runners can cover 2000 meters. Each set of runners runs sequentially, with the

© The Author(s) 2020

R. E. Wagner, *Macroeconomics as Systems Theory*,
https://doi.org/10.1007/978-3-030-44465-5_2

team's output measured as the elapsed time between the first runner's start and when the fourth runner crosses the finish line. Aggregation would be measured by adding the times it takes for each runner to cover the 500 meters. Each runner for each team might cover the 500 meters in 60 seconds, which aggregates to each team finishing in four minutes. Alternatively, each runner might have to pass a baton to the next runner of the team before that runner can continue. If the baton passes are swift and smooth, the team might finish the distance in less than four minutes due to the running starts the second, third, and fourth runners receive. But if those passes are rough and clumsy, the team will require more than four minutes to cover the distance. The different output of the two teams is not a simple aggregation over the speeds of the runners at covering 500 meters. That difference in times is a product of the qualities of interaction among the runners in passing the baton. The team's outcome includes emergent phenomena that lie beyond the reach of aggregation.

It would not lead thought astray to state that emergence starts where aggregation ends. Emergence pertains to situations where a union of two or more entities has properties that are not possessed by either of the individual entities. Water is a classical chemical instance of emergent qualities. As separate entities, hydrogen and oxygen can each support combustion. When these elements are combined to form water, however, fire can be extinguished. With respect to the humane sciences, two or more people living in close proximity will generate phenomena that would not be observed among a set of hermits. Most of those phenomena are features of everyday life because we all grow up in social groupings (Elias 1982 [1939]), and so understandably we think about these as some of the ordinary features of life. Yet these are features that we would not experience if we lived as hermits. These phenomena are products of emergence, just as the ability of water to douse fire is an emergent property of certain combinations of hydrogen and oxygen.

AGGREGATION VS. EMERGENCE: HOW MIGHT IT MATTER?

Someone who has chosen to place a bet on the outcome of a relay race and who has never seen the team members pass a baton would be well advised to bet on the team whose members can cover their assigned distances as individual runners in the least amount of time. In this case, aggregation over the individual runners would be a reasonable estimate of the team's performance when no information exists about the speed at which different pairs of individuals pass the baton. The members of a relay team comprise an exceedingly small society where social outcomes surely can be approximated with reasonable accuracy through aggregation over the individual members, recognizing that there will be some generally small residual in team outcomes that aggregation fails to capture.

While the speed at which a relay team covers its assigned distance depends in principle on the quality of interaction among pairs of the team in exchanging the baton, no one would claim that aggregation generally leads observers astray in forming expectations about the race's outcome. But the members of a relay team are among the smallest of all examples of social interaction, where the interactive part of social outcomes are dwarfed by aggregation over individual qualities. Technically, it is correct to say that the team's speed over its distance depends on interaction among the members, but little is generally lost in ignoring interaction and looking only at aggregation. Performance of the macro entity, the relay team, is reasonably estimated by aggregating individual performances. Relay teams, however, and athletic teams generally are social objects that can be reasonably controlled and directed by a coach or team manager. These objects correspond to the monocentric or homophonic network portrayed in Fig. 1.1.

A significant analytical difference comes into play once we distinguish between those social configurations that can be reasonably directed and controlled by someone's supervision and those that cannot. In the former case, a network's properties are largely a product of managerial supervision. In the latter case, network properties are not totally a product of some manager's choice and rather are to a significant degree a property of some system of interaction. There exists, in other words, a typology of societal configurations, some of which are subject directly to explicit supervision at the system-level and some of which are not, and in the latter case *supervision is a property of the system itself* (Pryor 2008). In the former case, system properties can be attributed to the qualities of management; in the latter case those qualities are emergent properties of a system of interaction that is too large and complex for the system to be assimilated to an organization. Figure 1.1 characterizes an organization which is subject to managerial control. In contrast, Fig. 1.2 characterizes a social order that consists of numerous organizations, each of which is subject to managerial supervision, and yet the system itself is not subject to managerial supervision.

PARADES AND PEDESTRIAN CROWDS
AS CONTRASTING SOCIAL CONFIGURATIONS

A large parade might be two miles in length and contain several thousand participants grouped into many dozens of such disparate organizations as marching bands, military units performing close-order drills, floats of great variety, and equestrian units. The parade is an organization of organizations. Each of the units in the parade is an organization that is subject to managerial direction and control. For each such unit, the quality of its performance can be attributed to the organization's management. To be sure, such attribution might not be wholly accurate. The quality of a marching band's performance will also depend on the musical abilities and marching talents of the band's members as these have been honed through rehearsal. It is the province of the band director to select music that its members can play well, but what they can play well also depends on the investment in practice the members of the band make.

Like the members of a relay team, a band's performance can be only approximately treated as an aggregation over musical abilities and time spent rehearsing. More highly skilled musicians and more time spent in rehearsal will almost surely yield a higher quality of performance. Similar statements can be advanced about the performances of all the individual units that constitute the parade. Each such unit is subject to managerial supervision and direction, as each constitutes an organization within the parade, and with the parade itself being an organization of organizations. As an organization of organizations, the parade is subject to the supervision and control of a parade marshal. In judging the overall performance of a parade, it will be reasonable to judge that performance according to the evaluative standard of the parade marshal, who occupies the apex of the parade as an organization of organizations along the lines that Fig. 1.1 illustrates.

Suppose there is an observer who stands in a hot-air balloon one mile above the parade. The parade obviously would appear orderly to the observer. There might be an occasional though only momentary disruption to the parade's flow. For instance, the engine on a float might stop running, with the parade being delayed momentarily until a tow vehicle is hitched to the float. Alternatively, a spectator might have thrown a firecracker into a passing equestrian unit, leading some of the horses to bolt which in turn led the riders to struggle to gain control of their mounts.

Again, the parade would be delayed momentarily until order within the unit is restored, after which the parade will continue. The parade could reasonably be treated as a system in equilibrium, and with that equilibrium established by the parade marshal who ordered the units within the parade and who had arranged to handle such exogenous events as the breakdown of a float's engine. If the parade started at 1000 and was four miles long, the initial unit would be rationally expected to reach the end at 1200 if the parade was planned to average two miles per hour. The final unit would likewise end its march at 1400. This timing of the parade viewed as a system is the property of the systemic planning of the parade marshal. That planned end to the parade would be a rational expectation that would be disturbed only by exogenous shocks to the parade marshal's plan.

Now change the scene observed below the hot-air balloon to several thousand spectators leaving an arena after watching an athletic event or theatrical performance. When the event ends, the spectators scatter for their various destinations. Those spectators are not reducible to a point of mass that can be spotted and followed along with a map. The observer surely would not describe those participants as illustrating a system in equilibrium. It would probably be described as being chaotic, at least at its early stages until many of the participants had arrived at their various destinations. To describe this scene as being chaotic is, however, to commit a *category mistake*, which arises when someone attributes properties to an object which that object cannot possibly possess. In this instance, the category mistake arises when a social configuration that must be polycentric is treated as if it were monocentric. To be sure, such erroneous treatment eases the theorist's analytical job because the centralized mindset (Resnick 1994) allows explanation to be reduced to the explanation of someone's plan or choice, in contrast to explaining interaction among individual entities. While a parade is clearly reducible to the planned choices of a parade marshal, the exit paths of the spectators are not so reducible.

For the spectators leaving the performance, the parade marshal and his or her choices is irrelevant because there is no parade marshal. Sure, it is rare that all the spectators would each travel as single entities. Some of the spectators would travel as single entities, but many would travel in small groups, including pairs. There might even be a few instances of groups that travel together in tour busses. The pedestrian crowd, in other words, is an *order of organizations*, which is an instance of what Warren Weaver (1948) characterized as organized complexity. It is a category mistake of gigantic extent to theorize about the systemic properties of a large society as if those properties were identical to those of such a simple organization as a parade.

From the perspective of an observer, it is easy to understand why orderliness as a social quality is assimilated to the presumption that the system exists in a state of equilibrium. The presumption of systemic equilibrium enables treatment of the crowd as if it were a parade because the presumptions of given preferences and technologies in conjunction with equilibrium prices locks the actions of all participants into a mutually consistent pattern of action. This set of assumptions effectively transforms a crowd of independent pedestrians into a parade—in the theorist's mind though certainly not in practice. In this respect, George Shackle (1974), in response to being asked what makes for a good economic theory, responded that a good theory eases a theorist's mind. One obvious source of mental comfort is the ability of a theory to answer questions the theorist poses to it.

At this point, we encounter the problem denoted as tractability, also known as Ockham's razor. While Ockham's razor has been given various formulations over the centuries, all of them countenance use of simpler over more complex explanations. There is surely much of value in Ockham's formulation, but that value is equally surely limited and not universal. Tractability comes at a price, and that price resides in the distortions in understanding that arise when the centralized mindset is invoked inappropriately. With respect to the humane sciences, one feature of a useful and accurate theory surely resides in congruity between the theory and known human capabilities as these are mediated through scientific equipment and instrumentation. For instance, a marksman could not reliably hit a bullseye a half-mile away with a rifle but can do so with a telescopic sight. To assume an isolated town of 20 people exists in a state of equilibrium is a reasonable use of Ockham's razor. To do so for a nation of several hundred million is not because it exceeds anyone's cognitive capacity. To be sure, there is theoretical room for developing explanations of how a situation resembling such an equilibrium might be a property of some describable process of social interaction, but that is a task for future work along the lines that this book undertakes.

Teleological Individuals Inside
a Non-teleological System

Figure 1.3 portrayed abstractly a relation between the action and the system-levels of society. Human action is the province of the micro- and meso-levels of society. No action occurs on the macro or societal level. To be sure, the characteristic features of the macro-level emerge from interactions among entities acting on the micro- and meso-levels, but the macro level is a combination of statistical artifacts of past action and ideas people hold regarding future possibilities, and with many of these being described as ideologies. The aphorism "think globally but act locally" expresses well the idea behind Fig. 1.3. Indeed, the construction of that figure entails recognition that genuine global action is not possible. There are global resultants of local action, but all action initiates locally where the actors are located. A foreign aid program might ship tractors and combines to other nations and those pieces of equipment might be used to increase agricultural yield which would be captured by the NIPA accounts. That increased yield, however, would be a macro-level portrait of micro-level actions stemming from legislative actions in the home country combined with the purchase of equipment from domestic producers.

The macro system looks differently in the presence of the foreign aid program than it would otherwise have looked. That different look, moreover, need not bear any direct relation to the micro action that led to the shipment of tractors and combines. The foreign aid program, or any program for that matter, can bring about numerous changes within a society's ecology of plans, and often with their being no direct or obvious connection to the original program. The foreign aid program enters the society at particular nodes within the ecology of plans and has similar impact on that ecology of plans within the nation where the tractors and combines are delivered. The initial impact is to increase profitability at the initiating node within the ecology. The increased demand for tractors and combines will in turn increase demand for some inputs engaged in producing tractors and combines. With higher prices being offered for those inputs, other producers within the ecology of plans will find their expenses for their inputs to be rising. In short, there will be rearrangements throughout the ecology of plans due to the connectivity among the nodes within the ecology.

All nodes or entities within the ecology of plans have teleology. The ecology itself, however, has no teleology. The society is not a thinking or planning entity. The persons within the ecology pursue plans and so have teleology, but there is no teleology at the system-level. At the system or macro-societal level, society resembles an improvisational cosmic drama. Individuals are teleological creatures who can form images of their present condition and compare that image with alternative images of prospective future conditions, and then seek to act now to attain one of those future conditions. Social systems, however, are not teleological, as distinct from containing numerous teleological entities. This situation surely often generates senses of exasperation or dissonance, and which surely is at work in promoting the efforts of numerous economic theorists to treat societies as if they were teleological creatures.

Indeed, the idea of economic reform mostly involves a treatment of societies as teleological, as can be seen by comparing Elinor Ostrom's (1990) substantial body of work on the governance of commons situations with the related literature on public goods and externalities. Commons settings generally entail situations where a set of people can fare better through cooperative action than through individual action with respect to various natural resource settings. Ostrom's approach to commons governance is to observe and examine how those sets of people work to fashion arrangements for governing their several actions as these pertain to the commons. One such commons might be the creation and maintenance of an irrigation project where water is diverted from a river to provide water for 100 farmers. Ostrom explores how those farmers establish and manage the irrigation project. Ostrom also notes that not all such efforts at commons governance are successful, and part of her analytical effort entails effort to understand when such efforts fail. Throughout her analytical efforts, Ostrom works within the teleologies of the participants. She does not imagine or impose a teleology on the collective body into which those participants might be aggregated.

Contrary to Ostrom, many theorists jump directly to attributing a teleology to the collective body. One common way of doing this is to attribute a common utility function to everyone. This common utility function can then be used to compute the benefit that the members of the group would receive from common action through some cost–benefit scheme of analysis. The analytical point of departure in this instance is to posit a state of market failure where people are unable to agree upon an irrigation project that would have been mutually beneficial. As to where that knowledge of the project's being mutually beneficial came from, that is typically an assumption that is invoked to illustrate the model. An existing situation is compared with a hypothesized situation, with the existing situation being inferior with respect to the evaluations of the participants.

In this case, the analysis starts from a situation where irrigation is not provided, and the theorist assumes that irrigated farming is superior to dry farming. As to why the inferior situation prevails over the superior situation, we arrive at one of those many analytical forks in the road. One fork in that road treats the claim on behalf of irrigated farming as a hypothesis, and a hypothesis that implies that some agreement among the participants is possible. If this hypothesis is correct, the participants should be able to develop an organization that would allow those mutual gains to be captured (Buchanan 1959). But that hypothesis might be wrong. In this case the participants would be unable to put together a mutually profitable arrangement and the irrigation project would be abandoned. Whether that project would go forward or be abandoned would be revealed through the actions of the participants.

To be sure, a theorist could posit a teleology on behalf of the group that would warrant an irrigation project on cost–benefit terms, in which case the failure to organize the project would reflect some such obstacle to securing agreement as high transaction costs or free riding. What should we conclude when we observe that no irrigation project has been established? The more common conclusion is that the theorist was correct in attributing teleology to the group and that the failure to provide the project was due to such obstacles as transaction costs or free riding. An alternative conclusion that is also consistent with the observed failure to pursue the project is that there was no mutually beneficial way of organizing provision of the irrigation project.

Conceptualizing Rational Action Without Imposing Societal Synchronicity

How can rational action be conceptualized within an ecology of plans without imposing the homogeneity that expected utility theory imposes? If the object of theorization is construed as a society in equilibrium, the presumption that individual actions are mutually consistent leads to explanation through presuming the presence of a common utility function. The individuals in the society are chained together by the presupposition of equilibrium, which leads to turbulence as being limited to exogenous shocks. By contrast, to treat turbulence as a systemic property of a society of relatively autonomous individuals requires a scheme of thought where the individual pursuit of plans can insert turbulence into the ecology as a by-product of creating connections within the ecology of plans.

Rational action conforms to the universal form of a person's acting to replace less desired states of being with more desired states. While form is sufficient for the efforts of an equilibrium theorist, substance must enter the theoretical efforts of the non-equilibrium theorist where turbulence is a systemic property of interaction among the members of a society. Within the scheme of personal probability, individual agents are captured reasonably well by the form of expected utility theory. But individual action is substantive and not formal. Among other things, this means that individual utility functions contain objects of particular interest for the agent's plan, as well as that plan being formulated through acts of imagination regarding future possibilities.

In his *Great Chain of Being*, Arthur Lovejoy (1936) explains that our thoughts often are grounded on presuppositions of which we are unaware. Two common presuppositions of most economic and social theories are universality and synchronicity. These presuppositions lead instantly to treating economies and societies through the image of a parade and most certainly not a crowd of pedestrians traveling to different places. These presuppositions lead immediately to an embrace of the centralized mindset even if explicit thought might have led a theorist to reject that mindset.

By universal, I mean the presumption of deep-level homogeneity among people. This presumption leads almost immediately to an embrace of holistic entities in social-level theories as reflected in such statements as "we all want the same things." More generally, it leads to the promiscuous use of a "we" language in place of one that distinguishes between you and me. You and three friends go camping for the weekend. When someone asks you next week how you spent the weekend, you would respond by explaining that "we" went camping. The plural pronoun is apt because its usage implies agreement among a plurality of minds.

Now suppose that as the four of you were loading your car, a stranger accosted you at gunpoint, forced you to drive to your camping site, then robbed each of you and drove away with your car and possessions, leaving the four of you tied up awaiting rescue or the arrival of four-legged predators. If you were subsequently rescued, you most certainly would not describe the five of you as a "we" who went for a drive. To the contrary, your language would distinguish between the four of you who were captured and the fifth person who abducted the four of you. In no way would a universal statement cover your actions in concordant fashion.

If antagonism is thought to occupy a significant position within human societies along with concordance, one of the challenges of a social theory is to explain the principles at work in governing the relative domains of antagonism and concordance within societies. Society as a concept can be invoked to pertain to organized humanity within some geographical territory. In this fashion society is used in a purely formal manner. But form does not dictate substance. There is a form to which an economic theory pertains, but there is also the substance which that theory is thought to illuminate. One prime lesson from the theory of markets is that people can use the same object to serve different purposes. There can be universal agreement that an object is desirable without there being any agreement over who is able to use how much of that object. This distinction between form and substance fits closely with Carl Schmitt's (1932 [1996]) invocation of the friend-enemy distinction as providing the linchpin for political action, as Chapter 7 shall examine.

Another and perhaps more significant dichotomy for macro-level theorizing pertains to the distinction between synchronic and diachronic action within society. Equilibrium theory reflects synchronic thinking. Whatever the size of the society, the plans of all the relevant entities are presumed to be synchronized with one another. To be sure, synchronization is a theoretical formalism and not a substantive proposition about reality. Synchronization was built into the foundation of general equilibrium theorizing by Léon Walras (1874 [1954]) when he invoked the image of an auctioneer who announced prices, received bids, and then revised the prices, and repeated this process until all markets cleared. Walras's auction was a fictional construction that placed a patina of reality over what otherwise would have seemed contrary to human experience. Ever since Walras, economic theory has proceeded under a presumption that an economy is a network of synchronized action.

To construct an economic theory within a non-equilibrium or ecological mode requires abandonment of synchronized action and its replacement with diachronic action within society. At any moment, a society can be characterized as possessing an ecology of plans (Wagner 2012a). Not all of those plans are equally robust. Some of them will be in the process of abandonment. Others will have just been set in motion. As the clock moves forward, some of those earlier plans will have been abandoned while other of them will have been revised. Even more, new plans will be inserted into a society's ecology of plans. Furthermore, those new plans will often interfere with earlier plans. In some cases, the interference will be positive or complementary. In other cases it will be negative. Either way, the ecology of plans will exhibit turbulence and not the placidity of synchronized action. A society is not a team of synchronized swimmers; it more accurately resembles the turbulence of playing water polo.

In referring to an ecology of plans in the absence of synchronicity, some special attention must be given to the idea of a plan along the lines of James Allen's et al. (1991) application of rational analysis to planning. While a plan is continuous from the time of its conception to the time of its liquidation or completion, a plan can be usefully decomposed into several stages, one illustration of which would distinguish between conception, initiation, execution, and revision. Each of these stages entails some duration of time. When people speak of forming a plan, they commonly refer to some combination of conception and initiation. Whether the formation of a plan entails one stage or two is immaterial. What is material for diachronic economic theory is that the formation of a plan entails the passing of time during which possibilities are explored and the ingredients necessary to execute the plan are assembled. This stage occurs against a background of knowledge being assembled that is relevant to the plan's success. A good deal of that knowledge concerns competitive and complementary activities elsewhere within the society. That knowledge is assembled at particular moments within the interval of plan formation and is subject to continual revision as other plans in the society are being expanded or collapsed. The executing stage entails some duration of time during which other plans are being injected into the catallaxy and yet other plans abandoned. All of this outside action might appear as just so much noise to the entrepreneur, but those affect the value of the entrepreneur's plan all the same. A time will come when that plan will be assessed, and perhaps expanded and revised or possibly liquidated. All such changes throughout the ecology of plans will create turbulence within the society. This situation means the capital gains and losses, along with associated output gaps, are a normal feature of the economic process, and not some sign of a poorly working system of societal interaction.

Within a diachronic scheme of analysis, the ecology of plans entails a birth-and-death process where within each discrete interval some plans enter the ecology while others leave it. This process of birth-and-death injects turbulence into the ecology of plans due to the ability of people to create their own plans as against being conscripted into someone else's plan. Such turbulence is data that stems from a social system that features individual liberty. In the presence of such liberty-induced turbulence, traditional macro theory looks to political measures to control turbulence, as illustrated by social insurance and claims on behalf of governments serving as employers of last resort. Political policy is thus portrayed as the means of limiting turbulence under orthodox macro theory. In contrast, Wagner (2012b) explains that it is the ability of people to fabricate contractual terms and organizational arrangements that moderates turbulence.

Theoretical Baselines for Establishing Systemic Normality

Recalling that no one has ever seen an economic system or society in its totality, as against experiencing pieces and parts, it is reasonable to wonder about the source of ideas regarding what is normal or attainable in human affairs. In this respect, social science serves two masters, just as do lexicographers. In large measure, dictionaries and grammars are compilations of how people use language. Practical usage is prior to compilation, necessarily so. Yet people also refer to those compilations as guides to their usage. Dictionaries and grammars originate in desires to describe how people use language, but they also serve normative purposes to the extent users refer to them in determining how they will use language.

Social theories entail the same duality. Most fundamentally, social theories originate in curiosity about observed patterns in the world of experience. Economic theories originate in perceptions of general orderliness within the realm of human affairs and social organization. But humans also have faculties of imagination that enable us to conceptualize what we regard as superior and inferior states of existence. Armed with such acts of imagination, it is natural for theorists to wonder whether their theories regarding their observations of orderliness can be used to improve the states of existence they experience. After all, one can easily imagine a superior state of existence without knowing how to attain it.

To declare some observed state of experience to be defective and hence remediable requires both some plausible baseline for establishing defectiveness and some plausible analytical framework within which alleviation of the defect can be rendered sensible. Aggregation as a framework entails neither of these features. To be sure, a flat-line measure of aggregate output is consistent with a steady state model of systemic equilibrium, where a system that has attained a state of equilibrium continues indefinitely in that state. But this system is a wholly imaginary construction that has been built on some theorist's whiteboard. The ability to construct such an imaginary system does nothing to bring that system to life.

Suppose we were to ask what it would take to bring that system to life. For a social system to maintain its parametric values indefinitely, it would be necessary for all individuals to repeat their activities indefinitely. This requirement contravenes so many facets we surely recognize as part of our worlds of experience as to be ludicrous. For one thing, it would deny boredom, imagination, and creativity to all individuals within the society. While there might be people who are pleased with simply duplicating their activities throughout their lives, there will also surely be people who will not, and who will seek to escape the boredom such duplication entails by doing such things as changing the products they buy, the jobs they hold, the enterprises they establish, or the supply chains in which they participate. In this respect, Nash equilibrium can be a property of individual action within an equilibrium model without allowing that property to contaminate our understanding of actual economic processes that operate in some non-equilibrium manner.

Even more, people learn from interaction with other people, which sets in motion sources of internally generated change that are excluded from consideration by orthodox macro models where the presumption of systemic equilibrium is used to reduce society to a representative or average agent. For interaction to have useful analytical work to do, it is necessary to avoid the analytical straitjacket imposed by the presumption that people have fully ordered utility functions along with possessing a full listing of their options over which they can choose. This standard presumption of expected utility theory necessarily renders individual action objectifiable and computable by some observer.

In contrast, a scheme of analysis that is suitable for theorizing about creative and open systems must contain individual agents who operate with only partially ordered utility functions. The presumption of partial ordering means that people can learn about the world and its options through their interactions with other people, and with different substantive interactions generating different pieces of knowledge. It is, in other words, through action and interaction that so-called utility functions take shape, as against being presumed to exist prior to choice (Buchanan 1982;

Emmett 2006). The point of this alternative formulation, moreover, is not that it is superior on some essentialist foundation, but that it is necessary for some such scheme of analysis to theorize in terms of open and creative systems of interaction.

Among most macro theorists, the DSGE framework treats economies as always being in systemic equilibrium, only those equilibrium states are continually disturbed by exogenous shocks. A time series of aggregate output would feature variability that resembled the teeth of a saw. Such variability, however, would be normal and not a sign of failures of market clearing. That variability would indicate continual changes in the rate of growth of aggregate output, due principally to changes in the stock of knowledge relevant to production, as sketched in such works as Kydland and Prescott (1982) and Plosser (1989). Volatility is a normal feature of economic systems and is not an indicator of some form of systemic defect to be corrected through appropriate policy measures.

The DSGE claims that systemic volatility, the turbulence associated with growth, is surely an advance in our state of knowledge when compared against formulations of flat-line equilibrium where volatility indicates systemic defectiveness. All the same, the DSGE theorists separate the micro- and macro-levels of analysis by postulating systems always in equilibrium, thereby enabling reduction of the system to the imagined actions of a representative individual. Within this analytical framework, all that exists of a theoretically useful form are resource allocations. Within this framework, those allocations are declared to be Pareto efficient. The institutional arrangements of human governance, both the sources of their emergence and their performance properties, are irrelevant for macro-level theory. By contrast, those institutional arrangements are of central importance within the scheme of thought that treats the entirety of an economic system within the framework of a theory of creative systems, as Fig. 1.3 illustrates and as Chapter 3 will examine.

METHOD AND SUBSTANCE: INTERACTIVE, NOT ADDITIVE

As already noted, theorists in the humane sciences are generally unable to observe directly their phenomena of interest, at least at the systemic level of analysis. There is plenty of room for observing individual action in laboratory settings, but systems of interaction among economizing individuals are not directly observable on large scales. So, theorists construct theories that they use to form their observations which they subsequently seek to explain. Intelligibility and fluidity, permanence and change, are two qualities of societies that everyone can appreciate in varying degrees. As a purely formal matter, there is nothing new under the sun; as a substantive matter, however, change is continually underway.

Intelligibility speaks to individual choices of plans and actions. Most theories of choice treat actions as being instantaneous, meaning there is no temporal gap between deciding to pursue a plan of action and observing the consequences of that plan. The presumption that our observations pertain to states of equilibrium renders this presumption plausible given that the theorist is willing to accept the presumption. There is, of course, no obvious reason for granting this acceptance. It is in no way intuitively obvious that the temporal lapse between planning an action and experiencing the outcome of that action is zero. Nor is it intuitively obvious that in social systems people are invariably successful in pursuing their plans. Quite the contrary, plans are often revised or abandoned.

Temporal gaps are inherent in all planned action. All the same, it is conceivable that the length of that temporal gap has no significant analytical work to do. In this respect, what Keynesian-inspired theorists describe as output gaps must be misidentified variations in the real rate of economic growth. For these theorists, macro-level outcomes are always Pareto efficient. To be sure, Pareto efficiency is a meaningful construction only within a model that has a position of long-run equilibrium built into it. Within a non-equilibrium framework of open-ended evolution, Pareto efficiency is undefined.

All forms of macro theory within the spirit of aggregative economics entail a focal point on the Pareto efficiency of resource allocation. Yet to pronounce on Pareto efficiency requires a presumption that a system exists in a state of equilibrium. If economies are thought to be non-equilibrium systems that undergo continuous evolution, a different approach to the examination of systemic qualities must be pursued. It could, of course, be recognized that economic systems do not truly exist in a state of equilibrium, and yet it could also be claimed that the presumption of systemic equilibrium is a sufficiently close approximation that does not lead thought significantly astray.

Possibly so, but this position could be held only as an article of faith and not as a conclusion derived from comparing alternative analytical frameworks. For to reach such a conclusion, it will have been necessary to develop an alternative framework that enables comparison. To get started in facing this challenge, the rest of this chapter will explore some standard formulations of macro theory that have been used to explain failures of systemic coordination within ordinary market processes. The central point of these explorations is to challenge the meaningfulness of macro theories that fail to recognize and incorporate complementarity between micro and macro theories. What appears to represent market failure within macro theories that treat micro and macro as independent and separate constructions are seen not to represent market failure when micro and macro refer to different levels of the same form of economizing action. To the contrary, those macro claims of market failure point to profit opportunities on the micro-level of action, and with exploitation of those opportunities operating to eliminate those profit opportunities along with the alleged market failure. The remaining sections of this chapter will examine some common macro-theoretic formulations that purport to characterize macro-level failure with respect to Pareto efficiency, and explain why these formulations do not show what they purport to show because they are conceptual illusions created by treating micro-level and macro-level theories as independent when instead they are complementary facets of the same societal process.

On DSGE and Maximizing Expected Utility

It will be useful to consider the widespread use of expected utility theory in economics as the primary element of the dominating presence of the orthodox macro model of dynamic stochastic general equilibrium (DSGE). It is easy to object to expected utility theory and DSGE on the grounds of the theory being unrealistic, for it is patently unrealistic to assume that people can list all possible states of the world and assign relative frequencies to those states. Without such assumptions, expected utility cannot be computed. But realism or its absence is not a definitive standard for embracing or rejecting a theory, for all theories entail simplifications from reality, as simple inspection of the value of a road map will show. We create models or maps that we think will allow us to pursue our thought in a useful manner, as Mary Morgan (2012) explains lucidly in her examination of many of the models that economists have developed over the years. The relevant question concerns not realism or its absence, but the usefulness of the theory relative to other possible theories in illuminating the objects we have chosen to examine, recognizing all the while that those objects have also been constructed through prior conceptual articulation.

Without doubt, expected utility does not mimic the mental states that accompany individual action. Equally without doubt, DSGE does not seem to describe the world we experience, though it should perhaps also be noted that this claim is at least modestly problematic once we recognize that no one can truly apprehend the totality of societal experience. The question at issue, though, is not whether those frameworks reflect some notion of reality but whether they are helpful in advancing our theoretical concerns and interests. In posing this question, we must confront that long-standing joke about the economist who was found searching for his lost car key beneath a lamppost. When asked what he was doing on his knees there, the economist told his inquisitor he was looking for his lost key. When asked if he was sure that was where he lost his key, the economist responded that this was certainly not where he lost the key. When further asked why he was looking where he didn't lose the key rather than looking where he did lose it, the economist responded that he had no option because there was no light where he lost the key.

This joke has an uncomfortable ring of truth about it, as it points to a possible disjunction between the models that theorists use and the phenomena they purport to characterize and explain. A model must be tractable if we are to use it, meaning that we must be able to manipulate it and to derive implications from our manipulations. But do our manipulations truly shed insight into our phenomena of interest? Or do we interpret our phenomena of interest as conforming to our ability to manipulate our models? Does the model of maximizing expected utility reflect a formalization of our recognition that we experience ourselves as calculating machines? Or is it that expected utility theory is embraced because its axioms are isomorphic to those of the calculus of constrained optimization, creating ready tractability, so long as issues pertaining to complexity and undecidability are avoided. In this regard, Chaitin et al. (2011) explain that many settings envisioned by models of optimal decision are actually undecidable, due often to the immense calculative complexity of the situation. It is easy to criticize a model on the grounds of its being unrealistic, for all models entail simplification to render them capable of manipulation. By contrast, genuinely informed criticism, which this book claims to advance, must be set forth within the context of some alternative conceptual framework that casts alternative illumination on the subject under examination.

An ancient adage claims that the proof of any pudding lies in the eating. This is surely wise counsel. Among other things, it implies that the value of a model cannot be determined by its internal or logical coherence. That a pudding is made according to its recipe does not make it valuable or good. The proof of the pudding lies in its eating, and this culinary judgment stands outside and above the degree to which the recipe has been followed. Similarly, the appropriate standard for judging economic models cannot be reasonably reduced to tractability and logical consistency, even though those are reasonable values with which to work. Nonetheless, our interest surely resides not in our models per se but in the ability of our models to illuminate phenomena of interest.

The DSGE model and expected utility theory combine to form a robotic model of social systems. This is a model of societies as mechanisms, and fits with common references to economic mechanisms. It is not, however, a model that assimilates to recognition of the emergent creativity that can arise through social interaction, or to recognition that different institutional frameworks can generate differing societal properties. A macro-level theory of this latter type cannot work with DSGE and expected utility, at least in the objective framework required for equilibrium mechanics.

It is possible to work with expected utility in a subjective or personalistic manner, along the lines that Leonard Savage (1954) sets forth. This scheme of thought opens readily into a distinction between micro-level action and macro-level explanation. This is a reasonable thing to do, though it also brings some implications in its analytical train that might not be readily digestible theoretically. A subjective theory of probability is consistent with Vilfredo Pareto's (1935) theory of human action, as Patrick and Wagner (2015) and Candela and Wagner (2016) explains. We can observe what people do but not the underlying motivation that drives their actions. Explaining action through postulating and computing expected utility is one possible approach to explaining action, though this approach flies in the face of any presumption that people operate with limited knowledge and, moreover, that interaction with others is a source of knowledge (Hayek 1937, 1945).

A subjective orientation toward probability starts with an acting individual who seeks more preferred over less preferred states of living but has no capacity to construct a complete listing of options and relative frequencies. Despite this limited capacity, people must choose courses of action, and must do so prior to experiencing the results of their choices. A person's choice among options can be rendered intelligible by an observer through invoking the categories of expected utility theory. Yet the person who makes that choice cannot use that theory as a calculative aid because complexity renders the situation undecidable. Decisions are reached all the same, only not through successful calculation but in response to animal spirits resident in the chooser, though without the consignment of animal spirits to the category of irrationality (Thaler 2015). To the contrary, animal spirits reflect phenomena that emerge through interaction with others, in contrast to the standard presumption of solipsistic individuals that commonly inhabit economic models, along the lines that Vernon Smith and Bart Wilson (2019) examine.

As noted earlier, there are two prime regularities that characterize all forms of economic organization outside of highly traditional societies. One is that societies can be said to work in the sense that people feed themselves, shelter themselves from the elements, and reproduce. In the limit, this characteristic can be captured by such a theory of equilibrium as that represented by DSGE. The other broad regularity is that societies are turbulent, meaning that they entail internally generated sources of change. These changes can be modeled as exogenous shocks to a previously equilibrated system. They can also, and alternatively, be modeled as phenomena associated with contestation among the members of a society for position and prominence within that society, as illustrated by Schumpeter's (1934) treatment of entrepreneurship as the locus of leadership within capitalist societies. To treat this kind of phenomena, however, requires stepping outside the DSGE framework to something like OEE and its focus on social systems that are open-ended and evolutionary as characterized by Devereaux and Wagner (2020a). Again, the proof of any pudding must lie in the eating. In this respect, the Keynesian formulation adduces two classes of market failure, price rigidity and failures of aggregate demand, both of which stand outside the DSGE model, but which can be incorporated into an OEE model, only with claims of market failure verging on vanishing within the OEE model because DSGE presumes for reasons of analytical tractability that history ends while OEE presumes that history continues indefinitely.

Stag Hunts and Game Theoretic
Explanations of Coordination Failure

In recent years, several theorists have advanced the stag hunt as a game theoretic framework for explaining how market processes might be characterized by low-level equilibriums (Bryant 1994; Friedman 1994; Young 1998; Skyrums 2004). The stag hunt represents a coordination game that has a simple structure, as Table 2.1 shows. Where Rousseau's original tale pertained to a tribe of hunters whose members could choose how much energy to devote to hunting animals, the stag hunt game reduces this situation to two players engaged in a cooperative enterprise where each can choose the intensity they devote to the hunt. Each hunter can devote either low or high effort to capturing game. However much effort individual hunters supply, what is caught is consumed in common. If each hunter supplies high effort, they catch a stag which yields each a net return of 2 to each hunter. Should they supply low effort, each of their net returns is 1, to indicate that they must feast on rabbit. Should one supply high effort and the other low effort, both will again eat rabbit; however, the hunter who supplied high effort will secure a net return of zero, to indicate that the marginal disutility of supplying high effort is offset by the value of eating rabbit.

This game framework has two equilibrium outcomes, one where they jointly supply high effort and the other where they supply low effort. Within the framework of this game, either outcome is possible. This framework has also been used to illustrate the possibility of underemployment equilibrium as an instance of coordination failure within a market economy. Consistent with Keynes-inspired analytics, an outside agency, the state, can be injected to assure attainment of the high-level equilibrium. This injection of the state is a classic illustration of conjuring a *deus ex machina* to escape an unpleasant situation. In actuality, there are no

Table 2.1 Stag hunt illustration of systemic coordination failure

	Low effort	High effort
Low effort	1,1	1,0
High effort	0,1	2,2

positions represented by Mt. Olympus from which the macro gods can intervene into society. All actors reside within society while occupying different vantage points within it, as Fig. 1.2 illustrates.

The outcome described as underemployment equilibrium in Table 2.1 is generated within an institutional framework that compels common consumption. Yet we know from anthropological research that even tribes that have common feasts typically have schemes by which some form of ownership is assigned over the game that will be feasted on, even though the feast will be enjoyed in common. Ownership might be assigned to the hunter who first sights the animal. Or it might be assigned to the hunter whose weapon first struck the animal. It might be assigned to the hunter who first arrived at the fallen animal. In any case, the assigned owner becomes the host of the feast. This institutional arrangement stands outside the framework of the stag hunt because it incorporates tribal approbation into the payoffs the hunters face. A supply of low effort is now accompanied by low esteem within the tribe; however, such interaction and its accomplishments are precluded from orthodox analysis based on effectively solipsistic individuals along the lines that Table 2.1 portrays.

Looking ahead briefly to Chapter 6, we might speculate on how we might incorporate a democratic arrangement into the stag hunt. Suppose hunting is done in several teams of five. Further suppose that two of those teams have by far the largest volume of success and, hence, approbation within the tribe. This arrangement would yield a skewed distribution of approbation. Suppose the larger number of relatively unsuccessful teams form a coalition and impose rules of "fair distribution" regarding the hosting of feasts. This might take the form of an automatic rotation of the position of host. In this setting, the game framework represented by Table 2.1 would become descriptively accurate, and the tribe in turn would become less well fed. This alternative situation, however, does not denote some form of macro-level failure independent of patterns of micro interaction because the macro pattern is inseparable from the pattern of micro interaction the dominant coalition was able to impose. Should the negatively affected members of the group succeed in overturning collective consumption, a higher standard of consumption will be attained along with a less equal distribution of esteem within the society.

Synecology as Interaction
with Divided and Limited Knowledge

John von Neumann and Oskar Morgenstern (1944: 8–12) opened their *Theory of Games and Economic Behavior* by contrasting the concept of rational action within a Robinson Crusoe economy with rational action within a social exchange economy. In making and pursuing this distinction between concepts of rational action, von Neumann and Morgenstern were pursuing the distinction Erik Lindahl (1919 [1939]) articulated in distinguishing between action and interaction as entailing different theoretical domains. The point of *Theory of Games* was to take some initial steps in shifting the theoretical focus of economics from a Crusoe economy to a social exchange economy. Neumann and Morgenstern did not intend to banish Robinson Crusoe from the economist's bag of tools. Rather they sought to supplement that bag so as to prepare economists for the numerous instances they thought reduction of a social economy to a Crusoe economy prevented economists from addressing many of the challenges they faced. Morgenstern himself warned theorists that it "is often easier to mathematize a false theory than to confront reality" (Morgenstern 1972: 1169).

While game theory has blossomed over the past generation to include endogenous institutional change, evolutionary pressures on strategy selection, imperfect information, deviations from rational choice theory, preference formation conditional on the preferences of others, and heterogeneous agents playing sequential locally constructive games, it still shows its beginnings as an alternative form of Crusoe-style economic theory, perhaps a result of its stubborn methodological adherence to the conventions of choice theory, only the objects of choice are rules for choosing actions where one person's best option depends on what that player anticipates the other player will do.

While game theory aspires to become a theory of social interaction, as illustrated luminously by Herbert Gintis's (2009) wide-ranging compendium of games, it falls short as social theory in one significant respect, a respect that hearkens back to the foundations of economic theory in the philosophers of the Scottish Enlightenment, as Aydinonat (2008) notes in exploring some of the difficulties economists have had in theorizing about invisible hands and spontaneous orders. While Cachanosky (2010) addresses concerns that spontaneous orders might not be representable within a game theory framework, Devereaux and Wagner (2020b) seek to integrate game theory with notions of spontaneous orders and invisible hands by carrying forward the concept of *synecology* from ecology. Synecology treats communities as arenas of interaction among species, and with ecologists contrasting synecology with *autecology*, which treats individual species as if members are duplicates of one another. To extend this biological image momentarily, macro theory of the DSGE variety proceeds in the image of autecology, whereas macro theory of the OEE variety proceeds within the image of synecology.

With respect to game theory as social theory, human communities are conceptualized not as a universal game played by rules somehow given in advance of play but as an ecology of interconnected games with heterogeneous players who are imaginative and open to experimentation. This shift in analytical orientation makes it possible to integrate principles of limited and divided knowledge into the social-theoretic framework of game theory. Central to this effort is recognition that the knowledge that is brought to bear on social processes exceeds the cognitive capacity of any player in the game. Societies work even though no person knows everything necessary for their working. A synecological orientation toward game theory combines social interaction with the generation and assembly of player-useful knowledge through social interaction. Within this synecological framework, societies are evolving ecologies of games that are not reducible to some representative game because no player participates in all the games that constitute a society. Figure 2.1 transforms the stag hunt game portrayed in Table 2.1 into a synecological game where the society is constituted through three subgames, denoted as hunting, butchering, and retailing. There is no entity in society that possesses all knowledge

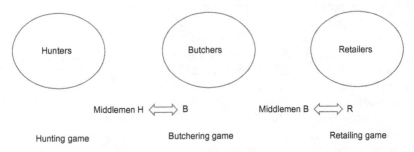

Fig. 2.1   Synecological decomposition of stag hunt with emergent coordination

necessary for coordination. There are three sources of specialized knowledge in this society along with two types of middleman knowledge that form connections among parts of that society.

The stag hunt game that Table 2.1 displays treats society as a universal game where all players understand the rules and the possible actions and probable payoffs. In contrast, the synecological game that Fig. 2.1 displays treats society as an ecology of three distinct but connected games. The hunting game deals with the hunting of deer and hares, the butchering game deals with the processing of game to render game suitable for consumers to process, and the retailing game deals with the placement of consumable game in homes and restaurants. The participants in each game are specialists in the activities associated with those games. There is no specialist whose knowledge encompasses all that is necessary to sustain life. There are specialists, typically known as middlemen, who intermediate between pairs of activities, as illustrated by agents H↔B and B↔R in Fig. 2.1. There is, however, no specialist who knows all that is necessary for the effective organization of social life. It is this distributed and divided quality of knowledge that the synecological orientation seeks to explore, especially for its systemic or macro-level implications.

Those who hunt and those who butcher game are specialists in their activities. The agents denoted as H↔B are middlemen who connect hunters and butchers, and in that capacity know something about each activity but not enough to replace a hunter or a butcher. Likewise, the agents denoted as B↔R are middlemen who connect butchers and retailers. Again, they know something about each activity but not enough to become a butcher or a retailer. Within Fig. 2.1, there is no person or organization that can truly apprehend the entire society, for the society is far too complex for anyone to possess such knowledge.

MACRO THEORIZING: ATOMIC VS. SUB-ATOMIC ANALYSIS

Equilibrium centered theorizing focusses on equilibrated relationships among economizing entities. This is economic theory conveyed in the passive voice, with consumers and firms responding to prices and perceived opportunities. By contrast, an open-ended theoretical scheme points toward the imaginative construction of courses of action. Most significantly, it is not organizations but individuals inside the organizations with which they are associated that are the carriers of imaginative action.

To illustrate this point, suppose we start with the standard articulation of the stag hunt that Table 2.1 presents. The orthodox game theoretic framework theorizes in an atomic or outside-in direction. The game matrix, with its strategic options and associated payoffs, is data to the players. Theoretical analysis concerns the implications of alternative matrices, but those matrices are data in any case. This analytical orientation denotes a type of atomic-level analysis, with a game matrix denoting a holistic entity whose properties remain for the theorist to explore.

An alternative direction of analysis would proceed in an inside-out direction, leading to a sub-atomic scheme of analysis where actions and interactions among participants conveys energy into the social world, similar to Ruth Kastner's (2015) exposition of the transactional interpretation of quantum theory. Within this scheme of thought, it is interaction among participants that generate the habits and conventions that are formalized by a game matrix. This inside-out direction is how lexicographers work in constructing dictionaries and grammars. It also describes the world of private ordering of social activity. In contrast, the outside-in direction reflects the consultation by users of dictionaries and describes the world of public ordering.

Suppose we start with a band of hunters who agree in advance that whatever they catch will be consumed in common. This situation corresponds to the standard expression of the stag hunt game. The inside-out, sub-atomic scheme of analysis asks us to consider the sustainability of some convention, as against simply asserting that it represents a Nash equilibrium. For instance, suppose one of the hunters comes across two hunters sitting in the shade, playing cards, and reports this back to the other hunters who are caked in sweat, laden with scratches from running through bramble, and yet have only a couple of hare for their effort. We might reasonably imagine that some such inside-out process as this would set in motion changes in the organization of hunts and the distribution of catch, and in the direction of injecting some form of private ordering into the institutional arrangement.

For an equilibrium centered theory using the method of comparative statics, the presuppositions of Nash equilibrium and outside-in modeling is effectively the only game in town. The rules of the explanatory game, as it were, are to explain observed outcomes based on the twin presumptions that people maximize given utility functions and that markets clear. This analytical framework, however, cannot accommodate action through time. Any effort, moreover, to accommodate action through time must recognize that people learn things through their actions, as well as through interactions with others. This recognition leads in turn to recognition that some non-equilibrium framework is necessary if economic theory is to give an account of the internal generation of change within societies, regardless of how someone might evaluate that change.

References

Allen, J.F., Henry A. Kautz, Richard N. Pelavin, and Josh D. Tenenberg. 1991. *Reasoning About Plans*. San Mateo, CA: Morgan Kaufman.

Aydinonat, N.E. 2008. *The Invisible Hand in Economics*. London: Routledge.

Bryant, J. 1994. Coordination Theory, the Stag Hunt, and Macroeconomics. In *Problems of Coordination in Economic Activity*, ed. J.W. Friedman, 207–25. Boston: Kluwer Academic.

Buchanan, J.M. 1959. Positive Economics, Welfare Economics, and Political Economy. *Journal of Law and Economics* 2: 124–38.

Buchanan, J.M. 1982. Order Defined in the Process of Its Emergence. *Literature of Liberty* 5: 5.

Cachanosky, N. 2010. Spontaneous Orders and Game Theory: A Comparative Conceptual Analysis. *Revista de Instituciones, Ideas y Mercados* 52: 52–55.

Candela, R., and R.E. Wagner. 2016. Vilfredo Pareto's Theory of Action: An Alternative to Behavioral Economics. *Il Pensiero Economico Italiano* 24: 15–29.

Chaitin, G., F.A. Doria, and N.C.A. de Costa. 2011. *Gödl's Way: Exploration into an Undecidable World*. Boca Raton, FL: CRC Press.

Devereaux, A., and Wagner, R.E. 2020a. Contrasting Visions for Macroeconomic Theory: DSGE and OEE. *American Economist* 65: 28–50.

Devereaux, A., and Wagner, R.E. 2020b. Game Theory as Social Theory: Finding Spontaneous Order. Manuscript, George Mason University, Fairfax, VA.

Dopfer, K., J. Foster, and J. Potts. 2004. Micro-Meso-Macro. *Journal of Evolutionary Economics* 14: 263–79.

Elias, N. 1982 [1939]. *The Civilizing Process*. New York: Pantheon Books.

Emmett, R.N. 2006. De Gustibus est Disputandum: Frank H. Knight's Response to George Stigler and Gary Becker's 'De Gustibus non est Disputandum'. *Journal of Economic Methodology* 13: 97–111.

Friedman, J.W. (ed.). 1994. *Problems of Coordination in Economic Activity*. Boston: Kluwer Academic.

Gintis, H. 2009. *Game Theory Evolving*, 2nd ed. Princeton, NJ: Princeton University Press.

Hayek, F.A. 1937. Economics and Knowledge. *Economica* 4: 33–54.

Hayek, F.A. 1945. The Use of Knowledge in Society. *American Economic Review* 35: 519–30.

Kastner, R.E. 2015. *Understanding our Unseen Reality: Solving Quantum Riddles.* London: Imperial College Press.

Keynes, J.M. 1936. *The General Theory of Employment, Interest, and Money.* New York: Harcourt Brace.

Kydland, F.E., and E.C. Prescott. 1982. Time to Build and Aggregate Fluctuations. *Econometrica* 50: 1345–70.

Lindahl, E. 1919 [1939]. *Studies in the Theory of Capital and Income.* London: Allen & Unwin.

Lovejoy, A. 1936. *The Great Chain of Being.* Cambridge, MA: Harvard University Press.

Morgan, M. 2012. *The World in the Model: How Economists Work and Think.* Cambridge: Cambridge University Press.

Morgenstern, O. 1972. Thirteen Critical Points in Contemporary Economic Theory: An Interpretation. *Journal of Economic Literature* 10: 1163–89.

Ostrom, E. 1990. *Governing the Commons.* Cambridge: Cambridge University Press.

Pareto, V. 1935. *The Mind and Society.* New York: Harcourt Brace.

Patrick, M., and R.E. Wagner. 2015. From Mixed Economy to Entangled Political Economy: A Paretian Social-theoretic Orientation. *Public Choice* 164: 103–16.

Plosser, C.I. 1989. Understanding Real Business Cycles. *Journal of Economic Perspectives* 3: 51–77.

Potts, J., and K. Morrison. 2007. Meso Comes to Markets. *Journal of Economic Behavior and Organization* 63: 307–12.

Pryor, F.L. 2008. System as a Causal Force. *Journal of Economic Behavior and Organization* 67: 545–59.

Resnick, M. 1994. *Turtles, Termites, and Traffic Jams.* Cambridge, MA: MIT Press.

Savage, L.J. 1954. *The Foundations of Statistics.* New York: Wiley.

Schmitt, C. 1932 [1996]. *The Concept of the Political.* Chicago: University of Chicago Press.

Schumpeter, J.A. 1934. *Theory of Economic Development,* 2nd ed. Cambridge, MA: Harvard University Press.

Shackle, G.L.S. 1974. *Keynesian Kaleidics.* Edinburgh: Edinburgh University Press.

Skyrums, B. 2004. *The Stag Hunt and the Evolution of Social Structure.* Cambridge: Cambridge University Press.

Smith, V.L., and B.J. Wilson. 2019. *Humanomics: Moral Sentiments and Wealth of Nations for the Twenty-First Century.* Cambridge: Cambridge University Press.

Thaler, R. 2015. *Misbehaving: The Making of Behavioral Economics*. New York: Norton.

Von Neumann, J., and O. Morgenstern. 1944. *Theory of Games and Economic Behavior*. Princeton, NJ: Princeton University Press.

Wagner, R.E. 2012a. A Macro Economy as an Ecology of Plans. *Journal of Economic Behavior and Organization* 82: 433–44.

Wagner, R.E. 2012b. Viennese Kaleidics: Why It's Liberty more than Policy That Calms Turbulence. *Review of Austrian Economics* 25: 283–97.

Walras, L. 1874 [1954]. *Elements of Pure Economics*. Homewood, IL: Richard D. Irwin.

Weaver, W. 1948. Science and Complexity. *American Scientist* 36: 536–44.

Young, H.P. 1998. *Individual Strategy and Social Order: An Evolutionary Theory of Institutions*. Princeton: Princeton University Press.

CHAPTER 3

Structures of Production and Properties of Social Order

In this book, spending is recognized to be a derivative and not a primitive variable. It is entrepreneurial plans and not spending that is the primitive variable through which economic organization flows. Observed spending is an output of a plan, and changes in patterns of spending reflect changes in the plans of economizing agents. To understand the macro-level properties of an economic system, it is necessary to understand the properties of the ecology of plans out of which economic observations derive. Plans, moreover, largely revolve around the mental images and perceptions people form, along with the institutionally governed relations that people develop as they interact with one another, both as individuals and as participants inside various organizations. This difference in conceptualizations of macroeconomics comes into the analytical foreground in contrasting two visions of a system of economizing action in its entirety: a circular flow on the one hand and a structure of production on the other, as Lewis and Wagner (2017) note briefly in contrasting what they regard as new and old versions of Austrian-style macroeconomics.

For a century or so now, economic theory has centered on the circular flow conception of a social economy. This conception requires that all economic activity be fully synchronized before any activity is actually undertaken. Within this DSGE conception, an economy is analogized to a parade or, equivalently, to a team of synchronized swimmers. In sharp contrast, this book embraces a diachronic vision of the economic process (Shackle 1972, 1974) where economic activity is not coordinated prior to any activity actually taking place. Outside of small tribes, the

© The Author(s) 2020 65
R. E. Wagner, *Macroeconomics as Systems Theory*,
https://doi.org/10.1007/978-3-030-44465-5_3

pre-coordination of economic activity is pure fantasy as conveyed by the image of the Walrasian auctioneer. Sure, auctions exist, many of them, but explicit auctions form but a tiny part of the economic organization of any contemporary society. A small society might conceivably organize its activities through auctions, but this approach to societal organization is impossible for modern societies. Sure, a theorist might treat auctions as a metaphorical form of theorizing through building black boxes. All the same, theoretical progress surely requires continual efforts to replace black boxes with plausible explanations. Any such replacement would recognize that social coordination is a never-ending process of births and deaths among plans continually injected into and withdrawn from society—and with those injections often affecting the performance of the other plans in society.

An economy is conceptualized as a continually evolving structure of production within the OEE motif that Devereaux and Wagner (2020) set forth. The source of evolution resides in the plans that people under-take, and with new plans continually being injected into society just as old plans sometimes are liquidated. Either way, it is plans and not spend-ing that is the prime primitive variable when society is conceptualized as an ecology of plans. Within this ecological conception, the analytical focus is placed on the institutional arrangements that the members of a society generate through their interaction, as these arrangements mostly reflect the unseen reality that are emergent and not chosen objects. In his presentation of the organization of economic theory, Joseph Schumpeter (1954) distinguished between economic theory and economic sociology. In this distinction, Schumpeter hearkened back to Carl Menger (1871) who distinguished between economizing action and institutional emer-gence. Theory is not divided into micro and macro, for it is rather divided between individual action and interaction among individuals, a theoretical movement that treats a theory of a social entirety as economic sociology. This chapter will plumb some of the depths of this alternative theoretical orientation.

THE CIRCULAR FLOW CONCEPTION
OF AN ECONOMIC SYSTEM

The circular flow conception of an economy is contained within Leon Walras's (1874) conceptualization of an economic system as existing in a state of systemic or general equilibrium. Within that conceptualization,

Walras characterized a society as organized through a set of factor markets and product markets. On factor markets people supply labor and capital for which they earn income. On product markets people spend their income on the products that were produced through the factor inputs that people had supplied to the factor market. What people earn is identically equal to what they spend, and this property of Walras's model became the income-expenditure model within the Keynesian framework of macroeconomics. Among other things, this circular flow conception yields four distinct measures of aggregate income, two pertaining to the factor side of the market and two pertaining to the product side. Those four measures are different ways of measuring the same set of transactions: on the factor market there is a measure of the incomes people receive from supplying inputs and there is another measure of the value of output those factors produce; on the product market there is one measure of what people spend in buying products and a second measure of the incomes that producers receive from selling their outputs. The macroeconomy is nicely balanced after the synchronized scheme of double-entry accounting within the circular flow conception.

In contemporary macro theory, the circular flow is conveyed by the reduction of society to an aggregate production function. With that aggregate representation, the economic activity of a society is reduced to some measure of aggregate output denoted as X, and with that output having been generated by employment of two types of input, labor and capital, denoted by L and K, yielding the representation $X = f(L, K)$. To be sure, this representation is purely formal, and most empirical work proceeds by postulating some particular functional relational relationship, with the Cobb–Douglass relationship, $X = L^{\alpha} K^{1-\alpha}$ being a common representation, surely due at least as much to the ease of using this functional relationship as to its empirical veracity and analytical tractability. At this point we must unavoidably face the question of what comprises a good framework for economic analysis. This question has been answered in numerous ways within the history of economics (Morgan 2012), and with no clear consensus having been formed.

To be sure, it is theorists through their patterns of usage who govern what makes for a good theoretical construction. Philosophers of science are prone to listing objective conditions that speak to the qualities of a good theory as it pertains to a system of economic interaction. And yet it is the theorists on the ground, so to speak, who determine what makes one theory superior to another. Moreover, there is no necessary reason to think all theorists would reach the same ranking of the merits of different theories because theories differ in what they highlight and what they neglect. George Shackle's (1974) recognition that a good theory is something that eases a theorist's mind affirms that it is theorists who decide through their practice in constructing theories what makes for good theory. Methodologists, like lexicographers and grammarians, can summarize practical usage, but it is theorists whose actions govern good theoretical practice. To be sure, multiple theories are typically in play at any moment, as Randall Collins (1998) explores lucidly in describing the organization of science as taking its shape through the efforts of scholars to compete for scarce attention space.

Theorists develop different formulations to illuminate their objects of interest. With respect to macro-level theories, the object of interest is the entirety of a society's economic activity. Since no one can truly apprehend that entirety, that entirety must be apprehended through the construction of theoretical representations. The circular flow is the most prominent option currently in play. Like all theoretical conceptions, this option focusses on some theoretically constructed phenomena while necessarily and simultaneously shielding from examination other possible phenomena. This situation is unavoidable, and it points to the competition for attention space that Collins (1998) describes as the process that drives science forward.

The circular flow conception invites the notion of an *output gap* which figures prominently in contemporary macro theories. The circular flow concept construes the aggregate of economic activity as if it was generated according to an aggregate production function. There is no presumption that such an aggregate function has literal existence, but only that it offers a useful way of accounting for the totality of economic output. At this point we come to another of those forks in the theoretical road. For given parameter values for an aggregate production function, a full employment rate of output can be estimated. Any deviation of actual output from the estimated full employment output comprises an output gap, with that gap serving to define an opportunity for political action to close the gap within the standard macro-theoretic framework where politics stands apart from economic organization and acts only in some socially perfecting manner as defined by the relevant theory.

Several things are notable about how this circular flow conception channels economic discourse. Perhaps most significantly, within this formulation there is no point of entry for lines of inquiry that treat output gaps as products of political action to do such things as increasing the costliness of market transactions. To the contrary, the central theoretical presumption is that observed output stems from market interaction pure and simple, which leaves by default any closing of that gap to the domain of political action. The portrayal of a circular flow through an aggregate production function maps readily into a market correction mode of analysis. Markets always perform up to their capabilities, which renders output gaps a reflection of the inability of markets to accommodate all mutually beneficial transactions.

Yet there is no such thing as a society that is fully governed by the principles of private property and freedom of contract. Market ordering and political ordering of economic activity are thoroughly entangled within contemporary systems of political economy (Wagner 2016). Sometimes political ordering might expand the extent of market interaction by protecting market transactions from invasion. But there is also plenty of analysis and evidence showing that political ordering often restricts the reach of market transactions. These possibilities, moreover, are hidden from view within the comparative static presentation of the circular flow and aggregate production function. Also hidden from view is the significance of the different institutional arrangements that might facilitate and protect market transactions, but which are also capable of impeding and preventing such transactions. In other words, the circular flow conception entails a subtext that confers on political entities the task of correcting market failures which manifest in output gaps. There is no good way within this theoretical framework that an output gap may illustrate either the creation of market failure as a by-product of the search for political gain or, and perhaps more significantly, serve as an inherent feature of any progressive society, and with political efforts to close such gaps serving to disrupt more than to facilitate mutually beneficial transactions. To explore these possibilities requires a different scheme of thought, one based on conceiving an economy as a structure of production that emerges and changes through continual interaction among economizing entities within society.

Economic Systems as Evolving Structures of Production

There is nothing wrong or illogical about the circular flow conception of equilibrium within a society of economizing agents. It is, however, but one reduction among a number of possible reductions of a complex social reality to a manageable model. A structure of production is another representation of that complex reality. Any such reduction can be manipulated by a theorist to probe and illuminate questions she or he seeks to examine. But different reductions direct the attention of theorists to different aspects of the entirety of a system of economic interaction.

In his *Theory of Economic Development*, Joseph Schumpeter (1934) illustrated how a structure of production could be reduced to a circular flow by adopting the Walrasian analytical motif. Schumpeter did this by invoking the image of trees that grow to harvestable maturity in 30 years. Imagine a grove of trees organized into 30 plots. Each year a stand of saplings is planted in one plot while the trees in the 30-year plot are harvested. This image illustrates a basic idea of a structure of production where the consumption of lumber today requires a duration of time during which capital is invested in immature trees and in which expenses are incurred in nurturing those trees to maturity. The essence of this process is that trees harvested today are a product of trees planted 30 years ago plus expenses associated with care and maintenance during the intervening years, and with Peter Lewin (1999) setting forth the structure of production model. By assuming that such a society exists in a steady state, however, the structure of production can be reduced to a circular flow where the harvest of trees today is a simple function of the volume of saplings planted today. The passing of time is eliminated through this reduction of a structure of production to a circular flow because the passing of time has been neutered by the presumption that all economic activity is synchronized. Within the structure of production, aggregate output must be represented by something like $X = f(L, K, t)$ where t pertains to the 30 years that separate the planting of saplings and the harvesting of mature trees. Many complexities accompany this formulation, not least of which is the determination and effect of the interest rate, of which several possibilities are in play among theorists. In short, the length of time between planting and harvesting is endogenous to the economic system and is not data that stands outside that system.

These complexities, and many more, can be avoided by assuming the economy exists in a state of equilibrium. This assumption eliminates everything associated with the passing of time, as well as requiring that all economizing action in society be synchronized because the passing of time has no analytical work to do, and with such authors as Currie and Steedman (1990), Vickers (1994), and Katzner (1998) exploring some of the analytical challenges that face any effort seriously to incorporate the passing of time into economic theory. In short, an economy can be described by the instantaneous aggregate function $X = f(L, K)$, and with modern macro growth theory inserting some shift function to convey technical progress. All that remains to do is to estimate parameters of the production function, compute output gaps, and then close that gap through appropriate policy action.

Once we recognize that a complex structure of production can be reduced to a simple circular flow, it is necessary to compare the analytical gain that reduction accomplishes with the analytical loss. The analytical gain is readily apparent in the ease of giving simple answers to questions regarding future economic activity. Those future activities can have a random component, for this is built into the DSGE model. All the same, the only variables of relevance are measures of aggregate activity. Complications that might arise because entrepreneurial insertions at one place within a structure of production can upset economic interactions throughout a structure of production can be ignored by embracing the circular flow model.

But much is lost by embracing this circular flow vision of the economic process. The circular flow vision centers on instantaneous action and reaction. A fall in private spending can be offset by an increase in private spending, and with little gap in time between detection of the fall in private spending and increase in public spending. In sharp contrast, the structure of production shows that the only way consumption can be increased today is by consuming capital that will in turn reduce future consumption as 29-year trees are harvested, leaving less wood to be harvested when the remaining 29-year trees are harvested along the lines that Fritz Machlup (1935) characterized for Austria between 1913 and 1930. Even more, the reduction in spending reflects changes within the ecology of plans. A plan that is liquidated today will rarely be replaced immediately by a new plan. In the interval between liquidating one plan and creating another plan, cash balances might be increased until the new plan is ready for insertion into the ecology of plans. An increase in cash balances does not correspond to common notions of idle balances but instead is a concomitant feature of the time-using character of all economic activity, both liquidating plans and forming new ones.

The structure of production model brings into the analytical foreground the strength of the self-corrective features of an economic system. Figure 1.3 describes a continual process of the birth-and-death of enterprises that is always underway at particular locations within the structure of production. The vision of the structure of production brings analytical attention to what might be called an economy's immune system, which addresses how an economic system responds to the births-and-deaths of enterprises. In contrast, the equilibrium vision of the circular flow is incapable of generating insight into the ability of differently ordered economic systems to repair themselves.

Schumpeter could not see how to incorporate a continual parade of entrepreneurial activity into his theory of development, so worked with a model of punctuated equilibrium where entrepreneurial acts inserted exogenous shocks into the economic process. All the same, it was clear that Schumpeter's intuition saw entrepreneurship as continuous and not sporadic, only the existing tools of thought did not provide a means to enable him to theorize in that manner. During the past half-century or so, however, tools of thought have been developed that render feasible some effort to resuscitate Schumpeter's vision of entrepreneurship as continual and not punctuated. It's doubtful that many macro theorists truly believe the simplicity of this standard theoretical framework where an aggregate production function is disturbed by exogenous shocks, and with there being some position of policymaker to guide the ship of state to close the output gaps that those shocks create within the DSGE model.

The challenge that a structure of production model faces is to explain in an analytically useful manner how such elements that are exogenous to a circular flow as time, expectations, animal spirits, and entrepreneurial plans are elements of ordinary economizing action that are continually entering into and changing the economic system and its structure of production. The analytical challenges are numerous and complex, which is easy to understand because it is far simpler to explain the orderliness of a marching band or parade than it is to explain the orderliness of a crowd of pedestrians along the lines of Norbert Elias's (1939 [1991]) insightful treatment of the individual-society relationship. Throughout our venture in theorizing, we should keep in mind the Janus-headed character of our theoretical conceptions: they focus our attention, yes, but they might focus it inaptly, in which case it is necessary to develop different theoretical conceptions that enable us to focus where we want to look.

INDIVIDUAL PLANS AND STRUCTURES OF PRODUCTION

Treating an individual as an active creator of plans is one of the prime points of entry into analysis of a structure of production. This conception differs sharply from the notion of passive individuals who operate inside

the circular flow. Within the circular flow, individuals are passive economizers who accept their preferences as data and who economize in two
ways. One way is by stepping into the product market to buy products;
the other way is to step into the factor market to earn income. Firms
are viewed as equally passive responders to those wants by organizing
production, and with the owners and managers of those firms receiving
their incomes from this activity. This scheme of thought assumes the prior
existence of the various social configurations with which theorists work:
markets, prices, property, contracts, and the like. By contrast, the order
of theoretical movement within a structure of production focusses on the
generation of structures of production through interactions among individuals who are pursuing plans they have created or chosen. Furthermore,
societies entail corporate existence in the sense that the individuals who
constitute a society are continually changing though births and deaths
which manifest in the continual injection of new plans and removal of old
plans, with the result being that micro-level change is continually in play
within the societal ecology.

Economic theory commonly works with a universal or generic model
of an individual as a bundle of wants and endowments. This model maps
directly onto a circular flow in equilibrium as befits the reduction of a variety of individuals to a representative individual. This reduction, however,
cannot accommodate a structure of production where the individuals who
act inside that structure differ in what they know and believe. Such differences among individuals point to a structure of production where a society is populated by a variegated array of economizing agents who know
different things and hold different desires. Sure, humans as the higher
mammals generally, have some common qualities that give some shape to
what economists describe as preferences. For instance, we all require food,
shelter, companionship, and such things. Yet even in the presence of such
commonality, we differ in many details regarding our likes and aspirations.
These details manifest differently within different types of social order. In
a collectivist order, styles of clothing might be proscribed, whereas in a
liberal order people might be free to choose styles of clothing, a situation
that in turn creates space for people to specialize in producing different
styles of clothing. In many respects, the ideal of a collectivist society is to
transform a pedestrian crowd into a parade.

Another fork in that long analytical road concerns the relation between
social systems and the individuals who inhabit that system. Equilibrium

thinking in this respect works to promote the fiction of an enduring relation between a social system and the personality or mentality of those who inhabit that system. In contrast, emergent or ecological thinking replaces a common individual with variegated individuals and treats the relation between system and individuals as an emergent feature of human interaction. In this latter case, individual choices and actions can be fateful through the ability of such actions to generate systemic changes that in turn can feed back to individual valuations. For instance, a social theory could be based on a presumption that everyone is naturally providential and hard-working. Alternatively, such a theory could be based upon a presumption that those qualities vary among the members of a society and, moreover, that the presence of those qualities can be strengthened or weakened through political programs of one type or another.

In Chapter 2 it was noted that a plan bridges time between its conception and its implementation, and with some further time interval being necessary to gain evidence about the success of the plan. Planning is not intelligible within an equilibrium-centric scheme of thought because there is no place in the theory for actions to bridge time. The closest to bridging time the circular flow can come is the DSGE presumption that present expectations of future system values are accurate on average. This theoretical scheme creates a pretense of intelligibility through invoking a generic or universal model of an individual that reflects abandonment of the distinction between *ex ante* and *ex post* appraisals of planned actions (Hayek 1989).

All plans bridge some interval of time. Often those bridges are of short duration and involve little capital investment, as when someone goes to a store to acquire items for a party to be given two days later. Even this short and simple plan might encounter obstacles that require a revision of the plan. For instance, a recipe might have called for salmon, but the store didn't have salmon, so you had to create a substitute menu on the fly. These kinds of plans are not even of sufficient theoretical interest for economists to theorize about them, though the anthropologist Mary Douglas (1979) has nonetheless sketched a potentially fruitful theoretical path to do exactly that.

There are commercial and industrial bridges that span large intervals of time and entail substantial capital investment. The typical theoretical approach to this situation is to invoke expected utility theory which requires in turn a frequentist approach to probability which analogizes commercial and industrial planning to playing roulette or craps. In this situation, any divergence between an *ex ante* belief or hope and the observed *ex post* outcome is computable from the start. This theoretical scheme forces the theorist to embrace DSGE. To avoid that embrace, the theorist must give scope for the individuals who inhabit the theory to form their own visions of what they are about, recognizing that those visions are only partly informed by observations of past experience pertaining to relative frequencies. After all, the present actor is not looking backward to repeat the past but is looking forward to implementing an imaginative vision regarding perceived future possibilities, along the lines that Ruth Kastner (2015) sets forth in her transactional interpretation of quantum theory. The actor is likely to entertain several possible outcomes in deciding how to set a plan in motion. That decision will likely entail some awareness of similar experiences from the past, but those experiences will not blindly guide the decision after the fashion of expected utility theory whereby an external observer can judge a plan to be either rational or irrational. To the contrary a plan is an expression of the opportunities a generally liberally governed society provides to people who live within its precincts.

Here it is important for clear thinking to distinguish between reason and rationality. Rationality is an ideological formulation that forces a theorist to conform to such strictures as those that inform expected utility theory. To be sure, rationality as ideology does not dictate particular theoretical conclusions. For instance, some DSGE theorists use rationality to claim that experienced reality is invariably Pareto efficient, and with so-called output gaps being but Pareto efficient changes in a rate of aggregate growth. Other theorists combine DSGE with a presumption that reality is but imperfectly competitive, which provides space in those models for political action to improve on experienced market outcomes. The use of rationality as ideology does, however, impose certain theoretical presuppositions on the theorist. For instance, all choice situations must be decidable. To treat all choice situations as being decidable, however, is to elevate rationality to ideological status as distinct from reason as being a human faculty that can be employed rightly or wrongly and with more or less dexterity.

Contrary to the presumption of universal decidability in choice situations, Chaitin, de Costa, and Doria (2011) explain that undecidability is widely present in situations requiring choice, due in large measure to the combinatorial arithmetic of situations requiring agents to make choices. The mere enumeration of possible outcomes of a choice might entail the evaluation of the more than 600 billion ways 13 cards can be selected from a deck of 52 cards. Calculation is costly in that all calculation requires time. If a commercial plan requires combination of 13 elements from among 52 elements and if each such plan requires one day to evaluate, it will take 1.6 billion person-years to compute a plan's expected value. If an entrepreneur hires 1000 people to construct and make those calculations, it will be 1.6 million years before the calculation will be completed. Expected utility theory is an ideological formulation that enables theorists to proceed under the banner of rationality.

In contrast to rationality as ideology, reason is a known human faculty. The products of human reason, however, are not wholly reducible to calculations that can be checked by external observers. Those products can be described or explained to external observers, but those explanations will not entail any complete enumeration or calculation. To the contrary, the explanations will be enshrouded in heuristics, and heuristics invariably entail idiosyncratic qualities and properties. Daniel Dennett (1978) coined the term "consideration generator" to indicate that there must be some mental process that is prior to the application of reason to a problem that requires a decision. It is that prior mental process that puts a person in the position of wanting to form a commercial plan. Uncountable are the number of ways that people can construct their lives within generally liberal societies, and however they construct them they are responsible for their construction. Some mentalities might crave variety and become easily bored; others might crave the warmth of permanent things. In his categorization of human sentimentalities in *Mind and Society*, Vilfredo Pareto (1935) distinguished between two primary forms of sentiment. Both of these forms Pareto denoted as residues, which Pareto regarded as the ultimate sources of human motivation and which varied among people. The two main categories of residue Pareto identified were persistence and combination. These residues referred to different personality types within a society. Persistence speaks to a proclivity toward permanence; combination speaks to a proclivity toward variety and change.

At this point Frank Knight's (1921) analysis of entrepreneurship and profit is relevant. Why are not all enterprises organized in a mutual form where all participants contribute capital to help form the enterprise and then live off the profits the enterprise subsequently returns. Some might object that many people might lack the capital to operate this way. But this is surely not a sufficient answer because such people could always borrow capital or go on their own as proprietors which would also require capital. As for claims that some people might lack capital even to go on their own, it should be noted that everyone begins as a member of a family. How a person might arrive at adulthood with no capital is a significant question to ponder but addressing it is extraneous to this book, though I address it to some extent in Wagner (1989, 2020). The conjunction of Knight and Pareto suggests that people vary in their willingness to take leaps of faith, which is what crossing a commercial bridge requires. In an earlier day when the instruments of navigation were crude, many people would set sail from shore. Only a few of those, however, would be willing to lose sight of shore to explore what might lie beyond shore. Those people would be among the builders of long and expensive bridges, desiring to initiate the journey without any way of guaranteeing either a return or a safe landing somewhere else. To induce others to participate in their entrepreneurial visions, they would have to pay people for their services prior to the success of the enterprise being determined. The entrepreneur pays wages based on his or her anticipation of hope regarding the success of the enterprise. Entrepreneurship is thus not an ordinary factor of production but is a human propensity of variable intensity among people and which is an internally generated source of change within societies.

Plans as Primitive, Spending as Derivative

The circular flow conception of an economic system reduces readily to flows of spending inside that system. What businesses spend to hire inputs to produce their products will translate immediately into spending by consumers on those products. Some of those consumers, moreover, might save some of their income to provide a capital fund to support investment in future activities. This analytical scheme accompanies the DSGE framework, with the circular flow being cut from the same analytical cloth as DSGE.

The structure of production presents an entirely different orientation toward the social organization of economic activity. This alternative orientation does not deny that the circular flow has some merit in its reductive presentation, but it rather recognizes that starting from a circular flow makes it impossible to arrive at the structure of production. By way of analogy, the two primitive algebraic functions $Y = X^2 + 10$ and $Y = X^2 + 100$ have the same first derivative $Y' = 2X$. Starting from the derivative $Y' = 2X$, it is impossible to reconstruct the primitive functions that generated the derivatives. To complete the analogy, starting with the equilibrated reduction of a society to a circular flow makes it impossible to construct the ecology of plans that generated that flow of spending.

Without an ability to construct that ecology, it is impossible to know what conclusions to reach about particular outcomes that emerge from the ecology. Suppose measured aggregate spending declines from one point of observation to the next. What, if anything, can be reasonably concluded about this observation? Within one form of DSGE model, this observation would correspond to an output gap. In contrast, another form of DSGE model would assert that there has been some shift in preferences or technology that has reduced potential output instead of signifying an output gap. In either case, what exists are dueling assertions, comparable to one assertion claiming that the observation $Y = 2X$ was generated by the function $Y = X^2 + 100$ while the other assertion was that $Y = 2X$ was generated by the primitive process $Y = X^2 + 800$. Absent an examination of the operation of the ecology of plans that generated the derivative observations, there is no option but to engage in duels regarding the making of arbitrary assumptions regarding phenomena the DSGE reduction is incapable of making.

In the following two sections, I shall amplify this point by exploring two common approaches to explaining what the DSGE model characterizes as output gaps, starting from the observation that aggregate output has declined between two points in time. observation. Within the DSGE framework, we face alternative explanations of some measured output gap. One line of explanation claims the gap reflects a failure of market clearing. An alternative line rejects any claim of market failure and holds instead that there is continual variation in an economy's underlying rate of growth. Yet neither form of DSGE provides a basis internal to the theory for choosing between those explanations because they provide no intelligible basis for understanding the genesis of the observations. Within a continually evolving ecology of plans, for instance, the ongoing birth-and-death of plans within the ecology will surely generate some expectation of variability or volatility as an ordinary feature of life inside an ecology of plans. Within the OEE modeling framework, continual variability within the coordinative quality of economic activity would be properties of the continual acquisition and use of knowledge. An entrepreneurial plan formed at some instant must reflect some belief or presupposition about future demands for the firm's product and about the future availability of inputs. Those presuppositions may prove to be erroneous, leading the firm to scale back its plans and even to liquidate.

This pulling back would ramify throughout the ecology of plans. To be sure, this death process will also be accompanied by births, but there is no good reason to presume that at the level of individual action these births-and-deaths offset one another at each time interval.

Instead, inputs that experience a decrease in demand may differ from those that experience an increase, due to the formation of new enterprises. It is possible to stipulate a setting where all prices are continuously variable, which leads to all markets continuously clearing, but to move in this direction is to theorize by stipulating answers to questions rather than explaining how changing knowledge and plans work their way through the ecology of plans. In other words, macro-level properties cannot legitimately be stipulated in advance of the human action and interaction that takes place within the ecology of plans that comprises a society. We start with the reasonable presumption that every entity in society seeks to do the best for itself that it can. To be sure, this presumption is purely formal and human action is always substantive. At the level of pure form, combinatorial arithmetic loses its bite and all questions appear to have exact answers mirrored by the mating of an objective function with a constraint. This is a world that appears to be readily amenable to systemic planning and guidance. This appearance, however, is a product of the stipulative character of a theoretical model and is not an implication of an analysis of the working properties of an ecology of plans.

The next two sections shall illustrate this contrast between addressing a stipulated model and exploring the inner workings of an ecology of plans where macro-level properties emerge through interaction among participants within the ecology. After doing this, the final section in the chapter will explore briefly some macro-like issues and questions that arise when social organization emerges not wholly through private ordering as guided by the institutional arrangements of private property and freedom of contract but is rather governed through some admixture of private and public ordering.

ILLUSTRATIVE MACRO PROBLEMATIC #1: MARKET FAILURE WITH PRICE RIGIDITY

Prior to the marginal revolution that began in economics in 1871, economists mostly regarded competition as a facet of human nature, as captured by simple recognition that generally having more of something that someone values is better than having less of that thing. This setting combined with scarcity created competition and struggle as conditions of life. With initiation of the marginal revolution through publication of Menger (1871) and Jevons (1871), along with Walras's (1874) statement of an economic system in general equilibrium, economists began to develop a more refined notion of competition. One facet of this refinement reached back to Cournot's (1837) effort to describe a systematic relationship between the number of sellers of an identical product and the price of that product. What emerged through the subsequent efforts of theorists was a statement of sufficient conditions for an economy to be in a state of perfect competition, which meant that it would be impossible for any resource reallocation to improve one person's situation without degrading at least one other person's situation, and with George Stigler (1957) surveying this piece of intellectual history.

One notable feature of this search for sufficient conditions for an economic system to be described as perfectly competitive was its implausibility, which suggested in turn that economic systems were almost invariably imperfectly competitive. In ordinary linguistic usage, a condition of imperfection is inferior to a condition of perfection. Economists, however, did not use their terms in this manner. Perfect competition was an absolute standard that was developed through demonstrative reasoning that pertained to a model where sellers universally were price takers, input suppliers universally received the values of their marginal products, and the total amount paid to input suppliers exactly equaled the value of aggregate output. The theory of perfect competition was thus a whiteboard exercise in demonstrative reasoning wherein it could be demonstrated that there would be no resource reallocation that could make one person better off without simultaneously making at least one other person worse off.

To state a theory of perfect competition in this manner is to invite acknowledgment that the world of experience must be imperfectly competitive. By linguistic convention, an imperfect state is inferior to a perfect state, though not by the conventions of economic theory. This problem arises in any effort to compare some ideal-type theoretical construction with some real world of practice and experience, as Frank Knight (1921) explained in his effort to bridge the gap between the demonstrable reasoning with which the theory of perfect competition was expressed and the plausible reasoning that must come into play in any effort to compare some record of experience with some idealized image of what might have been, and with George Polya (1954) setting forth a lucid contrast between demonstrable and plausible reasoning.

The theory of perfect competition entailed a presupposition that all market prices were fully flexible. This full flexibility was part of the Walrasian image of an auctioneer who continually revised price offers until all market cleared. While this conceptual proposition was necessary to demonstrate a set of conditions under which all markets must clear regardless of the states of demand in different markets, there is no sense at all that the world of experienced reality could possibly operate in this fashion. Hence, the world of experience must be but imperfectly competitive. This imperfect character of all market interaction is generally characterized as price rigidity. Once it is recognized that markets are networks of contractual relationships and that most contracts extend over some interval of time rather than being discharged on the spot, we are faced with comparing a model that posits an unattainable state of existence with an alternative and realized state of existence. A significant problem that arises in this respect is that the theory of economic equilibrium stands outside of time along with anything associated with the passing of time. Competition among people in searching for mutual gain through forming contractual relationships, moreover, will entail the establishment of prices that are rigid for some interval if for no other reason than for making calculations pertaining to the successfulness of plans. Instantaneous action is a convenient analytical fiction that allows reduction of actions to the differential calculus, but the experience of life and the evaluation of plans requires the accumulation of data which can only be done in a discrete manner.

The scheme of macro theory advanced in this book starts with plans, and with spending following in the trail of plans. The negative significance of price rigidity is surely exaggerated by economists, and in several respects. Absolute price rigidity for some considerable length of time would obviously impair the continual changes that accompany market economies. Since those changes do take place, however, it is also clear that price rigidity does not impede the insertion of change into economies. All that is necessary is that there exist at any moment some range of price flexibility, and not that all prices be flexible.

Further, the very idea of plans and the formation of contracts to execute plans requires rigidity over some interval of time. A plan entails combining inputs to produce some product or service that will be sold at some later time. Whether a plan is potentially worthwhile depends on projecting the expenses entailed in organizing production and the revenues anticipated to result from sale of the product. Those projects are based on numerous projections regarding such things as the terms on which people can be hired, the prices at which complementary inputs can be obtained, and the prices that people will pay for what is produced. Furthermore, the degree to which a plan performs as projected is knowledge that requires the passing of some interval of time even to acquire, possibly an extensive interval in the case of large construction-type or research-type projects. With a macro economy being an ecology of plans, most plans will be underway and subject to but marginal changes at any instant. To impose an abstract notion of an absence of price flexibility as denoting market failure, or at least as pointing toward its possibility, is to engage in "shadow boxing with reality" (Samuelson (1947 [1965]: ix).

Claims on behalf of efficiency wages are cousins to claims on behalf of price rigidity. These claims likewise seek to explain how commercial practice grounded in private ordering will create price rigidity and fail to achieve full social coordination of economic activity. According to the standard theory of perfect competition, all resource owners receive the values of the marginal products their activity generates. To be sure, there is no way this claim can be tested because values of marginal products are not directly appraisable. The theory of perfect competition holds that businesses will hire inputs so long as the price of those inputs is less than their cost. As a condition of competitive equilibrium, moreover, the aggregate of the payments that inputs receive must equal the aggregate output that is produced.

Within the framework of this theory, moreover, there is free competition to hire inputs, which means in turn that resource owners face multiple bidders to hire their services. An owner to chooses to supply service to one bidder could, alternatively, have supplied that service to another bidder. With respect to labor inputs, for instance, those inputs can choose among employers, and will select the one for which the value of their marginal product is highest, as judged by wage offers. Within the theory of competitive equilibrium where there exists a multiplicity of identical firms, we may reasonably suppose that these marginal products or wage offers are similar if not identical among firms. To the extent this is so, firms will be interchangeable from the perspective of workers, and workers will be approximately indifferent among firms. We can conceptualize an equilibrium allocation of workers to firms that equalizes marginal products across firms and maximizes aggregate output.

The theory of efficiency wages injects a consideration that stands outside the framework of competitive equilibrium by inquiring into the cost to firms of having to replace workers who choose to change jobs. Within the theory of competitive equilibrium, workers have no reason to change jobs, for the theory is in no way concerned with the process by which workers and employers become matched. Still, if we allow such inquiry, it is easy enough to see that an employer would rather maintain an existing worker than to replace that worker when, by implication of the theory of competitive equilibrium, all workers within the relevant set have identical marginal products.

Labor turnover raises the cost to the firm of maintaining a labor force of given size. Firms that face greater turnover will thus lose competitive advantage to firms that operate with lower turnover. The claim on behalf of efficiency wages takes this reasonable notion and deduces from it a proposition that a competitively organized economy will exist in a state of underemployment equilibrium because those firms will pay wage premiums above marginal products. Within labor markets of this type, workers will receive higher wages and aggregate employment will be less than the perfectly competitive level. Each firm seeking to maximize its net worth within an openly competitive labor market will generate a volume of employment that entails involuntary unemployment, and aggregate output will be less than potential output. An economy governed by private ordering will systematically entail involuntary unemployment, in contrast to the theory of competitive equilibrium. To remedy this situation requires political action within this scheme of thought.

The efficiency wage notion surely illustrates the ability of a suitably constructed model to explain nearly any imagined observation. After all, there is an indefinitely large number of functions that will fit any set of observations. Why would a theorist stop when a model has generated involuntary unemployment? This is surely an inadequate and incomplete way to end an economic theory. After all, all individuals are economizing agents who seek to do the best they can within the circumstances they face. An equilibrium with involuntary unemployment violates the presumption of economizing agents. We must ask what it is that such unemployed inputs would do when faced with their circumstances.

The efficiency wage claim precludes those unemployed inputs from securing employment by offering to work for less than what other workers receive because such workers would be less reliable and less productive within the framework of the efficiency wage notion. What might such unemployed inputs do? There would seem to be two prime options. One option would be to accept state payments for being unemployed.

We might wonder why a state would do this, and yet we can observe that states do this. This situation means, in turn, that employed workers are paying taxes to finance unemployed workers. The efficiency wage premium is a mirage that results from a failure to consider the full ramifications of the efficiency wage model. Stated alternatively, involuntary unemployment is a mirage because being unemployed does not mean going without income, but rather means receiving income from a different source.

The other option would entail exploring what such unemployed labor would do with their time if they were to forego unemployment compensation. Being economizing agents, we may presume that they won't choose to starve, but rather will undertake other activities to enable them to support themselves. One class of activities entails forming proprietary enterprises, or partnerships or other small-scale enterprises. If there is anything of analytical value to the efficiency wage notion, it is recognition that the theory is not a theory of involuntary unemployment. If it is anything, it is a theory of the size distribution of business firms. It is a theory that holds that as firms grow larger they experience a growing set of bureaucratic-like problems related to shirking which firms seek to counter by creating such relatively complex instruments as performance bonds that are forfeited upon termination.

The theory of competitive equilibrium is a model where prices are governed by the given data regarding consumer utilities and production techniques, as is the distribution of inputs among activities. This theory is not a theory of price or of pricing in any active-voice sense. It is not a theory where price is an object of choice that is part of an adventure into the construction of enterprises as going concerns. To the contrary, price is passive, as is the entire theory of competitive equilibrium. That theory is a passive voice construction that asserts what must be the case for a competitive equilibrium to exist. It does not truly generate insight into the activities that people undertake that in turn might lead toward such a macro configuration.

ILLUSTRATIVE MACRO PROBLEMATIC #2: AGGREGATE DEMAND DEFICIENCY

For Keynes (1936), it was deficiencies of aggregate demand and not price rigidities that were the prime source of market failure. Moreover, deficiencies in aggregate demand are not *ipso facto* correctible through price flexibility. Neither are they correctible through fiscal policy because changes in government borrowing exert no effect on aggregate net worth (Barro 1974). The genuine novelty of the Keynesian tradition resides in the rejection of generalized market clearing due to deficiencies of aggregate demand. At this point, the Keynesian theoretic blends into other process-oriented economic theories.

Within the classical scheme of thought, Say's law is a denial of any failure of effective demand. In the aggregate, a supply of commodities is simultaneously a demand for commodities. There is no disagreement among economists that Say's law holds within a barter economy because each transaction is simultaneously a demand and a supply. It is different within a monetary economy, where a demand to hold money is not a supply of anything (Clower 1977). An increased demand to hold money today might represent an increased demand for commodities tomorrow or, alternatively, an increased demand for labor tomorrow when an enterprise plan is put into operation. It is possible to posit conditions of intertemporal equilibrium where Say's law holds, but doing this is to replace an explanation of how coordination arises with an assertion that it does. Money is a form of loose joint within an analytical system of competitive equilibrium. In a barter system, all joints are connected tightly because an expressed demand for something is simultaneously an expressed supply of something else.

The presence of money and the loose joint it injects into an economic system makes possible the presence of some deficiency of effective demand. This possibility does not, however, imply that moving public ordering into the institutional foreground is necessary to secure a well-coordinated economy. Much depends on the operation of different institutional arrangements. Various analytical exercises can be performed to convey some of the issues and questions that are in play. One significant formulation in this analytical vein is Robert Clower's (1965, 1967) articulation of a dual-decision structure with respect to market analysis.

Starting from a position of systemic equilibrium, a general increase in the demand for money to hold would be accompanied by a fall in prices to maintain the equilibrium position, within the framework of equilibrium theory. This classical comparative static analysis, however, does not map directly onto any temporal process that would accompany movement from the initial state to the subsequent state. The standard analysis posits a type of black-box assertion which simply claims that a new equilibrium will eventually be attained subsequent to the increase in the demand of people to hold money balances. Clower examines the process by which this might happen, and attributes to Keynes (1936) this insight, though Yeager (1973) argues that this insight really belonged to Clower and Leijonhufvud (1975).

To whomever the insight might truly belong, it entails an effort to incorporate a temporal sequence into economic theory. Initially, there is an increase in the demand for money balances, which requires that people reduce their planned spending. Say's law asserts that this increased desire to hold money is consistent with equilibrium in the presence of lower prices. Clower, however, asks us to explore how an economy might move from its initial state to its new equilibrium. At issue here is the speed at which economic processes operate. Consumers reduce their spending to increase their money balances. What happens next? And how soon? Inventories accumulate, leading to workers being laid off. Personal incomes thus fall. Cutting prices in response to reduced demand might promote market clearing in the presence of unchanged consumer incomes, but those incomes have fallen by virtue of people being laid off.

Without doubt, Clower made an analytically progressive move by trying to incorporate the passing of real time into economic processes, though he did so with an eye to setting forth an alternative to the hydraulic version of Keynes represented by the IS–LM and income–expenditure frameworks. Clower sought to assert an analytical scheme of disequilibrium dynamics (Barro and Grossman 1971) which was subsequently abandoned because it proved incapable of generating substantive implications. The problem with this scheme of thought, in my judgment, is that it was articulated expressly as a *disequilibrium* theory. In contrast, this book is predicated on the usefulness of theorizing in a *nonequilibrium* manner. A nonequilibrium theory entails different analytical elements and structure than does a disequilibrium theory that must draw its bearings from a presumed state of systemic equilibrium, as Wagner (2012) explains in his presentation of Viennese kaleidics.

Looking ahead momentarily to Chapter 8, suppose a significant number of entities inside the ecology of plans decrease their current spending, perhaps as part of a process of liquidating failing businesses in preparation to creating new ones. This process of liquidation and redeployment of capital takes time to organize, leading to a decrease in spending and a building up of money balances. Within the income–expenditure framework, this situation could create an output gap, provided only that effort devoted to forming new commercial plans do not make the claims on material inputs that productive activity makes. A program of fiscal expansion might well increase measured aggregate demand, but that increase in aggregate demand does not duplicate the increases in demand that will be forthcoming when the new commercial plans are later put into action.

PUBLIC PROPERTY WITHIN ECONOMIC SYSTEMS

The archeological and anthropological evidence seems pretty strong that humanity originated in groups, and with the development of individual identity being an extraction from that tribal point of departure, as Henry Maine (1861) explains. To be sure, tribal groupings were small, with size not getting much above 100 before splits occurred (Schmookler 1984). It does not strain a theorist's imagination to conceptualize in some detail how a tribe could operate without private property and market-based relationships, save for tribe-to-tribe exchange. For large societies, however, truly collectivist planning is impossible. This situation doesn't mean that all large societies will be free-market societies. The Soviet Union was far from a free-market society. While it had instances of market exchange, those exchanges were terribly distorted in comparison to genuinely free exchange (Roberts 1971; Boettke 2001). For the most part, macro theory proceeds as though economies are privately ordered, with public ordering coming into play only to correct market failures. This claim about market correction through public ordering, however, is a product of theoretical stipulation and not explanation, as the latter part of this book shall examine. At this point, however, the deep presence of public ordering throughout modern economies warrants some preliminary examination of how public ordering might be incorporated into a theory of the economic organization of society when societal governance proceeds through some admixture of private and public ordering.

Economic theory gives us some reasonable though still incomplete idea about how knowledge gets transmitted and used within market-governed societies. When we come to politically governed societies, however, we come to a theoretical impasse. What we have in this case is an explanation of how coordination will break down as population grows. Even though the earliest societies may have been communal, the complexity of modern societies requires that much social organization be secured through the use of alienable property to form market-based relationships. For this reason, I set forth a model whose inspiration comes from Maffeo Pantaleoni (1911). Pantaleoni conceptualized societies as operating with two pricing systems, one was a system of market pricing and the other was a system of political pricing. In keeping with the model of competitive equilibrium that was in play when he wrote, Pantaleoni assumed that market prices were equal to marginal cost. Political prices, however, depended on the type of tax that generated political revenue. Pantaleoni assumed that political revenue was derived from a flat tax on all income. Hence, political prices rose directly with income. Pantaleoni also imagined a society as containing two bazaars, one a market bazaar and the other a political bazaar. Obviously, the political bazaar could not attract high-income buyers who could buy more cheaply from the shops in the market bazaar, and so would have to compel patronage. What is particularly noteworthy about Pantaleoni's formulation, at least with respect to the use of knowledge in political economy, is the parasitical character of the system of political pricing. Market enterprises generate their revenues directly from customers. Political enterprises don't and can't. Instead, they derive their revenue by making parasitical attachments to market transactions. Without market transactions, there would be no political revenue.

Figure 3.1 illustrates in a very abstract manner the commercial location of enterprises within a market system based on wholly private ordering along the lines of Edward Stringham's (2015) examination of the power

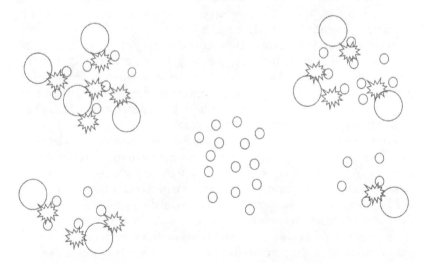

Fig. 3.1   Economic calculation and location of political enterprises

of private ordering to secure economic order, as adumbrated by Wagner (2018). Each circle denotes a firm, and the five distinct clusters of firms are meant to denote distinct industrial groupings. The industrial groupings differ in the number of firms as well as in the size distribution of firms. While this illustration contains only large and small firms, some process for generating firm sizes could be deployed. Figure 3.1 also contains several ragged-looking objects located beside some of the firms, and their significance shall be discussed momentarily.

The largest number of firms is in the center of the commercial space, where 14 small firms reside. The largest concentration of large firms is in the northwestern part of the diagram, where four of the 11 firms are large firms. At the northeastern part of Fig. 3.1, three of the 12 firms are large firms. At the southwest, two of the seven firms are large firms. While in the southeast, there is one large firm among the six firms. While there is much work remaining to be done in converting Hayek's intuitions into a generative explanation of the creation and transmission of knowledge and the resulting social order, at this point I will simply assert that some such process is at work, for it must be even if not much work has truly been done on how the fingers of the invisible hand do their work (Clower 1994).

Suppose we liken the distribution of firms over commercial space to the distribution of prospectors among potential sites. Just as prospectors will clump in some areas and avoid other areas, it is the same with the location of businesses. This location pattern shown in Fig. 3.1 is a summary snapshot at some instant of the commercially relevant knowledge that has been generated through market interaction. The center of Fig. 3.1 can support many firms, but the terrain is not capable of supporting large firms. In contrast, the terrain in the northwest supports four large firms. If we treat a large firm as equivalent to four small firms, the northwest supports the equivalent of 23 small firms. By similar construction, the southwest supports the equivalent of 13 small firms, the northeast supports the equivalent of 21 small firms, and the southeast supports the equivalent of 9 small firms.

Using Fig. 3.1 as an analytical point of departure to characterize the use of knowledge within a framework of wholly private ordering, and with the ragged objects momentarily suppressed, we can consider how public ordering might be introduced into a system based on private ordering. Figure 3.1 provides information about the pattern of human concerns, and with political enterprises adapting to the same general set of concerns as market-based enterprises. More particularly, market enterprises uncover knowledge about patterns of human concern, with political enterprises responding by inserting political programs and agencies into the same territory. The political enterprises are portrayed as porcupine-like to indicate they derive their revenue from attaching to market enterprises rather than generating revenue by selling services directly to customers. In this respect, firms located in the northwest and the northeast are particularly strongly implicated in dealing with matters of great human concern and interest. These are the activities that would attract attention in national newscasts, whereas goings on in the center or the southeast would attract less attention.

Market processes elicit valuation through the trial-and-error process of commercial competition. Can this knowledge about valuation be of any use to political enterprises seeking places to situate their programs? Much of the territory in Fig. 3.1 is vacant. Possibly this situation might be thought to exist simply because no one has yet explored that territory for its commercial prospects. This is possibly so, but it is surely more likely that vacancies exist because earlier explorations failed to yield commercial value. This line of consideration suggests that political enterprises and their programs will locate adjacent to successful commercial enterprises. With respect to spatial models of candidate location and political competition, candidates, programs, and other political entities will locate in the commercial vicinity of successful commercial firms. Commercial firms thus identify locations that are of most significant human interest and concern, after which political enterprises enter the territory looking for margins along which they can develop clientele and extract support.

This model of political location and the use of knowledge in political activity is doubly parasitical. First, there is the parasitical relationship that Pantaleoni (1911) set forth, where political enterprises attach their operations to market transactions. Second, the services that political enterprises supply and the activities they undertake likewise will largely be parasitical reflections of market interaction. Market entrepreneurs will identify the concerns and interests people have and will figure out how to commercialize those concerns and interests. It should perhaps be clarified that Pantaleoni used parasitical in the technical sense of an organism that is unable to support itself and rather requires a host for its support. The theory of public goods, for instance, holds that parasitical relationships have significant work to do in holding societies together.

Parasitical relationships can be mutually beneficial, but they can also be destructive. Much probably depends on relative numbers. A robust host can support a good number of parasites. As the parasites thrive and multiply, the host may eventually weaken and possibly even die, in which case the parasite too will die.

Suppose we now imagine the injection of several political enterprises into the enterprise map that Fig. 3.1 portrays. As will be explained more fully in Chapter 6, it is surely plausible to think political enterprises would locate their activities roughly in proportion to the density of private enterprises. In the center of Fig. 3.1, there are few market enterprises and their sizes are small. This situation is unlikely to attract strong interest from political enterprises. In contrast, the northwest of Fig. 3.1 contains numerous market enterprises, many of them large. It is surely reasonable to think that this situation will prove strongly attractive for the establishment of political enterprises. Political enterprises must do something. What they do, moreover, reflects concerns and interests present among some of the participants in those industries. Decisions regarding commercial location serve to order types of activity by their value to people, and political location acts parasitically to locate in the territories that commercial location have judged to be of relatively high value.

An appreciation of market interaction and the resulting spontaneous generation of social configurations that provide social benefits without being deliberately produced has surely been the primary contribution of social theorizing to human wellbeing. Jane Jacobs (1992) recognized that well-working societies required some reasonable mixture of commercial and guardian activities. She also recognized that excessive commingling between those categories of activity could have socially troubling consequences, what she described as "monstrous moral hybrids." Somewhat similarly, the classical Greek theorists recognized that democracy was a difficult form of government to maintain because of its strong tendency to erode the sense of personal responsibility that is bound up with the principle of private property and residual claimancy.

Vilfredo Pareto (1935) drew a sharp distinction between logical and non-logical action, and his distinction has much to offer regarding the assembly of knowledge in political contexts. At base, it would seem as though distributed knowledge would work in obverse fashion as between political and market settings, much as Pareto recognized. Market relationships are governed by private property and residual claimancy, and this is summarized by Pareto's use of what he described as the logico-experimental method. By this, Pareto meant that someone entering a market transaction is in the position of a conductor of a scientific experiment. A hypothesis is formed about the value of some object, money is paid, and then satisfaction with the choice is judged. In contrast, the logico-experimental method doesn't apply to politics. Without private property and residual claimancy, choice evaporates and is replaced by expressions of sentiment. Political competition, in turn, is propelled by efforts at ideological articulation that resonate more strongly with a selectorate than do other articulations.

It is still reasonable to speak of the use of knowledge within political processes. That use, however, is not at the level of electoral competition and selection. It resides rather at the level of actual, ongoing political activity, such as that illustrated by Fig. 3.1. That Figure asks the reader to imagine various kinds of negotiations among some of the political and economic entities within each of those enterprises. For instance, a failing corporation that fails to modify its products in ways desired by a neighboring political enterprise may well be allowed to fail, and perhaps with the political enterprise participating in reorganizing the corporation. Should that corporation provide the changes in its product line desired by officials of the political enterprise, the existing management might stay in place. In this and in numerous similar forms of relationship, knowledge is incorporated into political-economic interaction. That knowledge, however, is not the abstract knowledge about generic production and utility functions. To the contrary, that knowledge has a complex combinatorial quality wherein enterprises create myriad classes and categories of products, consumers, and workers, and engage in rent transfers among those myriad combinatorial margins that are too numerous to count, and so which disappear into the background, dwarfed by the electoral competition that is readily visible and yet of generally modest consequence.

In this regard, much of significance resides in the manner connections are established among enterprises. Some connections are established in a voluntary manner, as illustrated by ordinary commercial relationships. Other connections are established through some combination of duress and force. These are the connections of triadic exchange (Podemska-Mikluch and Wagner 2013) where an exchange is beneficial to a subset of participants, and with that beneficial quality made possible by virtue of other people being drafted into the exchange through taxation and regulation.

REFERENCES

Barro, J.J. 1974. Are Government Bonds Net Wealth? *Journal of Political Economy* 82: 1095–17.

Barro, R.J., and H.I. Grossman. 1971. A General Disequilibrium Model of Income and Employment. *American Economic Review* 61: 82–93.

Boettke, P.J. 2001. *Calculation and Coordination*. London: Routledge.

Chaitin, G., F.A. Doria, and N.C.A. de Costa. 2011. *Gödl's Way: Exploration into an Undecidable World*. Boca Raton, FL: CRC Press.

Clower, R. 1965. The Keynesian Counter-Revolution: A Theoretical Appraisal. In *The Theory of Interest Rates*, eds. F.H. Hahn and F. Brechling, 103–25. London: Macmillan.

Clower, R. 1967. A Reconsideration of the Microfoundations of Monetary Theory. *Economic Journal* 6: 1–8.

Clower, R. 1977. The Anatomy of Monetary Theory. *American Economic Review* 67: 206–12.

Clower, R., and A. Leijonhufvud. 1975. The Coordination of Economic Activities: A Keynesian Perspective. *American Economic Review* 65: 182–88.

Clower, R.W. 1994. The Fingers of the Invisible Hand. *Brock University Review* 3: 3–13.

Collins, R. 1998. *The Sociology of Philosophies: A Global Theory of Intellectual Change*. Cambridge, MA: Harvard University Press.

Cournot, A.A. 1837 [1995]. *Mathematical Principles of the Theory of Wealth*. San Diego, CA: James & Gordon.

Currie, M., and I. Steedman. 1990. *Wrestling with Time*. Ann Arbor: University of Michigan Press.

Dennett, D.C. 1978. *Brainstorms: Philosophical Essays on Mind and Psychology*. Cambridge, MA: MIT Press.

Devereaux, A., and R.E. Wagner. 2020. Contrasting Visions for Macroeconomic Theory: DSGE and OEE. *American Economist* 65: 28–50.

Douglas, M. 1979. *The World of Goods*. New York: Basic Books.

Elias, N. 1939 [1991]. *The Society of Individuals*. Oxford: Basil Blackwell.

Hayek, F.A. 1989. The Pretense of Knowledge. *American Economic Review* 79: 3–7.

Jacobs, J. 1992. *Systems of Survival*. New York: Random House.

Jevons, W.S. 1871. *The Theory of Political Economy*. London: Macmillan.

Kastner, Ruth E. 2015. *Understanding Our Unseen Reality: Solving Quantum Riddles*. London: Imperial College Press.

Katzner, D. 1998. *Time, Ignorance, and Uncertainty in Economic Models*. Ann Arbor: University of Michigan Press.

Keynes, J.M. 1936. *The General Theory of Employment, Interest, and Money*. New York: Harcourt, Brace.

Knight, F.H. 1921. *Risk, Uncertainty, and Profit*. Boston: Houghton-Mifflin.

Lewin, P. 1999. *Capital in Disequilibrium.* London: Routledge.

Lewis, P.A., and R.E. Wagner. 2017. New Austrian Macro Theory: A Call for Inquiry. *Review of Austrian Economics* 30: 1–18.

Machlup, F. 1935. The Consumption of Capital in Austria. *Review of Economics and Statistics* 17: 13–19.

Maine, H. 1861. *Ancient Law.* London: John Murray.

Menger, C. 1871 [1950]. *Principles of Economics.* Glencoe, IL: Free Press.

Morgan, M.S. 2012. *The World in the Model.* Cambridge: Cambridge University Press.

Pantaleoni, M. 1911. Considerazionisulleproprieta di un sistema di prezzipolitici. *GiornaledegliEconomisti* 42 (9–29): 114–33.

Pareto, V. 1935. *The Mind and Society.* New York: Harcourt Brace.

Podemska-Mikluch, M., and R.E. Wagner. 2013. Dyads, Triads, and the Theory of Exchange: Between Liberty and Coercion. *Review of Austrian Economics* 26: 171–82.

Polya, G. 1954. *Mathematics and Plausible Reasoning*, vol. 2. Princeton, NJ: Princeton University Press.

Roberts, P.C. 1971. *Alienation and the Soviet Economy.* Albuquerque: University of New Mexico Press.

Samuelson, P.A. 1947 [1965 reprint]. *Foundations of Economic Analysis.* Cambridge: Harvard University Press.

Schmookler, A.B. 1984. *The Parable of the Tribes: The Problem of Power in Social Evolution.* Albany: State University of New York Press.

Schumpeter, J.A. 1934. *Theory of Economic Development*, 2nd ed. Cambridge, MA: Harvard University Press.

Schumpeter, J.A. 1954. *History of Economic Analysis.* Oxford: Oxford University Press.

Shackle, G.L.S. 1972. *Epistemics and Economics.* Cambridge: Cambridge University Press.

Shackle, G.L.S. 1974. *Keynesian Kaleidics.* Edinburgh: Edinburgh University Press.

Stigler, G.J. 1957. Perfect Competition, Historically Contemplated. *Journal of Political Economy* 65: 1–17.

Stringham, E. 2015. *Private Governance: Creating Order in Economic and Social Life.* Oxford: Oxford University Press.

Vickers, D. 1994. *Economics and the Antagonism of Time.* Ann Arbor: University of Michigan Press.

Wagner, R.E. 1989. *To Promote the General Welfare.* San Francisco, CA: Pacific Research Institute. Mercatus Center Reprint, 2019.

Wagner, R.E. 2012. Viennese Kaleidics: Why It's Liberty More Than Policy that Calms Turbulence. *Review of Austrian Economics* 25: 283–97.

Wagner, R.E. 2016. *Politics as a Peculiar Business.* Cheltenham, UK: Edward Elgar.

Wagner, R.E. 2018. Trade, Power, and Political Economy: Reason vs. Ideology in Edward Stringham's Private Governance. *Review of Austrian Economics* 31: 245–55.

Wagner, R.E. 2020. Economic Theory and "The Social Question": Some Dialectics Regarding the Work-Dependency Relationship. *Journal of Contextual Economics* 139.

Walras, L. 1874 [1954]. *Elements of Pure Economics.* Homewood, IL: Richard D. Irwin.

Yeager, L.B. 1973. The Keynesian Diversion. *Economic Inquiry* 11: 150–63.

CHAPTER 4

Diachronic Action Within an Ecology of Plans

We all sense that we are encased inside of social systems that are not of our making, and which both provide us with beneficial opportunities and impose obligations on us. The French sociologist Emil Durkheim (1915 [1965]) explained that the religious concept of God was observationally equivalent to our concept of society. Human references to God have a duality about them. On the one side, God is regarded as a source of strength and solace, as when one prays and subsequently feels calmed by the action. Indeed, there is neurological evidence to this effect as Newberg et al. (2001) present in *Why God Won't Go Away*. The attributes that humans typically associate with God, Durkheim explains, are likewise typically features of the object we denote as society. The society provides us with numerous opportunities that we could never secure on our own. But societies are also sources of control and obligation. Furthermore, people can differ in whatever appraisal of costs and benefits they associate with membership in society. However wide these differences might be, it is surely rare to find people who would choose to live in what would surely be miserable and not splendid isolation. Judging simply by popular rhetoric and discourse, many people call for more societal control over their lives just as many others call for less. But society is what it is, a non-teleological entity that emerges in complex ways through interaction among people, though often in mysterious fashion. We all contribute to remaking society as we live, some more than others perhaps, though never in any way described or conveyed by orthodox theories of optimal choice.

© The Author(s) 2020
R. E. Wagner, *Macroeconomics as Systems Theory*,
https://doi.org/10.1007/978-3-030-44465-5_4

While social theorists generally acknowledge that society is a system constituted through interaction among myriad entities, they mostly recoil from recognizing that societies are not sentient creatures and so lack teleology. Individuals are teleological creatures, with teleology being manifest in the plans people form and pursue. Societies, however, do not have teleology, but rather are stages or platforms on which people participate in generating an ever-changing cosmic drama. Some participants in that drama, including social theorists and political figures, seem to find it useful for their teleological purposes to treat societies as having teleology, in contrast to recognizing that societies can serve as causal agents even though they are not sentient creatures. In this respect, Shakespeare had it right in *As You Like It* when he had Jacques aver: "all the world's a stage and all the men and women on it merely players." It is conceptually coherent to recognize that people recognize that they are born into a continuing cosmic drama in which they must participate in some fashion. The players have purpose; the drama itself does not.

For individual participants in the cosmic drama, it is often helpful to advance teleological claims as part of a strategy to capture larger shares of scarce attention space before an audience composed of teleological characters. Hence, that drama is organized around dueling teleological claims because it is dueling claims that make for drama in the first place. Those claims, moreover, are addressed to a non-teleological entity denoted variously as society or the public good. Yet neither society nor the public good are action-taking entities, but simply are complex reflections of societal interactions among teleological individuals seeking for their proverbial places in the sun. Winners in particular controversies speak on behalf of society or public good because humans can only speak in teleological terms, and the use of a teleological language enables speakers to feel good about their speech, as such noted Italian social theorists from a century ago as Gaetano Mosca (1947) and Vilfredo Pareto (1935) explained in their treatments of non-logical action. For instance, someone who favors open borders might participate in controversy over immigration by asserting that an increased supply of domestic labor might release a future Albert Einstein from domestic chores, providing more benefit for humanity through scientific discovery. Whether this proposition is true or false is probably undecidable. More than this, it mistakenly though understandably treats society as teleological. For teleological humans, this romantic presumption is surely more satisfying than recognizing explicitly that social-level outcomes emerge through complex interactions among conflicting teleologies.

ECONOMIC THEORY AND ECONOMIC SYSTEMS: AN IMPOVERISHED VOCABULARY

Economists commonly work with an impoverished set of concepts and vocabulary when they theorize about and compare systems of economic order. Those comparisons entail resort to such dualities as capitalism vs. socialism-communism or liberalism vs. collectivism. When proceeding in this fashion, economists also typically note that actual economies contain mixtures of polar types, as when modern democratic regimes are described as mixtures of liberal market principles and collective political principles that are typically classified as liberal democracies. Whether an economist thinks in terms of pure forms or mixed forms, the performance properties of an economic system are typically summarized by two or three aggregate variables collected within the NIPA and similar accounts. One variable is a gap between actual and potential output. Actual output is measured by GDP and similar variables. Potential output is a theoretical projection of what actual output would be if there were no involuntary unemployment. A second variable of strong interest to economists is the rate of growth in aggregate output. Also of interest to numerous economists is the distribution of output, with there being a presumption among many though not all economists that more equal distributions are superior to less equal distributions for any given output gap or rate of growth.

This conventional scheme of thought pretends that economic systems are simple entities whose systemic properties can be controlled directly through action by political entities, much as the engineers situated in Mission Control in Houston can guide a spacecraft to a rendezvous in space and then return it to Earth. In operating with such simplistic presuppositions, macro theorists mostly embrace the pretense of knowledge (Hayek 1989). This strikingly immodest stance of many economists stands in stark contrast to the efforts of ecologists to theorize about the complex patterns of interaction that emerge within such places as coral reefs or tropical rainforests, as can be seen readily by perusing the essays that Scheiner and Willig (2011) collect. It is widely though not universally acknowledged that the emergent organizational pattern of a market economy cannot be duplicated through political planning. Indeed, in a still cited essay, Leonard Read (1958) explains that it is not even possible for someone to set forth all the necessary steps in the proper temporal sequence to produce a pencil. Pencils emerge within an ecology of plans that generates numerous potentialities which some people inside that ecology can formulate particular plans to which other people can connect their plans, and with pencils emerging as one output within that ecology.

One significant line of economic theory explains that polycentric inter-action inside the private ordering principles of private property and free-dom of contract can yield such beneficial outputs as pencils even though no solitary individual could think through what actions would be neces-sary to produce a pencil. It would be in keeping with the modeling tradi-tions of macro theory to model a single-good economy. A macro theory of growth would thus describe expansion in the production of that single good, which might as well be described as pencils. Here again we arrive at one of those numerous forks in the analytical road. One branch of that fork explains the ability truly to produce pencils is too complex for any single human mind, so pencils cannot be produced within a monocentric societal arrangement. The other branch of that fork, the macro-theoretic branch, treats the production of pencils as a simple matter of following a recipe that requires only two ingredients, labor and capital, and possibly a third ingredient described as knowledge. Within the form of the theory, however, all these variables are simple scalars that can be located along the real line.

Many macro-theoretic models of growth have been constructed. Fun-damentally, they feature a single output produced by two inputs, typically labor and capital, and with data on output and inputs taken from NIPA-like data. Macro growth theory thus takes the form of a fable and should not be understood as a characterization of how life proceeds. Macro growth theory is wholly form; it lacks substance. As form, there is surely nothing wrong with saying that labor, capital, and knowledge produce growth when somehow combined. But this is form and not substance. The terms labor, capital, and knowledge give the illusion or pretense of substance, but there is no substance there, and in two distinct respects. For one thing, labor, capital, and knowledge pertain to abstract qualities. What matters, however, is not the fact that people are working but what it is that they are working on, and how well. It is the same for capital and knowledge. For another thing, great significance resides in who and how judgments are made as to the types of talents people acquire and the forms of knowledge and capital equipment people develop.

Economic systems do have performance properties, but those prop-erties emerge out of micro- or meso-level interaction. The qualities of labor, capital, and knowledge that might be projected onto the macro-level of society are emergent properties of micro- and meso-level actions and interactions. Without incorporating such prior interactions, ordinary macro theory is incapable of addressing the performance properties of different systems of social-economic order even though such properties are the prime analytical interest of those theories. Surely, the principle questions people seek to address and explore when using macro-level theories are the systemic properties of different social arrangements. A major difficulty with standard macro theory is that it is incapable of addressing such concerns because it is wedded to simplistic concepts of economic control that are suitable for a parade marshal but not suitable for facilitating a turbulent flow of pedestrians. Such an alternative theoretical scheme must bring individual interactions as mediated through institutional arrangements into the analytical foreground. This is the scheme of thought that Fig. 1.3 presented in a rudimentary fashion.

INSTITUTIONAL INCONGRUITY AND SYSTEMS PERFORMANCE

In his examination of the Legacy of Max Weber, Ludwig Lachmann (1970) claimed that societal governance occurs through a hierarchical arrangement of institutions that typically entail some degree of clashing with one another. That clashing portends internally generated change through forces set in motion by that clashing, thereby pointing toward an analytical framework based on emergent dynamics and not comparative statics, and where systems of human interaction themselves have performance properties. Recall Warren Nutter's (1962) explanation of why the Soviet Union would never surpass western economic performance despite near unanimity among western economists at the time Nutter wrote that the Soviet Union was quickly gaining on the western world and would soon surpass it, unless the western world adopted a greater measure of Soviet-style planning. For these western economists, the central challenge for the western world was how to embrace the central principles of collective organization while maintaining some semblance of traditional western liberties, perhaps as reflected in the soft communism of British-style Fabian socialism.

The central operating characteristic of private ordering is agreement. A social system that is organized through the private ordering principles of private property and freedom of contract generates a system of economic interaction that is commonly described as a market economy. Private ordering generates a network of dense and complex interactions based on transactions. Within this system, someone who can't find a buyer for a service he or she wants to supply will either have to lower the price of the service or find something different to offer. A liberal market economy offers no guarantee that entrepreneurial actions will be successful. Indeed, history suggests that many of them will fail. A market economy offers people opportunities to pursue their dreams, though in that pursuit they must secure the agreement of customers and suppliers; they cannot compel other people to support their dreams. This situation changes with public ordering. Public or political ordering opens new possibilities as a political sponsor might support the otherwise unwanted service, paying for that service through taxes imposed on people who would not buy the service on their own. With respect to Nutter (1962) and the Soviet Union, western economists almost universally denied Nutter's claim that the Soviet Union would never surpass the West. The prime difference between Nutter and those other economists was that Nutter was an incipient systems theorist. Nutter recognized that the Soviet Union was not an ordinary western society that just happened to face particularly cruel exogenous shocks. To the contrary, Nutter recognized that Soviet-style systems entailed such things as purges and famines as some of the properties that held the system together.

Most comparative analyses of economic systems conceptualize an entity described as an economy as operating independently of the entity described as state or polity. Thus, communism or socialism is described as entailing political ownership of the means of production, with the state assigned the task of making this system work. Just who assigns the state this task is left unstated, typically by asserting that "society" makes the assignment without, however, explaining how this might play out in practice. Yet action is a property of individuals and not of societies. While individuals can act collectively, there will be some structured pattern of interaction that enables such collective action, with some people exercising leadership in generating outcomes. A collection of individuals can act in the name of the collective, but that action will be sponsored by possessors of leadership positions (Sterpan and Wagner 2017).

Once we recognize that there are people who strive to attain positions of political power, we must also recognize that those positions are economically valuable. No one strives to attain power over an activity that no one cares about. Hence, political activity reflects the same logic of economizing action as does commercial activity. The efforts of people to attain political office and the efforts of people to create commercial enterprises both entail striving by the actors to attain what they regard as more desirable states of being. The holders of political offices will be economizing agents. Any conception of independent political and economic processes operating inside a society must give way to recognition that the political and the economic or commercial are both manifestations of economizing action that operates inside societies. The holders of political offices will be economizing economic agents, reflecting recognition that all action initiates at the ground or action level and not at the societal level of statistics, projections, and ideologies.

Similarly, political democracy is commonly described as the complement of economic capitalism, with both together constituting a political economy of freedom. This complementarity, however, is doubtful or at least disputable. Capitalism or liberalism is the name applied to a social system where relationships and interactions among people are governed by the ordering principles of private property and freedom of contract. When human interactions are governed by an institutional framework centered on private property and freedom of contract, we typically describe that social system as being one of liberalism, free enterprise, or capitalism. In contrast, democracy is typically construed as meaning that the desires of majorities of citizens trump the desires of minorities, though with the proviso often added that minorities are afforded constitutional protections over some domain of action. Democracy is not a simple manifestation of private property, for it establishes a realm of public or political property that impinges on private property. Those impingements might work for mutual benefit, as when a set of people form a partnership. Yet creation of the partnership creates relationships among the partners that might generate actions that some partners might find disagreeable. Without auxiliary legal protection, one group of partners could even systematically freeze-out another set of partners within the political rules of the partnership. This relationship of the many trumping the few conforms to the template of a mass of people trumping some oligarchs or a dictator, which fits a common stereotype of democracy being the political system of freedom. That relationship of the many trumping the few, however, also corresponds to the template of the less successful in any endeavor trumping the more successful, under conditions of skewed distributions of outcomes where those outcomes are subject to approval and revision through voting.

A systems-theoretic examination of systems of social order and organization points away from the conventional dichotomies. Perhaps most significantly, there is no independence of the political and the economic in societies, even though each has realms of autonomous presence. The economist Frank Knight (1933) famously summarized the challenges facing any economic system as being to determine what is produced, how it is produced, and for whom it is produced. The political scientist Harold Lasswell (1936) similarly declared that the central problem of politics is to address questions regarding What, How, and For Whom. Combining Knight and Lasswell arrives at recognition of the entangled nature of systems of political economy (Wagner 2016). Whether an action is denoted as being political or economic, we may be sure that the actor is seeking to attain states of existence that he or she regards as more desirable. To be sure, that actor can attain more desired states of existence only by advancing the similar desires of other members of the society. Here, differences can arise in the share of affected parties within the population. For market interactions, the immediately affected parties are those who participate in transactions. For political interactions, we can distinguish between those who choose to participate and those who are forced to participate, and with this difference creating second-order differences of some significance, as can be seen by contrasting the dyadic character of market transactions with the triadic character of political transactions (Podemska-Mikluch and Wagner (2013).

SYSTEMS AND INSTITUTIONS: THE PROBLEMATIC OF RULE-GUIDED GOVERNANCE

Walter Eucken (1952) described a market economy as the abstract noun that pertains to a society where interactions among individuals are governed by the institutional rules we denote as property, contract, and liability. While those rules obviously operate in the present world, equally obviously these are not the only rules that operate. The entire network of taxation and regulation, for instance, often operates to give advantage to some while imposing disadvantages to others. To be sure, democratic ideology often tries to hide this reality beneath an ideological fog that claims that all collective actions necessarily operate for general and universal benefit (Eisenstein 1961; Wagner 2018). Such claims might possibly enable those who make such claims to feel good about their actions, but such claims are clearly fictive all the same. Should collective action require unanimous consent, such action would surely operate to the anticipated net benefit of all members of society. But should such action require only majority approval, it is a plausible first approximation to assert that such measures provide net gains for a majority of citizens, and with those gains financed by imposing losses on the remainder of the citizenry. This first approximation, moreover, is only that—a first approximation. It is based on viewing taxes as imposed through referendums. Typically, however, taxes are imposed through legislative negotiations and bargains where the few can benefit at the expense of the many, generating increasing tax complexity in the process (Eusepi and Wagner 2013; Hebert and Wagner 2013).

In any case, the institutional rules that are in place within a society are typically described as comprising a society's rules of the game (North 1990). Any society must return answers to questions regarding what will be produced, how that output will be produced, and how that output will be distributed among the members of the society. No society can truly be planned by central authority, for there is no option to all members of society having regions of autonomous action. Genuine central planning would entail a society of puppets orchestrated by a puppet master. This is perhaps possible in small groups, but not in societies of the modern scale. To be sure, puppetry is surely present in all societies as people do experience some of their lives as responding to the demands of outside forces over which they have no option but to respond. But autonomous spheres of individual action also exist where people can choose their courses of action within a context of other people doing the same. Within this environment of autonomous action, the properties of societal interaction are influenced by the rules that shape and influence individual action.

In similar fashion, a set of people could split into two groups and engage in competition to move a ball up and down a field. The quality of the resulting social interaction will depend on the rules the players establish regarding the movement of the ball. There are numerous ways in which this society will exhibit different properties depending on the rules that are established. They could play with a round ball or an ovular ball. If a round ball, the players could select among various diameters. They could further select between directing the ball with their feet or with their hands. Whatever constellation of rules the players select, the players will conduct their actions within that framework of rules, and with the characteristic features of the game depending on the rules that were selected in conjunction with how the players act within that framework of rules. While the descriptive details of play will vary across rules, the participants will be fully employed in any case. There will be no systemic output gap, but some rules might lead to superior consequences as these are judged by the participants.

For simple games, we may be assured that people would prefer games that reflect competition among opposed interests than in games without contestation. For social-economic processes, whether competition is open to all or is restricted to a few contains domains of ambiguity. Requirements that commercial practitioners often must be licensed by a political agency is often justified by practitioners as necessary to protect against consumers being harmed, and without letting consumers say through their actions whether they agree with the political agency. In this respect, Carroll and Gaston (1981) found that the licensing of electricians led to an increase in the volume of electrocutions as significant numbers of people economized on the cost of hiring electricians by doing their own electrical work. Whether or not a simple game entails opposition is plain to see. Whether a complex social-economic process entails a coalition by which some people are able to dominate others, as against that apparent domination protecting values everyone would support upon careful reflection, will unavoidably entail ambiguity. Ambiguous nor not, the most significant social-economic questions at the systems level are surely not ones of output gaps, which pretty much are evanescent, but are questions concerning the properties of different systems of social interaction.

To be sure, games are never fully defined by formally selected rules of play. Those rules prohibit certain actions and compel others, but never eliminate autonomous imagination from the realm of action. This situation recalls the actions of lexicographers and grammarians. In a limited sense, lexicographers and grammarians provide rules by which people use language. This happens whenever people consult dictionaries or grammars in selecting among possible usages. For the most part, however, dictionaries and grammars are descriptions of action and not rules that govern action.

Similarly, in large measure people learn repertoires through action starting in childhood, as Norbert Elias (1939 [1982]) explains in exploring *The Civilizing Process* through which people acquire the capacities and outlooks of adulthood. While it is not wrong to describe institutions as rules of the game, it is an incomplete description unless primacy is given to the habits of heart and mind that are established starting in childhood. Any social system can be described in terms of a set of rules that govern individual action, though most of those rules are informally established and not deliberately adopted. In some cases, such informally established principles can be codified, and codification might take on a life of its own through a process in which periodic conventions are established to revise or amend the code. Whether they are codified or not, informal rules are adopted through interaction where the participants ratify those rules, and repeatedly through their actions. These informal rules give law-like character to patterns of human interaction within societies, and which in the limiting case those rules are denoted as constituting private ordering, recognizing all the same that societies also unavoidably entail contested zones of political or public ordering, along the lines that Carl Schmitt (1932 [1996]) sketched in characterizing the autonomy of the political in society.

PRIVATE ORDERING AND ECONOMIC INTERACTION

Legislation generates formal rules with different qualitative characteristics than informally emergent rules, particularly if those rules are selected through ordinary democratic procedures grounded in majority rule principles. Where informal rules emerge through usage and gain prominence as their usage spreads, formal rules are often established in a setting where some people favor the rule and others oppose it. All societies entail rule-guided governance, and with those rules emerging out of various social processes. What are denoted as informal rules emerge out of practical action, and with the types of practices relevant to the generation of rules depending on the techniques of production resident within the society. For instance, the practices that emerge within factories will differ in some respects from those that emerge within commercial fisheries due to different situations practitioners encounter and the repertories they develop to handle those situations. Among other things, larger teams of participants are often involved in assembling factory output than are involved in catching fish and transporting them to port. It would not be surprising to see subtle differences in the substantive character of rule-guided interactions resulting in response to these different situations, along the lines that Elinor Ostrom (1990) explores.

Setting aside this Ostrom-like point about the subtleties of rule-guided governance, a standard mode of economic thought asserts that societies require two sets of institutional arrangements, one appropriate for the organization of market interactions and one appropriate for the organization of collective activity. This dichotomy corresponds to the distinction between private and public goods. The typical presumption in this respect is that private goods can be organized successfully through market trans-actions, but public goods require political provision because market pro-vision will fail to secure full exploitation of the potential gains from social interaction. This claim is surely about as erroneous as it is common. It invokes a statement of what appears to be intuitively obvious when that condition is not at all so obvious.

Consider the widely repeated claim that lighthouses provided protec-tion to all ships that passed nearby even if the ships did not contribute to support the lighthouse. It is an intuitively obvious step to claim that this situation could be remedied by collective provision which could force contributions from people who might not contribute otherwise. Yes, the situation might be remedied in the manner, but it does not follow that collective provision would accomplish this. Nor does it follow that col-lective provision is even necessary to accomplish this outcome. The sit-uation the lighthouse example describes is one where there exist unex-ploited gains from trade among the affected parties in establishing a light-house. This situation means that some potential profit opportunity exists in developing some organizational arrangement for providing lighthouses (Coase 1974; Krause 2015; Candela and Geloso 2018).

For someone to build a lighthouse and then subsequently hope to receive voluntary contributions will not be an effective or wise entrepreneurial strategy. True, this strategy of building something first and then waiting for customers to come is a common approach to market-based activity. But it is not the only approach, and different settings call for different approaches. For instance, someone might think of build-ing a few lighthouses on the way to a harbor, figuring that most ships that use the beam might dock at the harbor. Rather than hoping that shippers would make voluntary contributions when they docked at the harbor, the lighthouse owner could purchase or lease docking rights to the harbor, and thus charge for lighthouse services through docking fees. Alternatively, a consortium of ship owners could secure docking rights and form a cooperative to build lighthouses. Yet again, the shippers or lighthouse owner could prevail on the public authority that operates the harbor to collect fees from ships, which is the situation Coase (1974) described. Whatever organizational scheme emerges, it would promote the securing of gains from social interaction. In short, any situation that posits unexploited gains from trade is simultaneously a situation in which entrepreneurial profits can be secured by developing some organizational or contractual framework suitable for capturing those gains.

To state the point differently, an output gap is not a useful concept for a bottom–up or emergent approach to social-level phenomena. Each agent in society will have strong reason for seeking valuable employment of the resources he or she owns. All agents are in the same position. An agent who thinks he or she has good value to offer to other agents is free to test that hypothesis, and with affirmation or rejection residing in whether an offer is accepted. True, this places the burden of finding contractual partners on the resource owners, but those owners are surely in the best position to bear that burden. Sure, there are politicians along with their supporters who will claim that they can better bear that burden by creating administrative agencies, replacing private with public ordering in the process. Here we must ask whether a public employment agency is truly superior to a private agency, or if the possible appearance of superiority is a manifestation of the tax-financed subsidization that public agencies receive. Public ordering, moreover, might also confer the advantages of power and compulsion that are not open to private ordering.

Public Ordering and the Generation of Societal Tectonics

Any situation for which it is claimed that unexploited gains from trade exist is simultaneously a situation where people can reap profits by developing new organizations or contractual forms. Nonetheless, public ordering may still arise not to secure those gains but to redistribute rents that might otherwise have resulted. Within macro-theoretic orthodoxy, spending is spending and that is all there is to the matter. Public spending is a perfect substitute for private spending within the income–expenditure framework. The two are not perfect substitutes, however, once organized activity is viewed from within a theory of economic organization.

A principle feature of private ordering is residual claimancy and individual responsibility or liability for actions undertaken. A cost function is defined as a combination of inputs that produces an output in the least costly manner possible. There is, of course, no way truly to know whether an output is produced in a least-cost manner. A cost function simply provides a boundary between what is possible and what is impossible. It is impossible for an output to be produced at less than its minimum possible cost. It is, however, always possible to produce at more than minimum cost. Economists typically locate cost at the boundary between possible and impossible because private ordering creates a situation where the owners of an enterprise can capture any residual difference between the revenue received from selling a product and the expenses entailed in producing it. Hence, there is a compelling logic to support the proposition that private ordering tends to generate least-cost modes of production. Sure, at any instant there doubtless will be firms that are producing in an inefficient manner, but we may reasonably expect that these firms will be on their way to extinction, either through being liquidated or being sold to another firm, as Henry Manne (1965) explains in describing how mergers operate as instruments for enabling better managed firms to take over poorer managed firms, capturing in the process some of the resulting increase in firm value.

The situation is different when economic activities are politically organized. A privately ordered lighthouse will have a position of residual claimancy; a publicly ordered lighthouse will not. A publicly ordered lighthouse will not have customers it must attract where those customers can choose whether to pay tolls in comparison with using their money differently. A publicly ordered lighthouse will have clients and patrons whose support it must receive, but those clients and patrons don't have alternative sources of supply against which they can compare the offerings of the public agency (Niskanen 1971). A publicly ordered lighthouse, or enterprise generally, will not have any market value, for there is no market for its ownership shares.

Public ordering replaces individual with collective liability in some fashion. For instance, publicly ordered enterprises operate without residual claimancy, which means that expenses and rents can be difficult to distinguish. A publicly ordered enterprise might operate with procedures that force it to operate slowly in comparison with how a private enterprise in the same situation would operate, thereby increasing its cost of doing business and failing to pursue commercial opportunities that a private enterprise would likely have pursued. This slower mode of operation might be a source of gain to executives of the public enterprise when that enterprise does not have market value and residual claimancy. What is excess cost to a private enterprise with transferable ownership and market value can thus be executive rent for managers of public enterprises where market value does not exist.

Recognition that some enterprises are privately ordered and others are publicly ordered, as well as recognition that there is also a good deal of entanglement between the types of enterprise, brings into the analytical foreground the character of interaction among the different types of enterprise. Within the standard macro-theoretic framework, the form of enterprise is economically irrelevant, due to the presumption that it is spending and not plans that is the primitive variable that moves the economic process. This presumption resides in various notions concerning the rule of law, where public ordering takes its bearings from private law. This relationship of a background of public law to a foreground of private law surely characterized western economies into the early twentieth century, and which Henry Maine (1861) stated succinctly in setting forth his oft-noted observation that up to his time the direction of social movement within the western world had been one where the domain of status-based relationships had been giving way to the domain of contractual-based relationships. Over the past century or so, however, the relationship between status and contract has been undergoing reversal as an increasing domain of social activity has come under the governance of status-based relationships. Relationships grounded on status can generate societal tectonics when they encounter relationships grounded on contract.

BRAIDED CHARACTER OF CONFLICT AND COOPERATION WITHIN SOCIETIES

To illustrate how societal tectonics can emerge in the presence of conflict among enterprises organized under private ordering and those organized under public ordering, consider the organization of public transportation within urban areas. We may start with the emergence of jitney service in the early twentieth century (Eckert and Hilton 1972). At the time, people mostly worked in the center of a city and lived outside the center. They traveled between home and work either by driving cars or riding in street cars and busses. Jitney service emerged as drivers started to carry passengers in conjunction with their trips between home and work. As jitney practice spread, jitney service became increasingly regular and systematic, coming to represent a free market in public transportation. In the process, jitneys competed with busses and street cars until jitneys were regulated out of business. In this fate lies a lesson about societal tectonics that comes about when private and public ordering occupy the same commercial territory, due to the inability of political enterprises to compete on equal footing with commercial enterprises.

Such political enterprises as busses and street cars have tools to promote their survival that commercial enterprises lack. Commercial enterprises must attract the capital necessary to supply their services in open competition with other uses of capital. The way they do this is to supply services to customers for which customers are willing to pay sufficiently to attract that capital. It is possible to imagine a political enterprise that is established within the same institutional framework as commercial enterprises. Such a political enterprise would receive its capital from investors and would generate its revenue from customers. Within such an institutional framework, political and commercial enterprises would operate according to identical principles, with enterprise success depending on the enterprise's ability to generate revenue larger than expenses to attract the necessary supply of capital.

But political enterprises don't receive capital from willing investors. They receive it from budgetary appropriations that are acquired from tax extractions. For commercial enterprises, the return to investors must be created through the revenues that customers provide. For political enterprises, there are taxpayers and not investors. This difference is huge. Investors face options among which they are free to choose. Hence, commercial enterprises must attract investors in open competition with other enterprises. Taxpayers have no option regarding the direction of their tax payments. They do not choose how much to contribute to political enterprises relative to commercial enterprises. Nor do they choose how to distribute their tax payments among political enterprises. Recurring to Henry Maine's (1861) distinction between relationships based on status and relationships based on contract, political enterprises exist within a sea of status relationships regarding budgetary politics. There are, to be sure, margins of contractual interaction within budgetary processes, but those marginal interactions are also shaped by given tax institutions that do not allow taxpayers to direct their tax payments to commercial enterprises of their choosing.

This situation means that political enterprises do not have to be directly concerned with maintaining investor presence in the firm because investors are irrelevant to the firm's success. To the contrary, political enterprises must be concerned with maintaining support from key players in the budgetary process. Without doubt, maintaining such political connections has some overlap with the maintenance of investor relationships by commercial enterprises, but that overlap is only partial and incomplete. Private ordering entails creation of a network of dyadic transactions whereby interaction among numerous people can be reduced to the simple logic of mutual gains from trade. By contrast, public ordering entails creation of triadic ordering where willing participants secure gains from unwilling contributors through taxation or regulation (Podemska-Mikluch and Wagner 2013).

Political enterprises, moreover, have tools at their disposal to promote their survival that commercial enterprises lack. Most significantly, political enterprises can use their regulatory powers to restrict the competitive ability of commercial enterprises and can do so in myriad ways. Jitney drivers could compete with political busses by picking up customers at their homes rather than requiring customers to get to bus stops. Through regulation, however, jitneys could be required to drive fixed routes, which would reduce the attractiveness of jitneys relative to municipal busses. Jitneys could be licensed at a sufficiently high fee that would reduce significantly the supply of jitney service, again increasing the demand for municipal busses. Taxes and other forms of restriction could be placed on downtown parking, which again would increase the demand for municipal bus service. In short, political and commercial enterprises are not independent of one another, but rather are entangled (Wagner 2016). There can be no level playing field that pertains to political and commercial enterprises that operate within the same territory, for enhanced success by one class of enterprise will degrade the success of the other class, and vice versa. Within an entangled system of political economy, competitive processes will be neither wholly cooperative nor wholly antagonistic. They will be some admixture of both, due to the different organizational imperatives generated by private ordering and public ordering.

RESPONDING TO PLAN FAILURE: BANKRUPTCY, BUSINESS REORGANIZATION, POLITICS

Equilibrium-centered economic theory characterizes a perfectly coordinated economy where no unexploited gains from trade are present. There is no way truly to know if such a situation exists or has ever been observed. All the same, that characterization is the central theme of the theory of competitive equilibrium. Most economists, and especially macro theorists, claim to the contrary that societies exist in various states of imperfectly competitive equilibrium. Theories of imperfect competition, moreover, recognize that societies generally entail significant degrees of coordination, only with that degree being less than what is implied by the theory of perfect competition. While those theories are incapable of identifying objectively actual instances and magnitudes of failure, they are used all the same to assert the presence of output gaps for political action to close.

By the law of the excluded middle, either a state of perfect competition exists or doesn't. As Chapter 1 explained, the law of the excluded middle is a piece of syllogistic logic that is relevant for a narrow range of situations, and complex processes of social interaction are not among them. Indeed, the law of the excluded middle does not even pertain to such a simple act as riding a bicycle. More significantly, it does not apply to processes of economic coordination within societies. This inapplicability of the excluded middle has two sources, one methodological and one substantive, recognizing that methodology and substantive are interdependent.

Methodologically, a phenomenon can never be satisfactorily explained by asserting its existence as part of some set of axioms. That phenomenon might be consistent with those axioms, but assuming the pertinence of those axioms is just an indirect way of assuming the existence of the sought-for phenomenon. The alternative to proceeding axiomatically is to proceed algorithmically. Through this alternative procedure, the phenomenon of interest can be generated, or not, through some process of interaction among simpler elements, similar to Bruno Latour's (2005) recognition that it is methodologically superior to explain social phenomena as emerging out of interaction among pre-social phenomena as against imposing a set of axioms contains the presence of those phenomena.

As a logical matter, interaction at the micro-level is prior to results of interactions that are projected onto the macro-level of societal interaction. Contractual forms, hiring practices, and commercial conventions are among the myriad institutional arrangements inside of which people act and interact. Those arrangements have a primary direction of causation that runs from actions to institutional conventions, which fits the motif of interaction among pre-social entities generating social phenomena. But there is also a reverse direction of causation which runs from arrangements to actions. This opposing direction violates the law of the excluded middle, for by that law either actions must cause institutions or institutions must cause actions. Contrary to the excluded middle, the dialectical process of yin-and-yang explains that harmonization emerges through interaction among contraries. Invoking insights from yin-and-yang enables us to recognize that orthodox dichotomies between perfectly and imperfectly competitive or coordinated outcomes lead social theorizing in a misleading direction. Dialectical principles enable us to recognize two enduring qualities of social processes that clearly violate the excluded middle: (1) a person cannot step into the same river twice and (2) there is nothing new under the sun.

With respect to social coordination, no one creates a plan with the intent of failing. And yet many people abandon plans they had set in motion at an earlier date, while other plans flourish. Plans are experiments people undertake with the intention of succeeding, for who ever heard of someone trying intentionally to fail? But failure is part of the experimental process of entrepreneurial action in a world where there exists no oracles or crystal balls. The failure of plans is an element of social reality, and this recognition brings into the analytical foreground the institutional arrangements through which the debris left by failed plans is cleared away to make room for new social configurations. Here, we can distinguish between private and public arrangements for social ordering.

An entrepreneur who abandons a plan nonetheless has ownership rights to some stock of assets that have salvage value, as Wagner (2012) explores in examining the ability of private ordering to overcome enterprise failures. Those assets owned by failed enterprises might entail real estate, inventory, and contracts for various inputs. Those assets will have value when incorporated into other entrepreneurial plans, but the entrepreneur who disbands the enterprise faces the challenge of liquidating the enterprise in the most valuable manner. After all, principles of profit maximization pertain as fully to abandoning enterprises as they apply to growing enterprises. Within a social system based on private ordering, the redeployment of assets from abandoned enterprises will follow the same commercial logic as pertain to growing enterprises. Indeed, we experience the redeployment of assets every day as we drive around our neighborhoods and observe the renovation of buildings. For instance, what had started as a bookstore in a strip mall might be undergoing conversion to a gym. Or what had been a fast-food place with drive-through service might be undergoing conversion to a bank. Most significantly, the principles and practices of private ordering apply just as fully to removing failures of economic coordination as they pertain to generating new instances of coordination.

The situation can change, and dramatically, when public ordering comes into play. With public ordering, political officials have some ability to govern how commercial debris from abandoned plans is cleared away, as DelliSanti and Wagner (2018) examine in comparing bankruptcy and bailout. With private ordering, business reorganization is often the most economical form of abandoning plans. But public ordering can prevent economical forms of business reorganization. For instance, under publicly ordered labor law union contracts cannot be breached, which leaves bankruptcy the only avenue for reorganization. And antitrust law can be employed to prevent the mergers that are often the most economical form of business reorganization.

A contemporary aphorism asserts that "when the going gets tough, the tough get going." This sentiment surely sounds fine to some, but we may wonder how strongly it is honored. Without doubt, it reflects the systemic logic of private ordering. At one time each person in a community of five people establishes a business. At some later time, two of those are successful and three are collapsing and about to be abandoned. According to the aphorism, those three will liquidate their businesses and start over again, either by creating new businesses or by offering to work for one of the two successful businesses. This pattern of response to success and failure reflects the operating logic of a market economy grounded on the institutional principles of property, contract, and liability (Eucken 1952).

We may wonder whether that institutional framework is robust against infringement from the institutions of public ordering. For instance, the owners of the three failing enterprises could form a coalition to impose a tax on the two successful enterprises, using the revenues to fund subventions for the creation of new businesses through some such agency as a Small Business Administration. Alternatively, the owners of the unsuccessful businesses might press legal action against the successful businesses by framing some form of claim grounded in principles of unjust enrichment and insider trading. In this instance, it could be claimed that the successful firms were privy to information of which the other owners were unaware, due to connections they didn't share with the other owners. Either path, if successful, would transfer support from successful to unsuccessful enterprises, and would wrap that transfer around some ideology grounded in claims of fairness, justice, or equal treatment.

QUANTITY, QUALITY, AND SOCIAL ORDER: THE EVANESCENCE OF OUTPUT GAPS

Zen and the Art of Motorcycle Maintenance (Pirsig 1974) unfolds around a controversy over quantity and quality as organizing concepts for human action, and with Matthew Crawford (2009) covering-related territory in his examination of *Shop Class as Soulcraft*. This controversy is as fully in play within economic theory as it is within philosophy more generally. The quantitative scheme of thought holds that societal success entails maximal output consistent with given labor–leisure preferences. In this respect, the most prevalent scheme of macro theory these days asserts that market economies are afflicted by output gaps which reduce the present value of lifetime aggregate consumption below its potential value. Within this scheme of thought and harkening back to the income–expenditure model, the shortfall in private spending can be offset by an increase in public spending, closing the output gap in the process.

The standard macro analysis of market economies afflicted by output gaps is a common form of whiteboard exercise. The cogency of that exercise is dubious and, moreover, that exercise elevates quantity over quality when there are good grounds for making the reverse elevation. The first thing to be said about any claimed output gap is that it is a product of some macro-level model. Yet, there is no way any output gap can arise independently of some micro-level process occurring that prevents or at least inhibits the full capture of gains from trade among market participants. System-level consequences must imply individual-level activities that generate those consequences, and it is both worthwhile and necessary to probe the individual-level activities that might generate the system-level consequences.

There are two paths toward theorizing in this manner, one fictive and one genuine. The fictive path ignores individual-systemic interaction by ignoring any interaction through which wholes emerge out of interaction among parts. The typical way of doing this is to assume the system is inhabited by people who are identical in all relevant respects, which enables reduction of the system to a representative agent. Whatever change in action a representative agent makes is thus identical to the same change at the system-level. An increased demand for leisure by the representative agent will reduce the supply of labor and create an output gap between the old steady state and the new steady state. We may doubt, however, that this situation calls for corrective action by a political agency, at least if political agencies are thought of normatively as conforming to individual desires. People want more leisure, for which they are willing to accept less consumption.

It could be claimed that there has been no diminution in the desire to consume, but this claim is incoherent within a representative agent model because the representative agent *is* the social system. To avoid being trapped inside this analytical box requires abandonment of the representative agent model and its DSGE cousin. Long ago, Leonard Read (1958) explained that no one could truly create the detailed set of blueprints and plans that would be necessary to produce an ordinary pencil. Yet many macro theorists stand ready to theorize in terms of output gaps for a pencil economy where the output is produced by some combination of labor and capital inputs. Within this conceptual framework, if the private production of pencils fails to secure full employment of inputs, public supply can close the gap. Within a representative agent model, however, there is no social interaction and, hence, no division and distribution of knowledge. The representative agent carries all the necessary knowledge required to produce coordinated social outcomes. The representative agent really exists in two distinct capacities in these models. One capacity is as a private citizen; the other capacity is as a politician. If the private citizen decides to spend less, the political self can decide to spend more, leaving the representative agent in an unchanged position.

Sure, representative agent models are not presented in such a fatuous fashion, but such models are fatuous all the same due to their elimination of all social phenomena from economic theory. If we wish to pursue economics from within a social-theoretic framework, it is necessary to work inside the contexts of such frameworks as against ignoring them. With respect to the production of pencils, we would thus recognize that our ability to use pencils is a product of a transactional nexus that enables someone to fabricate pencils from previously created materials, even though no one could truly describe all the actions stemming back centuries required to yield pencils today. Once again, the institutional arrangements governing human interaction replaces the actions of political figures as the linchpin for understanding the systemic properties of economic processes.

A non-fatuous manner of economic theorizing must be algorithmic and not axiomatic; it must reflect plausible and not demonstrative reasoning. It starts with an individual node at the micro- or meso-level of society and asks how changing the pattern of action within that node ramifies throughout the social nexus, with system-level observations emerging through social interaction. There are numerous reasons why private spending might fall without that fall denoting systemic failure as viewed by all the participants. For instance, the fall in spending might be initiated by the owners of failing firms who are liquidating their business prior to forming new businesses and getting back into the game. We currently have no useful means of theorizing in congruity with the passing of historical time, and the method of comparative statics is misleading by substituting a set of systemic axioms for an algorithmic process that mirrors action, as J. F. Allen et al. (1991) illustrates in his exploration into *Reasoning about Plans.*

Some contours of such an alternative scheme of thought can be set forth all the same. First, liquidation of a business will take time to find new buyers for the assets being disposed. Second, some of those assets might be deployed in the new business established after the old business is liquidated, in which case those assets will enter a period of unemployment. Third, businesses do not operate independently of all other businesses within the society. To the contrary, any business is engaged in a set of interactions with other businesses, both with respect to receiving inputs and supplying outputs. New relationships take time to form just as old ones take time to abandon. In consequence, we may reasonably expect output gaps to have irregular character and for them to be part of a well-working economic process in any case.

In other words, the orthodox macro concept of an output gap is a feature of one analytical model, and not a very useful one at that. It is not a feature of any reasonable concept of reality where economic activity is diachronic and not synchronic (Shackle 1972), recognizing that a synchronic process describes the members of a parade, but it takes a diachronic process to describe the members of a pedestrian crowd. With respect to the possible emergence of some output gap, we can usefully distinguish between two sets of entities at the micro- and meso-levels. One set pertains to those entities that are liquidating failed enterprises and preparing to create new ones. These entities will reduce their demand for inputs while they are creating new enterprise plans and contractual arrangements. In turn, those inputs might reduce their spending until they locate new sources of demand for their services. This output gap, however, does not point to some form of market failure that projects to the macro-level. Rather, it points to a response to new information by particular entities within the economic nexus, and with that information leading to changes in demands, both positive and negative, elsewhere within the economic nexus. Whether this output gap is Pareto efficient within a non-equilibrium scheme of thought is impossible to determine because it entails a hypothetical comparison of future possible actions.

What can be said, though, is that output gaps are not a persistent feature of a system based on private ordering. Someone who has too much leisure will simultaneously be motivated to exchange leisure for products. It doesn't follow that making such exchanges will be easy or simple, but it does mean that people who find themselves in this position will be motivated to obtain more consumption by reducing leisure. To be sure, the world we inhabit is not one of universal private ordering. In many ways public ordering restricts the range of contractual options, thereby restricting the scope for people to exchange leisure for commodities. Public ordering also entails subventions for being unemployed and having low consumption, which also diminishes the motivation to replace leisure with work. It is a category mistake to draw conclusions about present social configurations based on models of privately ordered economies when actual economies are riven with public ordering.

STRUCTURE OF PRODUCTION VS. CIRCULAR FLOW, REDUX

The circular flow model fits within the orthodox framework of macro theory where resource allocations occupy the center of the analytical stage and where the institutional arrangements of human governance reside somewhere on the analytical periphery. This scheme of thought divides a society as it operates into two capacities: one as consumers and one as producers. What people consume is produced by firms. People supply inputs to firms in exchange for which they payments for those services. Those payments to consumers enable the consumers to buy the products the firms produce.

The circular flow presents a clear view of a system in economic equilibrium in a highly aggregative manner. A circular flow is a form of textual characterization of a society, with that text dividing society into producers and consumers, realizing that the same people undertake both types of activity. Texts also often bring subtexts in their wake, and the circular flow certainly does this. Subtexts pertain to associations, sentiments, and intuitions a text might evoke. The text of the circular flow model is simple, for it says that all transactions are two-sided involving both production and consumption. Possible subtexts are less obvious but pertain to some of the mental or emotional predispositions that might accompany the notion of a circular flow. One possible subtext is a presumption that readjustments to new conditions can occur instantaneously, or nearly so. The income–expenditure claim that a fall in private spending can be quickly offset by a rise in public spending reflects this instantaneous presumption.

The structure of production entails a different textual description of the economic process, which in turn likely promotes different subtexts that inform economic understanding and intuition. Where the circular flow depicts the economic system from the top looking down, the structure of production depicts it from the bottom looking up. A structure of production is assembled from myriad activities by different economic entities. Where the circular flow presents an instantaneous view of an already organized economic process, the structure of production depicts that process both as operating with time delay and as reflecting emergent organization as entrepreneurs insert their plans for enterprises into the ecology of plans. This time delay starts from recognition that any act of planned production requires the passage of time before inputs have been converted into final products, sometimes a long interval of time.

With variable lengths of time involved in different production processes, the rate of interest becomes a central element of market pricing that ramifies throughout the economic nexus. Following in the demonstrative analytical tradition that Augustin Cournot (1837 [1995]) represents, consider the economic calculus of a supplier of bottled water from a mineral spring who is exploring possible options for increasing production from the spring. The simplest possibility would add a second station for pumping water. An alternative possibility might turn the spring into a reservoir, thereby enabling a greater amount of water to be captured by the bottler before the water moves downstream. A third possibility might sponsor research on techniques for reducing evaporation, thereby eventually bottling water that otherwise would have evaporated.

The question of economic calculation concerns the ranking of different ways of increasing the harvest of water from the spring. Building a second pumping assembly would require a relatively small capital investment and would yield its added output relatively quickly. Building a reservoir would require a larger capital investment and would require a longer passage of time before a larger volume of output materialized. Sponsoring research on retarding evaporation is more speculative than building a reservoir, as is the outcome of such research. In a large economy, we would observe all these activities and many more, often undertaken by different enterprises. One company might build bottling machinery, another might build reservoirs, and yet a third might conduct research into retarding evaporation.

What makes all these activities valuable is their connection with consumable product, water in this case. Producing bottling machinery will increase the yield of water in quick order. Building a reservoir, or expanding an existing reservoir, will yield a larger increase later. Research into retarding evaporation might produce considerable increases in yield without building dams, but the outcome is speculative. The central idea behind a structure of production is that entrepreneurs will be willing to invest in futuristic production activities so long as they judge that investment to be worthwhile. The willingness of entrepreneurs to undertake relatively roundabout means of increasing consumption goods depends significantly on their willingness to postpone present consumption in light of their beliefs or projections regarding the anticipated return to the postponement of present consumption.

The structure of production conception also entails recognition that an economic system is assembled through myriad decisions among economizing agents made in diachronic and not synchronic fashion (Shackle 1972). At one moment, there might be some businesses that bottle water and other businesses that produce assemblies for bottling water. At some later instant, some chemists might develop a plan to experiment with retarding the evaporation of water from mineral springs or reservoirs. This activity would change the structure of production by shifting the structure of employment toward evaporation research relative to bottling water. One significant feature of the structure of production is recognition that the amount of consumption available within a society is a product of a previously generated structure of production. In sharp contrast to the circular flow presumption that spending can be increased instantly, the structure of production recognizes that present consumption is determined by past production and is not subject instantly to change, other than by consuming previously created capital along the lines that Fritz Machlup (1935) explained.

Recognition of the primacy of plans over spending within a structure of production provides superior insight into political efforts to increase aggregate spending. The circular flow model makes it seem to be a simple matter of arithmetic to increase public spending to offset some perceived decline in private spending. By contrast, the structure of production model shows this arithmetic to be illusory because it is impossible to increase consumption today except through consuming capital, which entails a reduction in future consumption. The earlier illustration of a forest of trees existing in a steady state with the trees varying in age from one to thirty allows the point to be illustrated nicely. The amount of mature lumber available currently for consumption is determined by the number of saplings that were planted 30 years ago. The only way that consumption can be increased currently is to harvest immature trees, presumably starting with the trees that are 29 years old. Doing this, however, means that future consumption will have been reduced in consequence of the effort to increase consumption today. In other words, present consumption opportunities are governed by past entrepreneurial actions. The only thing present action can affect is future possibilities. This situation becomes readily intelligible through the structure of production.

With respect to thinking about the performance properties of different systems of social-economic organization, this book places primary emphasis on alternative institutional arrangements for governing economic interaction, thereby deemphasizing the place of public ordering out of recognition (1) that output gaps are evanescent and (2) that public ordering is incapable of operating in the so-called corrective fashion its proponents claim for it. The next chapter explores what might be meant by references to systemic normality when an economy is modeled as a structure of production and not a circular flow.

References

Allen, J.F., H.A. Kautz, R. Pelavin, and J. Tenenberg. 1991. *Reasoning About Plans*. San Francisco: Morgan Kaufman.

Candela, R., and V. Gelaso. 2018. The Lightship in Economics. *Public Choice* 176: 479–506.

Carroll, S.L., and R.J. Gaston. 1981. Occupational Restrictions and the Quality of Service Received: Some Evidence. *Southern Economic Journal* 47: 959–76.

Coase, R.H. 1974. The Lighthouse in Economics. *Journal of Law and Economics* 17: 357–76.

Cournot, A.A. 1837 [1995]. *Mathematical Principles of the Theory of Wealth*. San Diego, CA: James & Gordon.

Crawford, M. 2009. *Shop Class as Soulcraft: An Inquiry into the Value of Work*. New York: Penguin Books.

DelliSanti, D., and R.E. Wagner. 2018. Bankruptcies, Bailouts, and Some Political Economy of Corporate Reorganization. *Journal of Institutional Economics* 14: 833–51.

Durkheim, E. 1915 [1965]. *Elementary Forms of Religious Life*. New York: Free Press.

Eckert, R.N., and G.W. Hilton. 1972. The Jitneys. *Journal of Law and Economics* 15: 293–325.

Eisenstein, L. 1961. *The Ideologies of Taxation*. Cambridge, MA: Harvard University Press.

Elias, N. 1939 [1982]. *The Civilizing Process.* New York: Pantheon Books.

Eucken, W. 1952. *Grundsätze der Wirtschaftspolitik.* Tübingen: Mohr Siebeck.

Eusepi, G., and R.E. Wagner. 2013. Tax Prices in a Democratic Polity: The Continuing Relevance of Antonio De Viti de Marco. *History of Political Economy* 45: 99–121.

Hayek, F.A. 1989. The Pretense of Knowledge. *American Economic Review* 79: 3–7.

Hebert, D., and R.E. Wagner. 2013. Taxation as a Quasi-Market Process: Explanation, Exhortation, and the Choice of Analytical Windows. *Journal of Public Finance and Public Choice* 31: 163–77.

Knight, F.H. 1933. *The Economic Organization.* Chicago: University of Chicago Press.

Krause, M. 2015. Buoys and Beacons in Economics. *Journal of Private Enterprise* 30: 45–59.

Lachmann, L. 1970. *The Legacy of Max Weber.* Berkeley, CA: Glendessary Press.

Lasswell, H.D. 1936. *Politics: Who Gets What, When, How.* New York: McGraw-Hill.

Latour, B. 2005. *Reassembling the Social: An Introduction to Actor-Network Theory.* Oxford: Oxford University Press.

Maine, H.S. 1861. *Ancient Law.* London: John Murray.

Machlup, F. 1935. The Consumption of Capital in Austria. *Review of Economics and Statistics* 17: 13–19.

Manne, H.G. 1965. Mergers and the Market for Corporate Control. *Journal of Political Economy* 73: 10–20.

Mosca, G. 1947. *Elementi di scienza politica,* 4th ed. Bari: G. Laterza.

Newberg, A.B., E.G. D'Aquili, and V. Rause. 2001. *Why God Won't Go Away: Brain Science and the Biology of Belief.* New York: Ballantine.

Niskanen, W.A. 1971. *Bureaucracy and Representative Government.* Chicago: Aldine.

North, D.C. 1990. *Institutions, Institutional Change, and Economic Performance.* Cambridge: Cambridge University Press.

Nutter, G.W. 1962. *The Growth of Industrial Production in the Soviet Union.* Princeton, NJ: Princeton University Press.

Ostrom, E. 1990. *Governing the Commons.* Cambridge: Cambridge University Press.

Pareto, V. 1935. *The Mind and Society.* New York: Harcourt Brace.

Pirsig, R. 1974. *Zen and the Art of Motorcycle Maintenance: An Inquiry into Values.* New York: HarperCollins.

Podemska-Mikluch, M., and R.E. Wagner. 2013. Dyads, Triads, and the Theory of Exchange: Between Liberty and Coercion. *Review of Austrian Economics* 26: 171–82.

Read, L. 1958. *I, Pencil*. Irvington-on-Hudson, NY: Foundation for Economic Education.

Scheiner, S.M., and M.R. Willig (eds.). 2011. *The Theory of Ecology*. Chicago: University of Chicago Press.

Schmitt, C. 1932 [1996]. *The Concept of the Political*. Chicago: University of Chicago Press.

Shackle, G.L.S. 1972. *Epistemics and Economics*. Cambridge: Cambridge University Press.

Sterpan, I., and R.E. Wagner. 2017. The Autonomy of the Political in Political Economy. *Advances in Austrian Economics* 22: 133–57.

Wagner, R.E. 2012. Viennese Kaleidics: Why It's Liberty More Than Policy That Calms Turbulence. *Review of Austrian Economics* 25: 283–97.

Wagner, R.E. 2016. *Politics as a Peculiar Business: Insights from a Theory of Entangled Political Economy*. Cheltenham, UK: Edward Elgar.

Wagner, R.E. 2018. The Language of Taxation: Ideology Masquerading as Science. In *For Your Own Good: Taxes, Paternalism, and Fiscal Discrimination in the Twenty-First Century*, ed. A. Hoffer and T. Nisbit, 77–96. Mercatus: Arlington, VA.

CHAPTER 5

Kaleidic Economies and Internally Generated Change

All systems have performance characteristics that describe the features people can reasonably expect from a well-working system. For a coffee maker those characteristics might including grinding coffee beans to the proper fineness and maintaining the brewed coffee at the appropriate temperature. For a car's electrical system, those characteristics might include keeping the lights shining steadily and starting the car without hesitation. Sometimes mechanical systems don't work according to the expectation built into their design. This situation brings into play a mechanic to diagnose and repair the system's malfunction. Mechanical systems are built with a teleological purpose or objective in mind, and that purpose creates both an expectation of reasonable performance and recognition of when that system is failing to perform properly. To be sure, designed systems vary hugely in size and complexity. While malfunctioning may be easy to recognize, repair might be difficult due to the multiplicity of connections among the interacting parts of the system. All the same, the teleology that informs the construction of mechanical systems contains both an expectation of reasonable performance and elicits the diagnosis–repair template in response to a mal-performing system.

Economists have long-described economic interaction within an economy as constituting a system whose performance properties can work to variable effect. The development of economic theory has mostly pursued and amplified this systems image, illustrated in the late nineteenth century by such concepts as a price system or competitive system and more

127
R. E. Wagner, *Macroeconomics as Systems Theory*,
https://doi.org/10.1007/978-3-030-44465-5_5

recently by describing an economic system as one of dynamic and stochastic general equilibrium. The point at relevance for this book is that these various efforts to describe economic interaction as constituting a "system" are executed in a fashion that reduces those systems to a mechanical system, perhaps a relatively complex one, but a mechanical system all the same. As a mechanical system, it possesses a designer's teleology and is subject to the expectation–diagnosis–repair template.

SYSTEMS THINKING: MECHANISTIC OR VOLITIONAL AND CREATIVE?

Economists are prone to treating economic systems by the image of mechanism, as illustrated by the spate of references to "market mechanism" throughout the history of economics. The very concepts of perfect and imperfect competition convey this idea of mechanism, while also calling into play the diagnosis–repair template. With respect to economic theory, diagnosis was the province of economists and repair the province of the political administrators who supervised the economic mechanism. A theorist could accept this mechanistic mode of thought while doubting the ability of political administrators to repair that system effectively, perhaps operating under the presumption that the losses from impeded or imperfect performance would be less than the cost of repairing that mechanism. It might be possible to imagine a better performing economic mechanism without being able to improve performance without incurring more cost than the improved performance would warrant.

All the same, the widespread conceptualization of an economic system as operating in a state of equilibrium melds immediately into a vision of an economy as a mechanism. Economists may differ in their evaluations of the mechanism's performance as well as over the ability of political supervision to improve the mechanism's performance. All the same, there seems to exist nearly universal agreement among economists that their object of analysis is a mechanistic system that is subject to teleological examination as exemplified by such works on political administration of the economic mechanism as A. C. Pigou (1912), Jan Tinbergen (1952), and Nicola Acocella (1988). This image of economists as using their theories to advise political administrators is perhaps helpful if the theory of the system is apt; otherwise, those efforts might insert chaotic impulses into a system that has self-repairing properties.

This book embraces the claim that any description and appraisal of economic activity and interaction must entail the recognition that the operation of economic processes in historical time is necessarily characterized by turbulence, and not by steady states. This claim bears a family resemblance to real business cycle theories where an economy is continually buffeted by shocks to its rate of growth, and with those shocks absorbed in a Pareto efficient manner. But to have a family resemblance is not to be a twin. Real business cycle theorists treat the macro economy as directly observable by eliminating human interaction through embracing a representative agent as constituting macro reality. In doing this, those theories must further assume that economic activity is synchronic, for a representative agent has no option but to be coordinated with himself. In contrast, this book denies the usefulness of theories reduced to representative agents, which in turn opens into recognition that economic activity is diachronic in Shackle's (1972) frame of reference. In other words, economic actions are never fully coordinated because new actions continually are being injected into a society. That the institutional arrangements of a market economy generally operate to promote societal coordination is a historical observation that is open to theoretical explanation; however, an equally accurate historical observation is that market economies entail turbulence. That turbulence, moreover, is not suitably described as resulting from exogenous shocks. From the point of view of an individual, nearly everything in the world of experience arrives as an exogenous shock; however, from the point of view of a social system what are claimed to be shocks are actually clashes among plans that necessarily can never be fully coordinated. Recognition of this fact of social life gives especial significance to the institutional arrangements that govern the abandonment and liquidation of plans.

SYSTEMIC EQUILIBRIUM: MISLEADING BUT NOT WRONG AS SOCIAL THEORY

Orthodox macro theory takes its bearings from the Walrasian (1874) conception of general equilibrium. To be sure, the theory of general equilibrium has advanced far beyond Walras's counting of equations and unknowns, as illustrated by Arrow and Hahn (1971). While the form of the theory changed dramatically over the century between Walras and Arrow and Hahn, as Roy Weintraub (1993) surveys, the central idea of consistency among economic actions remains in place. For instance, an increase in the demand for one product must entail either a decrease in demand for some other product or an improvement in the technology by which a product is produced. There is general interdependence among economic activities that in the limit can be characterized as an equilibrium wherein there would exist no reallocations of resources that would increase some people's welfare without reducing the welfare of others.

To be sure, this claim about Pareto efficiency is a piece of demonstrative logic (Polya 1954) that provides order within a theorist's mind. As George Shackle (1974) explained, a good theory enables a theorist to feel good about his or her construction. Equilibrium theory pertains to a particular scheme of logic and is not a statement that in any directly observable way describes historical reality. There is no way a theorist can tell by observation whether Pareto efficiency characterizes reality, as Oscar Morgenstern (1972) explains. For instance, does a ship crashing on rocks point to Pareto inefficiency? We may reasonably presume that the owner of the ship and the cargo, as well as the shipmates would prefer not to crash. But they might have been compensated sufficiently to induce them to sail in the presence of the risk of crashing. Indeed, observation that they chose to set sail surely gives reasonable grounds for inferring that they agreed to bear the risk. While a lighthouse might have prevented the crash, those who were at risk might not have been willing to support construction of a lighthouse by taking a reduction in their payment for sailing. Further, the logic of gains from trade tells us that any situation that is described as being Pareto inefficient simultaneously means that there exist courses of action that would yield gains from trade, thereby eliminating the Pareto inefficiency in the process.

For standard macro theory, the equivalent of market imperfection is the presence of output gaps, as well as the existence of a rate of growth below some Pareto efficient rate. But is an output gap observable? Is a Pareto deficient rate of growth observable? Output gaps and deficient rates of growth are features of a particular analytical model, which enables a theorist to claim inefficiency *within the context of that model*. That model, however, is necessarily a reduction from a far more complex set of historical observations, recognition of which puts the question of Pareto efficiency back one level to examine the pertinence of the analytical model. It is easy to posit a model of competitive equilibrium that operates unchanged through time. Under such circumstances, aggregate output and employment will be constant and Pareto efficiency will prevail. No one, however, thinks this model provides a reasonable guide to the actual operation of economic processes. But what would be a reasonable characterization of an actual economy as societies proceed through time?

At this point we must recur to the law of the excluded middle and its assertion that a statement cannot be both true and false. Either reality is Pareto efficient or it isn't. Either an economy is in equilibrium or it isn't. Adherence to the law of the excluded middle forces a theorist to make a choice between two options. But the law of the excluded middle pertains to a syllogistic logic that is concerned with logical implications of sets of assumptions. To the contrary, a good deal of reality entails a form of tacking between opposing forces. For instance, economic reality entails a tension between the supporters of currently profitable enterprises and the supporters of plans who seek to insert those plans into the societal ecology, upsetting some successful plans in the process.

Within a framework of yin-and-yang, it is possible to recognize that there is nothing new under the sun while also recognizing that a person cannot even step twice into the same river. At issue in this aside about philosophy is the relation between structure and process within economic theory. There is a formal structure to all social relations and interactions that entail production and trade. There is also ever-changing substantive content to those relationships and interactions. Substantive content continually changes through entrepreneurial experimentation while the formal structure of inputs and outputs and of producers and consumers remains invariant. A theorist can recognize the wisdom Ecclesiastes expressed about there being nothing new under the sun while simultaneously recognizing Heraclites's different wisdom that you can't even step twice into the same river.

Here we must confront questions regarding the types of insight and illumination we hope to attain from our theoretical constructions. Once again, we stand before one of those numerous forks in the theoretical road. The DSGE model provides what is presently the primary branch of the theoretical road. The text of DSGE is clear: an economy exists in a state of equilibrium until it is shocked by some exogenous event. The text is silent about what happens next, other than asserting that a new equilibrium will be attained. DSGE provides no insight into how societies respond to the exogenous shocks that feature prevalently within the theory. By default within the DSGE framework, if there is to be any repair it is to be orchestrated by governmental entities which are assumed to stand outside the economic process. Not all DSGE models embrace political action to close the output gaps that accompany exogenous shocks. For models of New Classical vintage, the economy is always Pareto efficient, with shocks simply denoting a parade of changes to an economy's rate of growth due to changes in technology and preferences. For these models, an economy conforms to the model of perfect competition.

By contrast, economies are presumed to be imperfectly competitive within the DSGE models that maintain roots in the postwar Keynesian tradition of macro theory as concerned with systemic failure. Since the DSGE model has no internal source of restorative activity, the remedy for any claimed or perceived output gap must reside in political action, and with those who populate the political precincts within a society being forms of mechanic who repair the body politic. What arises at the level of subtext is an analytical framework that envisions people writing the first draft of the manuscript of societal life through their market activities, and with political entities then completing, amending, or otherwise revising that manuscript. In other words, the basic model is one of the societal failure when human activities are organized through consent alone. The state is thus treated as an entity that overcomes those failures.

Within this scheme of thought, "failure" pertains to transactions that would have been mutually beneficial within the context of some theoretical model, but yet those transactions were not undertaken, typically because some untestable claim was advanced about those transactions being prevented by high transaction costs. What is one to do in the presence of a theory that claims mutual gains from trade were prevented by high transaction costs? It is, after all, costly to put transactions together, and the cost of doing this to the organizer might be higher than what that organizer perceives to be the gains. In any case, a failure for such a transaction to be organized brings us to yet another of those forks in the theoretical road. One branch of that fork would claim that the theorist's claim is correct, which in turn might enable the theorist to feel good about supporting the use of power to impose a theoretical recommendation. The other branch would hold that failure to embrace the theorist's recommendation is evidence against the theorist's claim (Buchanan 1959). This is the impasse at which we arrive in pursuing the DSGE model of analysis.

OEE offers a way around that impasse by developing different theoretical insight, and here it is different insight and not superior insight that should be emphasized. After all, our statements are all products of the models we build, all of which are reductions from the reality inside of which we sense ourselves to be encased. DSGE characterizes an economic system as existing in a state of equilibrium until it is hit by an exogenous shock. DSGE then applies the method of comparative statics to the new data after the shock to assert the existence of a new equilibrium. The theory neither contains nor offers insight into the internal workings of the system. DSGE operates within a stipulative and not a generative mode of analysis. In contrast, OEE operates within a generative mode of analysis, which means that the theory captures the idea of a social system acting on itself to transform itself.

To speak of a system transforming itself opens into numerous forms of insight and illumination that are hidden from view within the DSGE vision. For one thing, transformation can be the province of anyone within the system. People are no longer treated as passive responders to systemic data, but rather are recognized as creators of data that enter into the system and may in some cases transform that system. All agents within a social system are potential carriers of transformative energy. How much energy they carry and to what effect is an open question that in any case carries systems-level analysis in a different direction from where DSGE macro takes it. To take note of transformation is not to assert that any transformation is of generally beneficial quality. Transformation might benefit a few at the expense of many. It might benefit many at the expense of a few. The main point in any case is that change always initiates with particular entities inside a society, and how fully or rapidly it spreads depends on the reception accorded by other entities within the society. For instance, a failing enterprise might create an output gap within an equilibrium theory. Within a process-oriented theory, however, where people continually are forming new enterprises, there will also exist potential markets for the assets and contractual relationships held by failing enterprise. Under a genuinely free economy, output gaps are evanescent.

NATURAL FLUIDITY WITHIN AN ECOLOGY OF PLANS

DSGE theory portrays an economy as existing in a steady state. The idea of a steady state as providing a sense of normality pervades attempts by both political figures and economists to determine whether downward deviations from some perceived steady state indicate some form of economic malfunction. For instance, the National Bureau of Economic Research has emerged as the entity that determines whether an economy is in a state of recession. Basically, the NBER defines a recession as six months of negative growth in GDP. To the sure, the NBER relies on more than GDP, including data on real income, industrial production, and retail sales, all relating to the NIPA accounts, and all pointing backward. For a recession to be declared, the aggregate data must have shown six months of decline. Those data, moreover, are collected with delay and, furthermore, often undergo revision in future months and years, sometimes of significant magnitude.

It is quite possible that a period that later is described as denoting a recession might be entering a recovery according to data that will be acquired in the future. There would thus seem to be some disconnection between the use of data to guide economic control after the fashion of mechanics working on faltering engines and recognition that economic activity is fundamentally forward looking. Macro theory of the DSGE form seeks to treat a national economy as an economizing entity instead of recognizing it to be an ecology of economizing entities. One significant question worth pursuing is what happens when a wrong-headed model is used to inform some effort at systemic control. For instance, and to use a different mechanical analogy, when flying a propeller-drive aircraft through a storm, reacting to a downward dip by pushing the nose upward can cause the plane to stall and possibly crash, because raising the nose interferes with the plane's natural stability properties. Might something similar be at work when political entities seek to regulate aggregate measures of economic activity when those measures are generated not by a DSGE system but within an open-ended and evolutionary ecology of plans?

One feature of ecologically grounded action is that action at one node typically complements some other nodes while interfering with yet other nodes within the societal ecology. The orthodox scheme of macro ignores the ecological and entrepreneurial processes through which plans are created or abandoned. Any statement about the macro level must be preceded by a micro-level analysis from which the macro phenomenon emerges. Recognition that societies are diachronic ecologies of plans entails recognition that turbulence and output gaps will be working properties of an enterprise economy. We might expect that turbulence typically to be moderate, but we would not expect it to vanish. Each instant will see the insertion of new plans into the ecology of plans, which unavoidably will unsettle some previously settled relationships within the societal ecology as some people change jobs and other people change the products they buy.

The so-called competitive model presents an idealized vision of a society as existing in a steady state (Mises 1966) of cooperative relationships. That vision, however, is historically unattainable, at least within liberally organized societies where people are at liberty to choose their activities. This liberty to choose will operate continually to inject novelty into society, which will unsettle some previously established relationships. Cooperative relationships are also established through a process that often entails quarrels and conflicts where peaceful relationships stand at the end of some settlement of those quarrels and conflicts, as Lewis Coser (1964) explains. The competitive vision posits the presence of "policy" as the instrument the state uses to prevent conflict, thereby maximizing the domain of peaceful interaction. This competitive vision, however, is deeply incoherent because without conflict is utopian and not an attainable reality. Orthodox theory personifies the state as an entity that acts to suppress chaotic forces latent within society, thereby expanding the range of peaceful cooperation. For the state to do this, however, requires talents and capacities that are nowhere present in society. The competitive vision might serve as some sort of ideal rallying point, but it is one that is historically unattainable and, moreover, one for which efforts to attain will be socially destructive by replacing voluntary with compulsory principles within the organization of social activity.

The competitive vision as commonly presented imagines action to take place at the macro or social level, which cannot happen. Even the claim that the state provides the framework for good public order must enter society at the ground level, and with system-level consequences depending on the properties of that ground-level action and how it is greeted by other nodes within the ecology of plans. To illustrate this point, compare the properties of litigation when both parties are private and when one party is a public entity. By now, a significant literature has arisen regarding the properties of a system of privately financed litigation to economize on litigation. The central idea behind this literature is that litigants own the enterprises they represent and that their expenses of litigation are part of their commercial operation. By the standard economic calculus, a litigant will increase spending on litigation so long as the anticipated return from doing so exceeds the added cost. Each party to the litigation is in this position. Furthermore, trial rules and procedures regarding such things as discovery operate pretty much to instill in the litigants similar anticipations regarding the outcome of any litigation because each party knows a good deal about the other party's evidence and theory of the case. This similarity helps to generate settlement of cases without trial due to the ability of litigants to economize on their litigation expenses.

The situation changes when the plaintiff is a public entity (Wagner 1999). A public plaintiff is not a residual claimant over the expenses of litigation. Public plaintiffs still face options, but they operate inside a budgetary process. This means that an Attorney General receives a budget which is better spent in some fashion than returned to the treasury and accompanied by a lower appropriation for the next year. All the same, the Attorney General and the staff attorneys must still exercise choices over how they use their budgets, only they can't retain what they don't spend and so face no reason to economize on the expenses of litigation. They are, however, in a position to capture benefits from pursuing one course of litigation over another course. Just how these benefits might manifest is a substantive rather than a formal matter. For instance, an Attorney General might be thinking of running for Governor or Senator and might be able to use the expenses of litigation as forms of investment in securing favorable publicity. Staff attorneys might similarly be able to use their selection among potential cases as vehicles for promoting their careers. In such instances as these, defendants become to some extent forced investors in the ambitions of public plaintiffs. Within the normal context of macro theory, such possibilities are of no relevance because they are swept into and lost amidst the NIPA-like measures. Within the social-theoretic orientation pursued here, however, we have yet another illustration of how micro- and meso-level interaction generates the systemic or macro-level properties inside of which we all reside, for better or for worse.

SYSTEMIC NORMALITY: TURBULENT AND DIACHRONIC

OEE-style theories treat economies as turbulent and diachronic, as befits the analogy of an economy to a crowd of pedestrians leaving an arena after an event. The crowd is orderly, just as is a parade. It is, however, a category mistake to treat parades as identical to pedestrian crowds. We would attribute the orderliness of a parade to the musical and marching abilities of the participants. These attributes are irrelevant for apprehending the orderliness of pedestrian crowds, for that orderliness is more a matter of some combination of rules of common courtesy and the desire of people not to treat their bodies as the equivalent of bumper cars at a carnival. To treat economies as naturally turbulent leads to curiosity about whether a society can avoid or at least mitigate turbulence. In this regard, Axel Leijonhufvud (1981) speculated that there was some corridor within which turbulence would be self-extinguishing, whereas self-extinction as a systemic property was not automatic outside that corridor. To be sure, Leijonhufvud's claim was speculation that all the same had a ring of plausibility about it due to recognition that false trading might become so widespread that chaos emerges. This claim about a corridor does not imply that political action might be able to offset chaos in such circumstances because no one might possess the knowledge necessary to do this.

Still, within a diachronic framework there is a stream of discrete periods and not a continuum, as Stephen Wolfram (2002) explains. Each period sees the injection of new plans into the ecology of plans, and these plans make claims on resource inputs and on consumer desires, thereby competing with previously existing plans and thereby unsettling expectations regarding the performance of those plans. It is these injections of new plans and liquidations of old ones that is the source of turbulence within a society. Turbulence stems from disparity between the *ex ante* vision that informed formation of an entrepreneurial plan and some subsequent *ex post* appraisal of that plan. At this point we must confront just what it might mean to claim that agents have or form rational expectations. Within orthodox macro theory, those expectations pertain to such aggregate system values as the data generated through NIPA and related accounts. By this formulation, people form their expectations about future system values as if they knew future solutions to the relevant economic model. To be sure, this is not a claim that people are omniscient, but is only a claim that on average they will be right in their projections about future values. This framework maps readily onto one well-cited situation where numerous people guessed the weight of a pig at a fair. While the guesses varied widely, the average of those guesses hit the actual weight nearly perfectly. This is what rational expectations within the DSGE framework accomplishes. Does this outcome make for a satisfying theory?

Does not answer to this question depend on the relevance to human action of knowledge that a large group of people guessing the weight of a pig will on average be accurate? Each such guess could be interpreted as that person's commercial expectation. While the *ex ante* expectations among the guessers will be all over the place, on average those expectations will be accurate *ex post*. To change the situation, suppose you were working in a field beside a target that was one-meter square. One thousand meters away, a large number of people shoot at the target, with the most accurate shooter winning a prize. You were, moreover, assured that previous experience showed that on average the shots would hit the center of the target. Does this assurance provide sufficient basis for feeling comfortable about working in the shadow of the target? Surely not. Even a set of shooters whose vision was 20–200 and not 20–20 would be accurate on average by the law of large numbers when pointed in the right direction. It is variance and not average that matters for turbulence.

All plans entail the commitment of capital in particular forms and manners. Commercial planning is specific and not generic. A building erected to house a restaurant will be configured differently from one erected to house a welding shop. Capital deployed in acetylene torches will not be suitable for baking bread. Guesses about a pig's weight or shots fired from a rifle do not map reasonably well onto any model of economic activity. In particular, the expectations that are commercially relevant are not of system variables of the NIPA type but are of variables suitable for someone's commercial plan. Aggregate variables of the NIPA type are general and undifferentiated; commercial plans are specific and aimed at particular targets. An aggregation over those plans might yield something that resembles NIPA accounts, but such an *ex post* summary would be just dead statistics. Within the OEE framework this book carries forward, economizing action is always aimed at particular objectives and never at some NIPA-like aggregate. Projected prices of particular products and inputs are surely relevant for someone's commercial plan, but aggregate price levels are surely irrelevant to anyone's commercial plan. True, they might have some significance to such financial organizations as commercial banks, but even banks will be far more interested in such micro-level data as their projections about attracting depositors and finding customers to whom to supply loans. Within the OEE framework, human action can originate only on the micro and meso levels of society; macro-level statistics can be compiled, of course, but these are inert with respect to initiating action. Here again, we encounter the wisdom behind that old aphorism: "think globally but act locally" but with the proviso added that local action is the only possible type of action there is.

Turbulence is an abstract quality that derives its meaning in opposition to steadiness. The intensity of turbulence, however, can vary over time, and with several possible sources of variation. Most of that variation is what would reasonably be described as a natural product of a social system grounded on freedom of enterprise. Such variation, moreover, will generally feature self-mitigating properties. Accordingly, it is doubtful whether there are policy measures beyond the standard vision of government as helping to secure rights of property and obligations of contract that can reasonably calm turbulence (Wagner 2012). All new plans entail the *ex ante* projection by the owner that the present value of that plan will exceed the alternative return that the capital invested in that plan would yield. As an *ex post* matter, plans often will fall short of what their owners anticipated, which at some future moment of realization will lead to liquidation of such plans. Indeed, it has long been regarded as an open question whether entrepreneurial profits in the aggregate are positive or negative. If all enterprises were proprietorships and if the owner provided all inputs the firm used, entrepreneurial plans would operate independently of other plans. Typically, however, plans are interdependent, and in several ways, each of which can contribute to turbulence. Instead of proprietorships, corporate forms of organization might be used, thereby enlisting other people in the service of the entrepreneur's plan. Each of those participants, moreover, is an owner of his or her own plans, of which participation in this plan is but one piece of that plan.

Further, at different points subsequent to the initiation of the plan, the entrepreneur will need to hire inputs and pay them based on what market competition requires relative to the value that the entrepreneur anticipates those inputs will create. Even more, the output must later be sold, at which time the value of the preceding hire of inputs will be revealed. Any plan can be described as a directed graph that runs from the present into the future. Plans entail inputs and outputs, along with a temporal gap during which product matures. The simplest models work with discrete points, with inputs applied followed after some duration by outputs. This model mirrors planting-and-harvesting processes. Things get more complicated with continuous applications of inputs and outputs, which is generally the case, though accounting conventions and requirements also create discrete periods inside continuous processes, as Jack Hirshleifer (1970) illustrates.

In any case, the challenge is to illustrate the generation of turbulence as a feature of normality—and also to illustrate how entrepreneurs have good motivation to calm turbulence through their residual claimant status. In contrast, so-called "policy makers" lack residual claimancy and operate instead on other people's accounts. Within an ecology of plans, there would seem to be two categories of turbulence. One source resides inside the entrepreneur's sphere of action, for an entrepreneur might not achieve least-cost combinations of inputs. The other source resides elsewhere in the ecology as other entrepreneurial plans turn out to be more attractive. Political processes can also come into play. Political agencies without residual claimancy might advance the plans of their executives by supporting enterprises that would fail on their own weight, as DelliSanti and Wagner (2018) examine in comparing bankruptcy with politically organized bailouts.

Also relevant is the distinction between quantity and quality which Robert Pirsig (1974) explores in *Zen and the Art of Motorcycle Maintenance*. That book's narrative unfolded in conjunction with a motorcycle trip from the Midwest to the west coast, but it was really a meditation on the ancient discourse on quantity and quality in human effort. Economic theory mostly takes the side of quantity, as illustrated by the macro discourse on output gaps where what matters is the fact that people are working and not on what they are doing. In contrast, quality surely deserves a hearing. With respect to macro theory, the kinds of activities people pursue and not just the fact of their being employed is significant. Political ordering changes the pattern of human activity relative to private ordering, recognition of which brings forward the quality–quantity distinction, which Alasdair MacIntyre (1988) explores luminously in contrasting alternative conceptions of justice and rationality. In other words, a higher rate of economic growth is not identical with enhanced human flourishing, and this book stresses flourishing relative to growth. This is not to say that growth and flourishing are opposed but is rather to claim that there is a distinction between foreground and background that is significant for analytical clarity.

OUTLIERS, MASSES, AND THE RELEASE OF SOCIETAL ENERGY: A QUANTUM-LIKE VIEW

It is surely plausible to think that conservation dominates change in typical societies. Most people most of the time continue to established practices and patterns as they move forward in time. But not everyone does, and probably no one does all of the time. At any instant we may be sure that some people are taking their various practices into new territory. Most people surely want calm most of the time, but some people want movement. How might these different desires resolve themselves within a society? In posing this question, once again we come up against recognition that the answer varies depending on the conceptual framework with which we work. In this respect, two classes of conceptual model can be put in play. One class looks at masses; the other looks at outliers. Neither is right or wrong, for they address different questions and cast their illumination differently.

Orthodox macro theory looks to masses. The representative agent model does this directly by collapsing an entire society into a single individual. This isn't a real individual but is a virtual or constructed individual that is described by the average features thought to be pertinent for that society. This construction reduces what might otherwise be complex societal interaction to simple choices by what the theory has constructed as the representative individual. Alternatively, societies can be portrayed through averages without constructing a representative agent on which comparative statics can be performed. Under either approach, relationships and interactions among individuals disappears from the theoretical framework, and the theory proceeds either by theorizing about the representative agent or the societal average.

An alternative theoretical vision looks to outliers and explores the impact that outliers can have on social masses. In the spirit of Thomas Schelling (1978), suppose 1000 people are arrayed on a grid. Those people follow two rules. One is that they do not invade another person's location. This rule corresponds to the principle of private property. The other rule is that no player allows more than three squares to separate that player from the nearest neighbor. This rule corresponds to the principle that the individuals constitute a society, to indicate that our theoretical object is society and not rational action per se. The stipulation of such rules is a common feature of equilibrium theories where the properties of stipulated configurations of rules is the object of explanatory interest. Within the purview of this book, however, it must be recognized that the rules that appear to govern social interaction at any moment emerged through prior interaction.

Within any instant, suppose 50 of the persons change location. The remaining 950 have no desire to change location. Nonetheless, the movement of the 50 will induce movement among the remainder to maintain the rule of allowing no more than three squares to separate any person from his or her nearest neighbor. By standard statistical conventions, this society is static because the hypothesis of stasis cannot be rejected at the 5% level of significance. Yet the model is based on perpetual change, with 5% of the society inducing adaptation within the rest of the society. This setting reflects Joseph Schumpeter's (1934) recognition that entrepreneurship is the source of leadership in a capitalist society. Should this experiment be continued over a sequence of periods, time-lapse photography will show a society on the move, and with the direction of movement generated by entrepreneurial action.

In this respect, it is the outliers who propel societal change. While masses are content to conserve what is established, outliers seek to inject new ideas and social configurations into society. To be sure, the 5–95 dichotomy was selected to conform with standard statistical conventions and was not selected because it conforms to evidence about human sentiments and moral imaginations. Most people most of the time continue mostly to do what they have already been doing. But what matters for change and what is the source of turbulence are actions by entrepreneurial outliers. With respect to plausible reasoning (Polya 1954), both static structure and emergent process have explanatory value for thinking about social systems in their entirety.

This situation doesn't mean, however, that each theoretical scheme brings equal value to the scholarly enterprise of thinking about the systemic properties of societies. The question here is whether some reasonable priority regarding structure and process can be assigned. Over short intervals of time, structure has much to commend it as a point of priority because of the long-standing recognition that nature doesn't make leaps. But leaps do occur, as anyone who grew up before cell phones will realize. More significantly perhaps, process entails relationships among persons, whereas structure can be described wholly in terms of relationships among things. For economics conceived as a social theory centered on the ubiquity of economizing action, process would surely take precedence over structure in the generation of theoretical frameworks. While the qualities of social life depend on the availability of resources, those qualities are surely more significantly influenced by the pattern of relationships that are in play within a society, for resource allocations emerge through human interactions and relationships, as conveyed by George Shackle's (1972) recognition that economics is about thoughts more than about things.

Exogenous Shocks as Misidentified Conflict Among Plans

Standard macro theory starts with systemic equilibrium, then imposes an exogenous shock which is analyzed by the method of comparative statics. Joseph Schumpeter (1934) set forth one version of this approach, as did Ludwig von Mises (1966). This analytical method could be described as "punctuated equilibrium," in congruence with some formulations of evolutionary biology. At any instant, some set of tools for thinking exist for working with intuitions and extracting their implications. A thinker's ability to work with his or her intuitive hunches depends on the tools of thought that are available at the time. At a later instant, new tools might have come into play that render worthwhile a revisiting of older formulations. For instance, Nicholas Vriend (2002) asked "Was Hayek an ACE?" By this question, Vriend was asking whether Hayek would have been a theorist who worked with agent-based computational models. Obviously, Hayek could not have done that because agent-based platforms were not available to Hayek. Vriend's point, however, was to explain how agent-based modeling could have allowed Hayek to convey his thinking about distributed and incomplete knowledge more fully and thoroughly than he was able to do. In this respect, Devereaux and Wagner (2020) carry forward this idea by moving the traditional stag hunt onto a synecological platform where no entity in society can apprehend the entirety of that society.

It is reasonable to presume that at any instant new commercial experiments are being planned and set in motion. Those experiments are not set in truly unexplored commercial territory because humans are incapable of thinking without making some connections with what is familiar. Most work by economists that makes spatial references to treats the relevant space as Euclidian, along the lines that Fig. 3.1 illustrates. Yet, different conceptualizations of space will lead spatial thinking in different directions. Euclidian-inspired thought entails continuity over space, and lead to simple concepts of distance which enable statements to be made that some entrepreneurial acts differ more from what is familiar than other entrepreneurial acts. There are, however, non-Euclidian geometries that aren't easily visualized but which can map onto discrete combinatorial spaces, as illustrated by movement among discrete tiles that have some network pattern of connection. Whatever the model of space a theorist employs, an entrepreneurial experiment will seek to locate a product or service at some position in that commercial space where it will attract sufficient attention to become commercially viable. The form that commercial success takes is always the same: the product or service attracts revenue in excess of what must be spent to provide the service. But form is not substance, and the substance of success will be known only after the plan has been in motion for some time.

What exists in any case is a continual competition for commercial space along the lines that Fig. 3.1 sketched, recognizing that Fig. 3.1 presents a Euclidian conception of space. Business firms are the carriers of competition within society. While equilibrium theory assumes that firms combine inputs in a least-cost manner, this assumption is one feature of the claim that a competitive equilibrium is Pareto efficient. This is a piece of demonstrative logic that is necessary to support the claim of Pareto efficiency. In no way is that claim subject to independent verification. There are reasons grounded in plausibility to recognize that private property generates incentives for owners to try to operate their firms in least-cost fashion. To do that substantively as distinct from the formal level of pure theory requires recognition of the complexities of commercial management, and which is the obverse side of economic calculation.

To describe output as produced by two inputs with given prices trivializes the substantive difficulties of commercial management. For purposes of stating sufficient conditions for Pareto efficient allocations of resources, this standard theoretical framework does the job. But for understanding and explaining the turbulence that accompanies any enterprise system, it is deficient in the same manner that flat-line portraits of macro equilibrium are deficient. Furthermore, turbulence at the level of commercial enterprises can project onto macro-level turbulence. In other words, firms are continually engaged in experimentation, and with firms varying in the success they have. With knowledge continually being created, moreover, there is no sense in which an efficient input mix can be discovered for all time because new managerial insights, procedures, and techniques will continually be discovered within the combinatorial space that is relevant for entrepreneurial action.

Within standard theory, the problem of locating a production frontier amounts to finding the right a/b input combination for given prices for those inputs. This formalization is a necessary piece of the demonstration of the Pareto efficiency of a postulated competitive equilibrium. In no way, however, is this formalization pertinent to the practical actions of entrepreneurs and managers who are seeking to thrive within an ecology of enterprises. Those managers face challenging combinatorial problems of choosing among procedures, contractors, personnel, and the like to establish a going concern within the ecology of enterprises. Suppose the manager must select 10 such elements from among 50 possibilities. This situation yields over 10 billion ways of operating the firm. And if the possible elements were 100 in number, the firm could be constituted in over 17 trillion ways.

Truly exogenous shocks to a society are surely rare. A strike by a meteor would certainly qualify, as would the burning out of the Sun at some distant future. Such instances as these aside, what are commonly called exogenous shocks get their name with reference to the presumption that a flat-line equilibrium constitutes societal normality. They also reflect recognition that most change in the external world appears as exogenous shocks to individuals. In any case, flat-line normality is unchanging and dull, with all excitement and change coming from outside the society. Within the ecological framework, however, change originates within the society, and takes the form of injecting new experiments of various types into the society. The creation of new enterprises is one major category of experiment. Those experiments are always injected into an ongoing ecology, which means the new experiment must capture operating space for itself within its desired commercial territory. Whether the new experiment is successful or not, it will unsettle some established commercial relationships in the effort to capture operating space. Volatility and not placidity will characterize systemic normality within an enterprise-based economy.

MODERATING TURBULENCE
THROUGH PRIVATE ORDERING

To recognize that turbulence is a normal phenomenon to be expected within a well-working enterprise economy raises many questions concerning the use of political power to promote economic stability. One significant question is whether there is any basis for distinguishing between turbulence that is good and beneficial in some generally recognized sense and turbulence that is harmful and destructive. The qualifier "generally recognized sense" is vital in trying to make this distinction and may in turn be a qualifier whose applicability cannot be identified, especially in societies where enterprises are governed by admixtures of private and public ordering. We should also recognize that private ordering and public ordering are both abstractions, neither of which are found in pure form.

For this reason, it is misleading to refer to observed systemic outcomes as denoting the properties of a privately ordered market economy. All observations pertain to variable admixtures of private and public ordering.

Within an institutional arrangement governed by private ordering, an entrepreneur decides to create a menagerie of solar-powered yard equipment to replace such gasoline-powered engines as lawn mowers, leaf mulchers, and snow blowers. The equipment would be lighter, quieter, and cheaper to operate and maintain—or at least these presumptions reflects the entrepreneur's thinking. The institutions of private ordering provide a framework within which the entrepreneur can construct an experiment to test his belief in the value of the enterprise. This framework, moreover, is abstract and not specific, in that it operates within a generalized rubric of consensual interaction without specifying actions that must or must not be undertaken. The entrepreneur will have to amass sufficient capital to fund the enterprise, without specifying whether the entrepreneur is the sole supplier of capital or, alternatively, creates a corporate structure with shareholders or bondholders. The entrepreneur will also have to create a presence for the products in the minds of potential buyers, though there are many different channels along which the entrepreneur can try to do this.

The central point is that an enterprise economy allows people to pursue their commercial dreams to the extent they choose to do so, enlisting other people in that pursuit to the extent those people are willing to do so. Within private ordering, no one can be enlisted in the support of someone else's commercial dream. Not all dreams end happily. Indeed, entrepreneurial profits in the sense of Knight (1921) may well be negative in the aggregate. If so, this would surely indicate that the society contains a good number of people who are pursuing commercial dreams even though many entries into the ecology of plans will fail. Indeed, one could develop a model of welfare economics wherein the utility losses from failed plans exceeds the utility gains from successful plans and use this model to argue in support of public supervision over commercial investment. While failed plans impose capital losses on those who have invested in the plan, including those who have changed jobs and possibly changed residences as well, failed plans still have commercial value through liquidation. The owners of failed plans thus have incentive to secure the highest value they can obtain from liquidating the enterprise, which requires finding those buyers who value those assets most highly in their own commercial enterprises. While the liquidation of failed enterprises is unlikely to forestall any output gap, it is nonetheless likely to lower that gap as compared with a situation where liquidation requires participation by and permission from political entities who do not operate with direct residual claimancy over their actions.

While the economic theory of an enterprise economy has concentrated on the coordination of economic activities among enterprises, another significant facet of an enterprise economy is the way the enterprise system accommodates commercial liquidations. An enterprise that ceases operation to undergo liquidation has the inverse problem of the enterprise that is seeking to get established in commercial space. The enterprise to be liquidated has a stock of assets that might include real estate, inventories, and vendor relationships. The entrepreneur's problem can reasonably be posed as one of securing the maximum present value from liquidating the enterprise. In many cases, that highest value will belong to similar enterprises that might value equipment and inventories more highly than less similar enterprises, as Henry Manne (1965) explained in his examination of mergers. While mergers can mitigate turbulence within a system of private ordering, they can have the opposite effect in the presence of public ordering. For instance, antitrust legislation is often used to oppose reasonable commercial liquidation, increasing the degree of turbulence in consequence of reducing the efficiency of commercial liquidation.

Equilibrium theory stresses the coordination of economic activities; indeed, it focusses exclusively on such coordination, as illustrated by statements of the necessary conditions for competitive equilibrium. Historically operating economic processes, however, entail the creation and testing of entrepreneurial experiments in an environment where the outcome of an experiment cannot be determined prior to conducting the experiment. A theorist can assert that an entrepreneur forms a judgment about the probable outcome of the experiment, and with respect to frequentist probability assert that the entrepreneur's estimated outcome is an unbiased estimate of a probabilistic process. This procedure enables elimination of the distinction between *ex ante* and *ex post* orientations as an expectational matter. Even with this theoretical procedure, however, variance has significant work to do once it is recognized that *ex ante* entrepreneurial anticipations create specific capital configurations *ex post* to carry forward the entrepreneur's plan. The greater that variance among entrepreneurs, the larger will be the commercial debris created through the abandonment of commercial plans.

At this point, we enter the realm of personal probability. The standard reference to unbiased estimates corresponds to frequentist images of entrepreneurs treating their experiments as equivalent to rolling dice. All entrepreneurs recognize they are rolling dice, and so make the same calculations. This framework yields the DSGE model; however, that model leaves no room for entrepreneurs to believe in the special character of their individual qualities. If those entrepreneurs were surveyed, half of them would say they expected their plans to perform in a below-average manner. Such observations are unlikely to manifest in societal settings. To the contrary, most if not all entrepreneurs will think their plans will perform in an above-average fashion. To be sure, the share of the population that believes they possess above-average entrepreneurial qualities can vary through time, and with such variation in what might be called confidence often being described as a waxing and waning of animal spirits. In no way, however, should animal spirits be consigned to the realm of mystery and irrationality. All action must bridge a temporal gap between a choice to act and the experiencing of the consequences of that choice. In many cases the gap is narrow, and its depth is shallow. In some cases, however, the gap is wide and the depth deep. Whatever the state of animal spirits, commercial debris will be created by failing enterprises. Private ordering provides a framework for clearing away that debris and converting it to alternative commercial uses. The same can't be said for public ordering, or at least not so strongly and assuredly.

Intensifying Turbulence Through Public Ordering

Public ordering is typically defended as reducing and not promoting turbulence, only this defense is portrayed against the background of output gaps, income–expenditure types of theory, and DSGE modeling. Once a macro economy is recognized as an ecology of plans and not as a homogeneous field of spending, the comparative properties of private and public ordering come into better focus. The key feature of private ordering is consensus among participants. An enterprise to be liquidated has owners of the assets to be liquidated and potential suitors for those assets. There can well be instances where an owner will prefer some suitors over others, and thus liquidate for a lower price to reflect that preference. This ability is within the ownership rights of the owner, unless the owner is a corporation which has a fiduciary duty to its shareholders to liquidate for the highest price. Recognizing the truth in the aphorism "it's the exception that makes the rule," we don't go far wrong in claiming commercial liquidation tends to shift resources toward higher-valued uses as those values are judged by market participants.

Consensus is the central operating principle of private ordering, as a generalization of the principle of gains from trade. For the most part, two-person trades are used to illustrate how both participants gain from trade. The same thing can be said about the complex, multi-person trades that typify much commercial interaction. There is no essential difference between two people who form a partnership and 1000 people who form a cooperative or commercial corporation. Sure, there will be institutional details that distinguish the partnership from the cooperative or the corporation. Among other things, the cooperative and the corporation will have a more elaborate set of governance arrangements than will a partnership. With respect to essential features, however, all three of these social configurations operate through consensus among participants. For the partnership, that consensus is more of a daily occurrence, where for the larger organizations there are agent–principle relationships in play that can enable some modicum of deviation away from pure consensus. All the same, two is the magic number for private ordering, in that the variety of organizational arrangements established through private ordering can be reasonably reduced to a simple model of trade, as Richard Epstein (1995) explains in *Simple Rules for a Complex World*.

In contrast, three is the magic number for public ordering, as Podemska-Mikluch and Wagner (2013) explain. Three people are necessary to illustrate the institutional framework that governs democratic processes. This framework conveys the 2:1 split that reflects the majority–minority split within democratic processes. Within the logic of this split, public ordering will prove beneficial to a majority of people on that issue, while also proving detrimental to a minority. To be sure, this 2:1 split reflects the simplest and most literal model of majority rule. There are many models of democratic process that recognize that minorities can dominate majority-rule processes, as instances of democratic oligarchy (Michels 1912 [1962]). For instance, suppose a bloc of 50 people vote as a unit within a 1000-person polity, where the other members are indifferent between two options. If indifference is modeled as voting by flipping a coin, the block of 50 people will be on the winning side over 80% of the time. And that winning percentage will exceed 99% if the block contains 75 people. In other words, public ordering can promote organizational arrangements that can yield positive value to relatively small numbers of people by imposing net losses on larger numbers of people.

While private ordering might not support the development of solar-powered lawn equipment, public ordering might do so. Everything depends on how public ordering affects enterprise survival relative to private ordering. For private ordering, survival depends on the willingness of investors to provide capital when they are free to direct their capital to other uses. It also depends on the willingness of customers to buy the products and also on the prices that will compensate investors and input suppliers. It is the entrepreneur who ultimately determines the survival of the enterprise, at least over some interval of time, though ultimately even the wealthiest entrepreneur will give up supporting an enterprise that isn't paying its way.

Once the survival of an enterprise falls within the precincts of public ordering, we enter a different social reality. With public ordering, some political enterprise or agency becomes a peculiar type of investor or sponsor (Wagner 2016). Political enterprises still have budget constraints, but they are loose and peculiar. While there is a constraint of some form, it doesn't pertain to any right of ownership. A political enterprise that supports a market enterprise has no one inside the enterprise who provides that capital, for that capital comes from taxpayers who have no direct say in the transaction. Without the presence of transferable ownership, political support of the solar enterprise will not appear, positively or negatively, in the capital accounts of sponsors of the political enterprise. This is not to say that returns to sponsorship won't appear in some manner. It is only to say that they won't appear in the form of increased market valuation of enterprises. As to where they might appear, there are numerous substantive possibilities covering a wide range of degrees of venality. A relatively low degree of venality could be illustrated by ideological or personal zealots who are strongly animated by the possibility of reducing the noise associated with yard equipment. A relatively high degree of venality could be illustrated by a public executive who leverages the contacts made in working with solar equipment into a lucrative position with a trade association. Whatever the degree of venality, we would expect to see public ordering retard the liquidation of enterprises because those enterprises are advancing interests in play within the relevant public agency.

Private ordering and public ordering entail use of two different languages, or two dialects of the same language. Either way, it is costly to translate between the languages or dialects, as the earlier discussion of settling legal disputes illustrated. Within private ordering, the principles of private property and freedom of contract supply the language of profit and loss inside of which commercial transactions are organized. This language is used in the construction of commercial enterprises; it is also used in the liquidation of those enterprises. Public ordering, however, operates within a different language or dialect. It is likewise a transactional language, but that language is one appropriate for creating and maintaining coalitions, in contrast to the consensual character of private ordering. Furthermore, the transactional language of public ordering is grounded on non-logical action and not logical action, recalling Pareto (1935) along with Patrick and Wagner's (2015) amplification. With reference to the preceding discussion of spatial modeling in economics, private ordering occurs on Euclidian-like surfaces that are twice differentiable while public ordering occurs on discrete, non-differentiable surfaces where movement occurs through jumps and failures to jump far enough.

MACRO GROWTH THEORY: SHADOW BOXING WITH REALITY?

Starting with Solow (1956), macro theorists have shifted a good deal of their attention away from stability in resource allocation to the rate of growth. Simple reflection on the arithmetic of compound interest will show the attention-arresting power of this alternative focal point. A cardinal presumption of most formulations of macro growth theory hold that it is simple for public ordering to increase the rate of growth. Indeed, it could be no other way within the standard theoretical formulation. The aggregate rate of growth is a function of three variables: the size of the labor force, the size of the capital stock, and a productivity variable that operates to increase output from any given stock of capital or labor—and with most of the work being done by the productivity variable. Furthermore, that productivity variable is identified as knowledge which in turn is related to education and spending on education, as illustrated by Paul Romer's (1986) treatment of endogenous growth theory.

Returning once again to the canonical statement of the alternative micro–macro conceptualization described by Fig. 1.3, the standard formulations of macro growth theory entail a form of shadow boxing with reality. The growth equation asserts that the rate of growth can be increased by increasing any of its three arguments. It sounds like a recipe, but it isn't. It has the form of a recipe, generic ingredients, but it isn't a recipe because actual ingredients are not specified nor are instructions offered about how to combine those ingredients. Those macro-level variables are derived from micro-level interactions, and in no way are the primitive variables that accommodate human action. Setting labor and capital aside and focusing on knowledge, the central questions become where within the abstract space of human activity is knowledge generated and within what kind of organizational arrangement is it generated. Neither of these questions are relevant to macro growth theory, but it is questions like these that are necessary truly to understand the generation of knowledge. Knowledge always pertains to some identifiable subject, and it occurs within some organizational and institutional arrangement. Figure 3.1 asked us to conceptualize people as choosing locations for their enterprises. It could just as well have asked us to conceptualize people as choosing subjects to think about. Just as we can imagine a distribution of enterprises across abstract commodity space, so can we imagine a distribution of inquiry across abstract topic space. Some people might inquire into high energy physics, others into linguistics, and so on.

Similarly, people might finance their inquiries from their own resources, either through equity or through debt. They might also receive support from external sources. Those sources could be nonprofit organizations organized inside the precincts of civil society or they could be political organizations. Within orthodox macro theory, the only object of interest is the volume of spending. Anything else is irrelevant for a line of inquiry devoted to quantity. In contrast, for a qualitative line of inquiry what would matter would be the ability of different lines of inquiry to support the interests and concerns that various inquirers have. Any aggregate measure of a rate of growth would be a by-product of the interactions of the inquirers within the social nexus. A rate of growth would not be a direct object of choice made by some person or agency. To the contrary, it would be an emergent product of interactions among people at the action level as data from the ecology of plans is projected onto the macro level.

To treat growth as emergent and not chosen is not to deny that government can influence growth. To the contrary, any participant within the ecology of plans can influence growth. The point is simply that growth is a product of interaction among plans within the ecology of plans and not a direct object of choice. Any measure of growth described in terms of a system of interacting entities must be and can only be some composite of measures of growth that pertain to the myriad entities that comprise the system. A set of people in their capacities as political officials might promote solar-powered lawn equipment. Those people would have both regulatory and financial instruments at their disposal for doing so. Legally, it could exempt those enterprises from the jurisdiction of labor legislation. Financially, it could offer some long duration of tax exemption which, of course, would be accompanied by taxes on other enterprises that would necessarily be higher than they would otherwise have been. Perhaps some systemic measure would show increased growth, but perhaps it wouldn't. Either way, growth would be an emergent feature of interaction among enterprises within some governing institutional framework and would not correspond at all to the image of following a recipe.

Once we consider the differing institutional and organizational imperatives that operate within the frameworks of private and public ordering, we may doubt the general ability of increased public ordering to promote human flourishing, though here we enter the realm of plausible and not demonstrative reasoning. Some public ordering conforms to the image of providing a general and nondiscriminatory framework inside of which people can pursue their desired activities, corresponding to Richard Epstein's (1985) image of forced exchanges that he used to describe some but by no means all instances of eminent domain. To the extent governments support such non-discriminatory activities, there are reasonable grounds for thinking that public ordering contributes to progress. We may be sure, however, that the range of such activity is narrow, and with most governmental activity these days supporting some plans while impeding other plans, and probably retarding flourishing because of the resulting taxation of entrepreneurial activity.

In any case, we return to the distinction between quantity and quality, which mirrors the distinction between growth and flourishing. Macro theorists seem to have a fetish about growth, possibly betraying the Marxian roots of their materialist philosophy, though it could also be just a matter of the habit of conventional patterns of thought and expression. In any case, the distinction between growth and flourishing pertains to the distinction between the foreground and the background of a theory, recognizing that all theories have both. For OEE-style theorizing, the foreground is populated by a concern with the societal organization that reasonably accompanies human flourishing. While human flourishing within societies is not a simple concept to articulate, it can surely be assimilated to such qualities of character as rectitude, cooperativeness, self-restraint, politeness, and caring for others. Going back to Montesquieu, the claim has often been advanced that the world of commercial practice tends to operate in a civilizing manner, and with growth flowing from the personal qualities that are cultivated within a social reality dominated by private ordering.

Yet it is doubtful that organized social life can proceed wholly on the basis of private ordering. Human nature won't allow it, and for several reasons. For one thing, societies are rife with antagonism. While private ordering might suppress antagonism, it won't eliminate it. Envy (Schoeck 1969) seems to be a durable feature of the human predicament, as the example of Cain and Abel shows and in recognition that in most homicides the victim knew the perpetrator. Force will surely be a durable feature of human societies, at least as far as anyone can see looking forward. And with force comes its social organization along with the moral imaginations necessary to provide intelligibility to those who participate in the social organization of force. In her lucid treatment of *Systems of Survival*, Jane Jacobs (1992) explained that well-working societies unavoidably had to combine carriers of two types of moral sentiment: commercial and guardian. She further noted that it was difficult to keep the two sentiments separate, and that failure to do so generated what she described as monstrous moral hybrids where guardians invaded the commercial world while those who populated the commercial world acted in guardian fashion. Such considerations might lead to more acute recognition and appreciation of the complexity and difficulty of securing good societal governance because such governance requires maintaining a tension between opposing proclivities. Even more, the relevant societal setting is one where everyone exhibits a natural partiality to his or her view of reality when there is no one who inhabits that proverbial Mount Olympus despite the large number of people who claim to have visited there.

REFERENCES

Acocella, N. 1988. *The Foundations of Economic Policy.* Cambridge: Cambridge University Press.

Arrow, K.J., and F.H. Hahn. 1971. *General Competitive Analysis.* Amsterdam: North Holland.

Buchanan, J.M. 1959. Positive Economics, Welfare Economics, and Political Economy. *Journal of Law and Economics* 2: 124–38.

Coser, L.A. 1964. *The Functions of Social Conflict.* New York: Simon and Schuster.

DelliSanti, D., and R.E. Wagner. 2018. Bankruptcies, Bailouts, and Some Political Economy of Corporate Reorganization. *Journal of Institutional Economics* 14: 833–51.

Devereaux, A., and R.E. Wagner. 2020. Game Theory as Social Theory: Finding Spontaneous Order. Manuscript, George Mason University.

Epstein, R.A. 1985. *Takings: Private Property and the Power of Eminent Domain.* Cambridge, MA: Harvard University Press.

Epstein, R.A. 1995. *Simple Rules for a Complex World.* Cambridge, MA: Harvard University Press.

Hirshleifer, J. 1970. *Investment, Interest, and Capital.* New York: Prentice-Hall.

Jacobs, J. 1992. *Systems of Survival.* New York: Random House.

Knight, F.H. 1921. *Risk, Uncertainty, and Profit.* Boston: Houghton-Mifflin.

Leijonhufvud, A. 1981. *Information and Coordination.* New York: Oxford University Press.

MacIntyre, A. 1988. *Whose Justice? Which Rationality?.* South Bend, IN: University of Notre Dame Press.

Manne, H.G. 1965. Mergers and the Market for Corporate Control. *Journal of Political Economy* 73: 10–20.

Michels, R. 1912 [1962]. *Political Parties: A Sociological Study of the Oligarchical Tendencies of Modern Democracy.* New York: Collier Books.

Mises, L. 1966. *Human Action*, 3rd ed. Chicago: Henry Regnery.

Morgenstern, O. 1972. Thirteen Critical Points in Contemporary Economic Theory. *Journal of Economic Literature* 10: 1163–89.

Pareto, V. 1935. *The Mind and Society.* New York: Harcourt Brace.

Patrick, M., and R.E. Wagner. 2015. From Mixed Economy to Entangled Political Economy: A Paretian Social-Theoretic Orientation. *Public Choice* 164: 103–16.

Pigou, A.C. 1912. *Wealth and Welfare.* London: Macmillan.

Pirsig, R. 1974. *Zen and the Art of Motorcycle Maintenance: An Inquiry into Values.* New York: Harper Collins.

Podemska-Mikluch, M., and R.E. Wagner. 2013. Dyads, Triads, and the Theory of Exchange: Between Liberty and Coercion. *Review of Austrian Economics* 26: 171–82.

Polya, G. 1954. *Mathematics and Plausible Reasoning*, 2 vols. Princeton, NJ: Princeton University Press.

Romer, P.M. 1986. Increasing Returns and Long-Run Growth. *Journal of Political Economy* 94: 1002–37.

Schelling, T.C. 1978. *Micromotives and Macrobehavior.* New York: Norton.

Schoeck, H. 1969. *Envy: A Theory of Social Behavior.* New York: Harcourt Brace.

Schumpeter, J.A. 1934. *Theory of Economic Development*, 2nd ed. Cambridge, MA: Harvard University Press.

Shackle, G.L.S. 1972. *Epistemics and Economics.* Cambridge: Cambridge University Press.

Shackle, G.L.S. 1974. *Keynesian Kaleidics.* Edinburgh: Edinburgh University Press.

Solow, R.M. 1956. A Contribution to the Theory of Economic Growth. *Quarterly Journal of Economics* 70: 65–94.

Tinbergen, J. 1952. *On the Theory of Economic Policy.* Amsterdam: North-Holland.

Vriend, N.J. 2002. Was Hayek an Ace? *Southern Economic Journal* 68: 811–40.

Wagner, R.E. 1999. Understanding the Tobacco Settlement: The State as a Partisan Plaintiff. *Regulation* 22 (4): 38–41.

Wagner, R.E. 2012. Viennese Kaleidics: Why It's Liberty More Than Policy That Calms Turbulence. *Review of Austrian Economics* 25: 283–97.

Wagner, R.E. 2016. *Politics as a Peculiar Business: Insights from a Theory of Entangled Political Economy.* Cheltenham, UK: Edward Elgar.

Walras, L. 1874 [1954]. *Elements of Pure Economics.* Homewood, IL: Richard D. Irwin.

Weintraub, E.R. 1993. *General Equilibrium Analysis: Studies in Appraisal.* Ann Arbor: University of Michigan Press.

Wolfram, S. 2002. *A New Kind of Science.* Champaign, IL: Wolfram Media.

CHAPTER 6

Entangled Political Economy Within Human Population Systems

For the better part of a century, macro theorists have been in the fore-ground of creating the image of an inherently unstable market economy that requires political guidance and correction if people are to live well together inside the confined geographical spaces they inhabit. The first five chapters of this book have explained the inaptness of this orthodox presumption that macro theory provides a reasonable framework for pro-viding societal guidance in any way similar to the engineers who launch spacecraft and return them to Earth. With respect to this orthodox image, Gregory Mankiw (2006) presents the sharply contrasting visions of macro theorists as scientists and as engineers. An economy, however, is nothing like a spaceship. A spaceship is a robotic system that is designed by engi-neers following scientific principles and laws; an economy is a creative system that is continually emerging through the ability of humans cre-atively to imagine new options and to inject them into history, along the lines that Henri Bergson (1911) set forth in *Creative Evolution.*

Economic theory took a fateful turn in the late nineteenth century within the crucible created through the conjunction of Marxist theories of the exploitive character of market transactions and the neoclassical reduc-tion of market economies to exercises in constrained maximization where exploitation vanished in the presence of aggregate production functions that were presumed to be linear and homogeneous. In taking this analyt-ical turn, the mainline of economic theory was shunted onto a theoret-ical sideline, replaced by what became the neoclassical mainstream, with Peter Boettke (2007) presenting a luminous portrait of this shunting of

© The Author(s) 2020
R. E. Wagner, *Macroeconomics as Systems Theory,*
https://doi.org/10.1007/978-3-030-44465-5_6

157

the engine of economic analysis. Perhaps the most fateful element of that shunting was the abolition of the theme that liberally ordered societies had generally beneficial qualities so long as public ordering remained small and in the background. This theme about spontaneously ordered societies was central to the scholars of the Scottish Enlightenment, as well as being preceded by the Spanish Jesuits associated with the University of Salamanca (Grice-Hutchinson 1978). Indeed, Simon Bilo and Richard Wagner (2015), in their treatment of monetary non-neutrality, offer the speculative aside that had the Spanish Crown invested the inflows of gold and silver in the century preceding the defeat of the Spanish armada in the creation of academies to study explosives, ballistics, navigation, and the like, along with political economy in the tradition of Salamanca, Spanish could well now be the lingua franca of economics and we would be speaking of the Spanish Enlightenment.

The central concern of economic and social theory prior to the neoclassical period had been to deepen our understanding of the hidden ordering principles that undergirded the experienced orderliness of the social world, as well as to understand possible sources of disruption to that orderliness. To recognize possible sources of disruption and to think that it might be possible to mitigate such disruption is in no way identical to thinking that a society can be designed. There is a world of difference between tinkering with some perceived social object and seeking to create that object anew. The central concern of economics prior to the neoclassical reduction of an economic system to an aggregate production function had been to deepen our understanding of how the members of a society are able to generate complex economic ecologies within an institutional framework dominated by private property and freedom of contract. Within this mainline scheme of thought, politicians were treated mostly like stagehands in the cosmic drama of social life. In contrast, the emergence of the present mainstream of economic thought brought politicians onto center stage of the cosmic drama that society represents, changing in the process how that drama subsequently unfolds.

But what kinds of contributions do political figures make to this drama? Unsurprisingly, they and their allies tell us that they are pivotal figures in improving the quality of the drama. Without politicians and their supporters coming increasingly to occupy center stage, sympathetic economists claim that the drama would descend into chaos without the political guidance offered through bureaucratic agencies using data supplied through the NIPA and similar accounts to overcome the chaos that otherwise

would threaten. Politics is thus overwhelmingly construed as a beneficial force in the cosmic drama in which we are all inextricably bound, as
against representing a Faustian bargain that inserts the evil of force into
society, hoping that the good that arises thereby will outweigh the evil
that also will result (Ostrom 1984, 1996). It is easy enough to understand why political figures and their allies would push a vision of social
life operating on the edge of chaos, and with politics and political institutions, aided by economist advisors, bringing their intelligence to bear on
staving off the ever-looming chaos. This view of our world seems to have
attained the status of being intuitively obvious.

Considering the long and rich history of mainline economics going
back to the Spanish Jesuits of Salamanca in the sixteenth century (Grice-
Hutchison 1978), it is worth questioning the political presuppositions
that have informed what has become the mainstream of economic
thought (Boettke 2007). Those presuppositions are that we live on the
edge of chaos and that politics is the instrument for staving off chaos.
Two schemes of analysis are in play in exploring whether politics offers
an antidote to chaos or whether it might offer an avenue into chaos. One
line concerns the nature of social and economic processes and institutions
which the first five chapters of this book have explored. The other line of
examination concerns the actual as distinct from idealized operating properties of political processes and institutions which the remaining chapters
explore.

The theoretical analysis of the relationships between political processes
and macro-level variability presents an analytical fork in the road, similar to the fork James Burnham (1943) presented in contrasting Dante's
idealism and Machiavelli's realism in the opening two chapters of *The
Machiavellians*. This fork was characterized nicely by Herschel Grossman
(1975) in his review of the collected works of James Tobin:

> Tobin presumes that the historical record of monetary and fiscal policy
> involves a series of avoidable mistakes, rather than the predictable con-
> sequences of personal preferences and capabilities working through the
> existing constitutional process by which policy is formulated. Specifically,
> Tobin shows no interest in analysis of either the economically motivated
> behavior of private individuals in the political process or the behavior of
> the government agents who make and administer policy. (pp. 845–46)

One fork in the theoretical road points toward orthodox macro policy which treats polities as acting independently of economic interests, and with good policies reducing economic variability while bad policies fail to do so and may even increase variability. The other branch of the fork points in the direction of political imperatives promoting economic disturbances rather than smoothing them. Those disturbances, moreover, can be direct consequences of political programs or indirect by-products of the pursuit of political gain.

On Some Conventional Welfare Economics of Economic Stabilization

Macro theorists typically assume both that stability is desirable and that it can be attained through policy. As Chapter 5 explained, turbulence is surely a natural condition of a free economy. It could, of course, be granted that some degree of turbulence is a feature of a well-working economy, and that as a pragmatic matter the claims on behalf of stability pertain to turbulence outside that degree of normal turbulence (Leijonhufvud 1981). This type of claim is similar to claims that blood glucose levels in humans entail turbulence within some range, with glucose becoming undesirable only outside that level of normal variability. This would be a reasonable claim to make, both for blood sugar and economic indicators, but it also points to some problematical matters concerning both technique and politics. With respect to technique, issues arise concerning the ability of political entities to promote stability even if political persons operated with a single-minded devotion to stability outside some normal range of variability. With respect to politics, issues arise regarding the intensity of political devotion to the pursuit of stability.

To posit a single-minded devotion to promoting stability is an assumption that theorists make to close their models. Single-mindedness surely cannot be a substantive as distinct from purely formal property of democratically organized political regimes where candidates compete among themselves to attain office. Candidates cannot compete for attention space by duplicating what other candidates propose. Competition requires differentiation, and differentiation undermines claims of substantive single-mindedness. The claim of single-mindedness, moreover, is a common piece of ideology that asserts something like "we all want the same thing," so we should get along together. Behind this oft-heard assertion resides the reality that the speakers all want different things because competition among political programs will divide the world between winners and losers in the competition for office and power. Ideology in this instance serves more as a smokescreen than a source of illumination.

With respect to economic activity, there is no clear notion of a boundary between normal and abnormal variability in measured output once the presumption of flat-line equilibrium is abandoned. There are perhaps some grounds for thinking that natural volatility will vary with the intensity of animal spirits within the society, but this possibility does not provide some line of demarcation between normal and abnormal volatility. To work with this distinction, some arbitrary selection must be made, similar to asserting that a normal glucose measure ranges between 70 and 100 milligrams per deciliter. Even assertion of a flat-line measure of output growth leaves open the necessity of arbitrary choices because pragmatic considerations regarding measurement are unavoidably present.

Suppose two percent is thought to be an appropriate measure with respect to some aggregate accounting data. These measures pertain to some interval, perhaps three months, but economic processes operate continuously without respect to calendar intervals even if accounting works with discrete intervals in reporting results of operations. There is, moreover, an unavoidable absence of knowledge in judging whether the data between two periods indicate stability, and with that lack of knowledge being compounded by recognition that the data assume economic processes are synchronic when they are not. If the numbers are identical, the data have answered in the positive. But almost never would this be the case. One quarter might show growth of 2.365% while the next shows 2.361%. Pragmatically at this level of aggregation, these measures would be regarded as identical. What extent of divergence would lead one to conclude stability does not characterize the observations is a judgment call, both as a statistical matter and with respect to one's thinking about the magnitudes of error involved in aggregate data. Considering those errors in measurement, a measure that shows growth at two percent could well reflect growth at three percent just as well as it could reflect growth at one percent. Aggregate measures, moreover, are revised continually, often for several years, and sometimes with those revisions being significant relative to the original estimate.

Aggregate data, moreover, are always estimates. No one is measuring the height of Mt. Everest in estimating GDP or its growth. To the contrary, they are constructing images and estimates, that at best are approximations of something that seems intuitively plausible. For instance, governmental activity within the NIPA accounts is entered by the amount spent on those activities, reflecting the presumption that spending is spending and that is all that is relevant. Yet there is good reason to think that governmental activities are inputs into market activities and so should not be entered as if they were final products. In this respect, Forte and Buchanan (1961) set forth a coherent argument that double counting is involved in entering governmental activity at budgetary expense and that public expenditure should be neglected when those expenditures provide inputs into private production because their evaluation is incorporated into market prices.

Suppose we distinguish between two types of output gap. We could call these good gaps and bad gaps. Good gaps would reflect variations in the activities people choose to pursue during any interval. Bad gaps would reflect variations that are forced on those individuals. Good gaps would arise from voluntary unemployment. Bad gaps would arise from involuntary unemployment. It is easy enough to work with this language, but the ease of doing so does not render that language meaningful. A so-called output gap represents some observer's point of view and does not speak to the perceptions held by economic actors because an output gap implies that those actors are failing to pursue profit opportunities.

It could be claimed that people would prefer a pattern of stable consumption over their lifetime to a pattern with variable consumption. This claim is a straightforward presumption of people being presumed to have declining marginal utility at any instant. While this claim is commonly made by economists, its veracity may be doubted. This claim is derived from the St. Petersburg Paradox where some people are observed to reject a fair gamble, and with the rejection attributed to winnings having lower marginal utility than losings. To be sure, not everyone rejects fair gambles. Even more, people continually play games for which they want a clear demarcation between winning and losing. Yet the St. Petersburg formulation would surely hold that people would prefer that their games end in ties. Suppose we characterize games as bringing glory to the winners and shame to the losers. Within the St. Petersburg framework of diminishing marginal utility, the marginal gain in added glory from winning would be less than the marginal loss from increased shame. This situation would lead to a preference for games that end in ties.

One can, in other words, posit a social welfare function in which the promotion of aggregate stability is superior to volatility in output gaps, and could appeal to St. Petersburg logic in doing so. Doing this would be simple within a representative agent model because one utility function would drive the result of stability being superior to volatility, with stability dominating volatility as a solution to the representative agent's intertemporal utility maximization. As a general proposition, however, stability cannot invariably dominate fluidity. Stability entails the absence of change, including the absence of new entrepreneurial ventures. To the contrary, incipient entrepreneurs would surely prefer a world that entailed fluidity within an ecology of plans to one that entailed stasis within that ecology.

Conventional welfare economics accepts as gospel that people prefer stability to variability, with variability being acceptable only to the extent that it is offset sufficiently strongly by an increase in the expected return. Return is good and variability is bad, and this relationship follows from economics focused wholly on quantity. When economics is used to address matters of quality, one vital feature of a free enterprise system of social relationships is the ability of people to choose their paths in life and pursue their dreams. In any social system, people start a week with 168 hours at their disposal. Within a system grounded in private ordering, people choose how they will use their time. When public ordering is present, people have only incomplete control over how they use their time because political processes also influence how people use their time. In the limiting case of a socialist or communist society, people have no choice over how they use their time because their activities are dictated to them through some planning process, recognizing all the same that actual processes of collectivist planning never operated in the manner the idealized descriptions portrayed them as operating. In any case, experimentation and variability are among the operating properties of an enterprise-based economy. To eliminate experimentation and variability is to eliminate enterprise by regulation and political control.

MARKET, POLITY, AND ENTANGLED POLITICAL
ECONOMY WITH SOCIETY AS ARTIFACT

To repeat a theme that an earlier chapter set forth, human societies have but one foot in the natural world. That foot places the study of human societies within the purview of ethology, which is the science devoted to the study of the higher mammals. Indeed, the oft-cited manifesto advanced by Stigler and Becker (1977) would seem to locate economic theory fully within the province of ethology, for that theoretical framework has humans, like the higher mammals generally, working with their genetic endowments to cope with their environments that they necessarily treat as data. Within this theoretical construction, society comprises a natural environment inside of which humans live with their given preferences and genetic endowments.

By contrast, to treat human societies as artifacts recognizes that economics is not reducible to physics or biology or that social science is not reducible to ethology. That humans exist in the natural world is undeniable. As higher mammals, humans have many characteristics in common with the higher mammals. But we also have characteristics that so far as we know are not possessed by those other mammals, at least so far as we can tell without engaging in some form of anthropomorphism. To be sure, humans often engage in anthropomorphism by attributing human-like qualities to the other mammals and even to our concepts of God. Yet we don't have interior knowledge of what it's like to be one of the other mammals, or God, though we often seem to be eager to mirror our images of God, as illustrated by Newberg et al. (2001) using neuroscience to address the persistence of God in human perceptions.

Our interior knowledge is limited to what is entailed in being a human living in society with other humans. We can observe limited features of society and we construct theories that we think will help us to understand what we can't see directly because the enormous complexity of our object vastly exceeds our observational capacities. It is here where recognition of the artifactual character of society comes into play. Society is an artifact that humans create through interaction just as surely as the language they use and the tools with which they work. Those artifacts, in turn, remake what we perceive to be our natural environment. Language and tools are artifacts that help people to get along better in life, but these are not naturally existing objects. To be sure, Ilya Prigogine (1997) advances good reason for being skeptical that the natural world is truly a piece of data. One of the artifacts of the social world resides in the theories we create and the stories and myths we tell about that world.

For purposes of the macro- or social-level theories with which this book is concerned, theories of political economy can be separated between two-level and single-level theories. Using the vocabulary that Wagner (2016) sets forth, two-level theories reflect the feudal era practices where lords governed their manors in the manner that shepherds guide sheep. This is the vision of additive political economy that Fig. 6.1

Fig. 6.1 Feudalism vs. liberalism in political economy: panel A

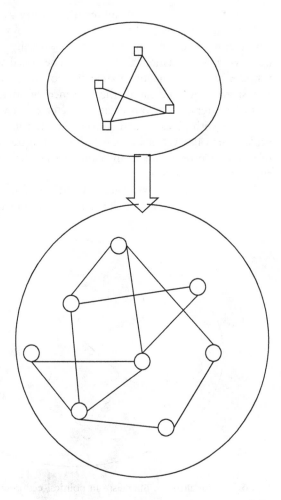

portrays. This Figure shows a set of lords who are fully connected to one another, to indicate that they act as a unity. The downward arrow shows that this polity sits above the eight members of the society who are connected in polycentric fashion with no entity among those eight being in charge of the others, but with all of those entities being directed by the unified political entity. Figure 6.1 presents a reasonable though idealized model of feudal governance as an artifact generated through particular patterns of human interaction where some people exercised dominion over others.

Liberalism arose in the eighteenth century as the feudalistic form of collectivism disintegrated as changing technology induced the creation of new forms for organizing production whereby people moved much of their work from manors to factories. The social world is still an artifact, just as a backhoe is as much an artifact of the social world as are pickaxes and shovels. All the same, the presence of backhoes changed patterns of social interaction from what characterized a world where all digging was done with pickaxes and shovels. Liberalism arose as a philosophy to explain the observations connected with the transformation of the social relations of production from manor to factory and beyond through an ever-expanding division of labor.

Figure 6.2 portrays an idealized version of a liberal system of political economy. Shown there are the same 12 entities that Fig. 6.1 portrayed,

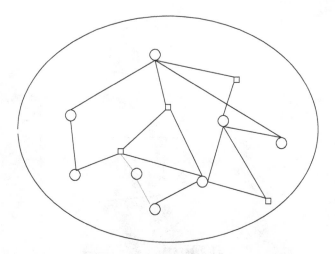

Fig. 6.2 Feudalism vs. liberalism in political economy: panel B

only those entities are organized in wholly polycentric fashion, in contrast to Fig. 6.1 where the eight market entities were organized polycentrically but the four political entities were organized homocentrically and, moreover, exercise supervision over the market entities. With the disappearance of feudalism, political entities were submerged into the general society as governance became the province of "the people" within the context of democratic ideology. Figure 6.2 shows the four political entities as submerged within the market arrangements of a liberal system of political economy. Within this idealized system of political economy, there were no positions of lords of the manor. Political entities were still identifiable within the society, as squares rather than circles, but they were selected from the general population to hold their positions, in contrast to the feudal inheritance of positions by birth. This setting illustrates Henry Maine's (1861) oft-cited recognition of a progressive society being characterized by status-based relations giving way to contract-based relations.

Both Figs. 6.1 and 6.2 depict societies in terms of civilizational artifacts and not features of some reality given by nature, and with Erwin Dekker (2016) presenting a masterful examination of how economic analysis has great relevance for the properties of civilizations. Both Figs. 6.1 and 6.2 are static representations of civilizational realities that are artifacts of evolutionary processes of continual change. Those evolutionary processes are not adequately characterized as stochastic within the spirit of DSGE and its Mt. Olympus orientation because that orientation denies any place where people can be said to participate in the creation of civilizational artifacts. Yet those artifacts are created, typically through competition among people competing for attention space. By no means does this competitive process mean that people create whatever civilizational artifacts they might prefer because the outcome of any competitive process will be unknowable without that process taking place. Again, OEE and DSGE do not offer contrary claims about the perceived structure of reality, for their claims can be reconciled. DSGE advances the unchallengeable recognition that history can't be repealed and replayed while also maintaining that the participants in that historical episode must have operated on the basis of intelligible beliefs. OEE accepts this recognition, only it seeks to transform the cosmic drama of social life from one told in the passive voice of people reacting to changes in data to one told in the active voice where people generate relevant data through forming and pursuing plans. In the end, all humans are mired in inevitability, of course, as our place in life's drama must end; however, OEE seeks to provide meaningful orientation with respect to that drama whereas DSGE denies the meaningfulness of any effort to attribute meaning to humanity's cosmic drama.

Is Economic Stabilization Technically Attainable?

Orthodox macro theory presumes that political agencies have the tools and knowledge necessary to promote systemic stability in the face of looming chaos from market interactions. Some of those theorists question whether politicians and their supporters have the will required to promote stability, but the underlying theoretical framework suggests that the knowledge required to do so is available. Sure, numerous pragmatic reasons can be advanced to explain why closing an output gap is a more difficult accomplishment than landing a spacecraft on the Moon. Engineers have accurate data sufficient to direct a spacecraft to the Moon. Economists don't have comparable data. A gauge on a spacecraft might malfunction, creating problems of guidance in the process without built-in redundancies, but gauges do not have willfulness and minds of their own. Data from the NIPA accounts and estimates of output gaps have subjectivity that engineered machines lack. Stimulating a faltering economy to close an output gap fits readily within the orthodox theoretical framework, and it seems to resemble guiding a spacecraft. But it isn't. Suppose we postulate the existence of an agency devoted to maintaining aggregate output at some fixed magnitude or, equivalently, rate of growth. Is this something this agency can truly accomplish? The short answer is no as a general proposition. The agency might be able to do this if everyone in the society had identical preferences, for then we have eliminated the problem by replacing society and its myriad minds with a representative agent where society has been reduced to a single person. In this situation, it is easy to envision the representative agent giving himself instructions to keep the output gap at zero.

Once we replace the representative agent model with a genuine society of individuals after the fashion of Norbert Elias's (1939 [1991]) examination of the individual–society relationship, the epistemic status of an output gap vanishes because that gap was a feature of a particular theoretical model and not some universally recognizable fact. For instance, just who determines the size of an output gap? There would seem to be two possibilities. One would be a choice by some arbitrary authority, perhaps an economist who makes econometric estimates to arrive at a measured output gap. The other would be treat an output gap as an expression of the desired labor–leisure preferences throughout a population. In this case, an output gap would not be determined by some economic theorist but would require a polling of the population. To be sure, no one knows truly how to do this, as distinct from posing questions to some sample of the population and constructing some estimate, which is likely what the econometrician would do in any case. There is, however, no way of directly measuring an output gap. Indirectly, a measure can be acquired through observing the labor–leisure choices people make. So long as there are people who value the gain from work to exceed the gain from leisure, there will be a positive output gap. This gap, moreover, is simultaneously an excess supply of labor, and that excess supply will find employment within a regime of private ordering even if not within one of public ordering.

Public ordering can thus create output gaps while also preventing their closure. For instance, an increase in a required minimum wage will increase the amount of labor people are willing to supply. Actual employment, however, will fall because the increased minimum wage makes it more expensive for people to hire other people. Hence, the minimum wage will create a positive output gap, in that people are willing to supply a greater quantity of labor at the minimum wage than other people are willing to hire at that wage. In this instance, an output gap can reasonably exist, but that gap is a product of public ordering and its ability to deploy power to prevent people from making mutually profitable transactions. Within a system of wholly private ordering, there will be no output gap because the presence of a gap implies that people knowingly are failing to exploit gains from trade. Output gaps can appear in the presence of public ordering; however, it is unlikely that public ordering can close output gaps short of Soviet-style conscription. In short, political agencies have limited ability to stabilize an economy outside the range of outcomes that reflect individual preferences and market interactions. Even more, output gaps are incoherent as persistent features of a privately ordered economy. Output gaps are features of public ordering, recognition of which surely gives one pause in advocating more public ordering to close output gaps.

Is Stabilization Politically Supportable?

To observe that a political agency has been instructed to stabilize an economy does not imply that this agency knows how to do this. Nor does it imply that political agencies would choose to do so even if they knew how. Politics is a peculiar business (Wagner 2016). Politics is a business, for it serves as a source of livelihood for many people. Politicians create programs that appeal to clients and they create bureaus and agencies to undertake numerous activities. People invest in politicians and their campaigns to seek office, and political agencies advertise their services. Politics is a competitive activity like any other form of business, only it is not subject to the capital market discipline that operates for ordinary businesses. Ordinary businesses have market value which allows them to be bought and sold, and which provides a vehicle for relating executive compensation to firm performance. Politics lacks these capital market tools, which leads to some peculiar performance characteristics, some of which were explained earlier with reference to Fig. 3.1. With respect to political-economic interaction, markets play a leading rule with politics following the path of successful commercial enterprises in locating topics of deepest human interest and concern.

Macro or system variables are nondiscriminatory at their core. Aggregate values pertain to no identifiable entity and are rather some amalgamation across individual entities. It is doubtful whether a genuinely nondiscriminatory political program would have much attractiveness within a competitive system. Suppose a small political system contains 99 members and makes decisions by majority voting. A truly nondiscriminatory political program would provide net benefits for all 99 members of the polity. It is possible to find programs that are dominated by these qualities, though perhaps not as many as people might think. For instance, much of the prison population these days is apparently inhabited by dealers in recreational drugs, which is a line of commerce of which some people approve and others don't, meaning that imprisonment of such offenders is a program that only a part, though likely a majority part, of the population approve.

We may question whether there can be a nondiscriminatory program of economic stabilization. The alternative is that what is described as economic stabilization is a type of ideological smokescreen that hides the conferral of benefits to favored interest groups, financed by general tax revenues. Suppose a macro theorist asserts that $100 billion measures the size of some output gap. This theory claims that added spending will close the gap, with details about that added spending being irrelevant to the theory. At the macro level, this theory would surely imply that a politician who supported the added expenditure would not care about the objects on which that program was spent. Such a person would be pleased to approve the appropriation to close the output gap, then let someone else determine how to spend the money. We may doubt that such a person would have much of a political career in the face of competition from those who have strong preferences how the money would be spent. Such a program could well carry some such title as an Economic Stabilization Act, but that program would entail a structured pattern of expenditure that would correspond to the requirements of political rationality (Bueno de Mesquita 2003). Such requirements of political rationality undergird the emergence of a contemporary literature on political business cycles, where the theoretical trust explores the claim that political rationality might operate to promote volatility, in contrast to orthodox claims about promoting stability.

The possibility that politics might be a source of economic variability goes at least as far back as Kalecki (1943) and Akerman (1947), and with Feiwel (1974) building expressly on those earlier Marxian efforts, though these efforts seem to have gained no analytical traction. Starting with Nordhaus's (1975) Keynesianesque formulation, a substantial literature on political business cycles subsequently emerged, much of which is surveyed in Hibbs (1987), Willett (1988), Keech (1995), and Wagner (2001). The central idea behind this literature is that whether political processes promote variability or stability depends on the relative payoffs from different policies to those who conduct the affairs of state. The initial literature largely developed under the presumption that states have the competence to promote macro-level stability but might choose instead to promote variability because doing so offers political gain. The starting point for such PBC theorizing is the presumption that an incumbent's electoral success is influenced by such macroeconomic conditions as rates of inflation, unemployment, and growth prior to an election. A further presumption of standard PBC theorizing is that politicians can truly choose the values of macro-level variables.

Figure 6.3 illustrates the various threads of the arguments that comprise PBC models. There are two components to Fig. 6.3, and these correspond to preferences and opportunities within a framework of constrained optimization. Preferences are expressed by votes or, alternatively,

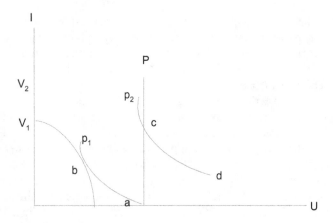

Fig. 6.3 Orthodox political business cycle model

by measures of candidate popularity. The quite reasonable presumption is that politicians would rather win an election than loose it. The PBC literature presumes, based on econometric evidence as well as on intuition, that increases in inflation and unemployment each exert negative effects on the popularity of the governing party. These presumptions are represented in Fig. 6.3 by the iso-vote functions described by v_1 and v_2, and with the value of those functions increasing toward the origin: if v_2 denotes, say, 48:52 odds of electoral success for the incumbent party, v_1 might denote 52:48 odds.

The opportunities facing an incumbent party are described by a Phillips relationship between inflation and unemployment. Figure 6.3 shows an exploitable relationship in the short run, as illustrated by p_1 and p_2, but not in the long run, as illustrated by the natural rate of employment, P. Contained within this description of opportunities is the presumption that an incumbent party can use its budgetary and regulatory powers to enhance its electoral prospects by acting on those opportunities. In Fig. 6.3, the preelection position is denoted by a, which lies on v_2. Under the assumption that there is an exploitable Phillips relationship denoted by p_1, the incumbent part is presumed to use its control over budgetary and regulatory policy to shift the economy to b, where it faces more favorable odds of electoral success described by v_1. Under the assumption that there is no permanently exploitable Philips relationship, the economy subsequently shifts to c, where Fig. 6.3 shows restoration of the preelection odds of success at the next election; moreover, a third iso-vote could be added to Fig. 6.3 to illustrate lowered odds of success.

Examination of the pattern a-b-c-d shows an election-inspired cycle. Starting from zero inflation and full employment at the natural rate, inflation is used to increase employment to increase electoral prospects. If the incumbent has good timing and the powers of policy presumed by the model, the reversion to the natural rate of employment will happen after the election. At this point the incumbent party faces a choice. Down one path it can continue with the permanent inflation and try yet another inflationary episode before the next election. Following this path, however, will generate decreasing political return from inflation. Down the other path, the incumbent runs a deflationary policy that lowers its popularity as shown by the move to *d*. If this is done sufficiently far in advance of the next election, the economy will have returned to *a*, and the incumbent party will be poised to repeat the policy cycle.

POLITICAL BUSINESS CYCLES: A REASONABLE IDEA, TERRIBLY ARTICULATED

Macro theorists have mostly stayed away from PBC ideas, and for readily understandable reasons grounded on a sense that those ideas entail presumptions of voter irrationality. If Fig. 6.3 is thought to describe accurately the mental pictures people form about the actions of political candidates, the PBC claim entails the presumption that incumbents do favors for voters prior to an election, remove those favors after the election, and then restore them before the next election. This version of the PBC idea portrays the economy as a balloon which the incumbent inflates prior to an election, deflates after an election, and then reflates before the next election. With this theoretical depiction, the PBC idea surely violates the canons of rational action held by most economists. It is, however, worth asking whether the PBC idea has been abandoned because it is conceptually incoherent or because the DSGE formalism rendered the idea incoherent.

The original PBC construction was developed to show a possible disparity between some normative prescriptions of activist macro policy and the incentives contained within political processes, as illustrated by the dichotomy that Grossman sketched above. The original PBC formulations were based on a simple Keynesianesque formulation of the income–expenditure type, which likens an economy to a balloon and envisions government acting to inflate or deflate the balloon. Those formulations were also based on adaptive expectations, meaning that people look in their rear-view mirror to form judgments about where they are going. The original PBC formulations accepted the circular flow conception of the economic process and asked whether the insertion of periodic elections into a political economy would have any systematic effects on expansion and contraction of the circular flow.

Roughly coincident with the development of PBC theorizing came two developments in macro theory that neutered the PBC formulations. These developments were the replacement of adaptive expectations with rational expectations and a whole-hearted embrace of the presumption that our observations are always of equilibrium states. These alternative presumptions rendered nonsensical the PBC formulations. If the PBC is modeled as a repeated game between a representative politician and a representative citizen, the actions described by the PBC violate ordinary canons of rationality, unless rapid and significant loss of memory is assumed to plague citizens. Furthermore, the reduction of complex polities to a representative politician and complex economies to a representative agent or citizen is rendered sensible by the presumption of systemic equilibrium but would not be sensible otherwise.

The idea that political processes might allow the opportunistic pursuit of gain to generate macro-level variability was excluded by methodological construction of the DSGE analytical framework. What replaced the notion of opportunistic cycles was the notion of partisan cycles, as exemplified by Alesina and Roubini (1992), Drazen (2000), and Besley (2006). When electoral competition, general equilibrium, and rationality in expectation are combined, the possibility of partisan cycles is all that is left standing from the original notion of political business cycles.

Partisan cycles are anemic relative to opportunistic cycles. They are founded on the presumption that politicians are indifferent to opportunity and care only about some pristine purity of some pre-political objective function that they seek to enact through political action. In competition between two such politicians, say with 50–50 odds, the actual, post-election policy will necessarily impose shocks to the expectations that were held prior to the election. For example, people might generally expect one party to operate with four percent inflation and the other to operate with zero inflation. Prior to the election a rational expectation would call for economic calculation based on a two percent rate of inflation. After the election, one or the other rate of inflation will prevail, and everyone's prior expectation will have been shocked. Hence, elections can serve as sources of cycles. Those cycles, however, are inherent in the electoral process in a setting where politicians act with purity and not opportunistically. What we have is a methodological hard core that renders the partisan framework grounded in rectitude as the only sensible formulation of the relation between politics and macro variability. Opportunistic cycles are neutered by the methodological framework, leaving partisan cycles as the only sensible option within that framework.

As a metaphysical proposition about human nature, the animating idea behind opportunistic cycles seems unassailable. After all, it is the same idea that animates economic theory generally, which is that as biological organisms we have a partiality to our own projects and will use the means at our disposal to advance those projects. Yet the hard core of partisan-type theorizing enervates this possibility, though I say this not as an act criticism per se because any analytical framework rests upon some such hard core, as Lakatos (1970) and Latsis (1976) explain. Several conceptual elements comprise this hard core, and which act together to neuter the prospect that opportunistic political conduct can generate macro-level variability. Stated in obverse manner, opportunistic theories of macro variability require an alternative analytical framework to give them room to breathe and to release their analytical energy.

AN ALTERNATIVE FRAMEWORK FOR PBC RECONCEPTUALIZATION

The macro framework conveyed by Fig. 6.3 cannot bear the analytical weight necessary to carry forward the claims about opportunistically generated variability. An alternative theoretical framework is required to carry forward those ideas. Here I will explore some of the contours of an alternative line of examination in a manner consistent with the preceding chapters of this book. To start, macro variables are not direct objects of choice but rather are statistical traces of those direct objects. To claim otherwise is to assert that a politician who desires to spend a trillion dollars to shift electoral prospects as described by Fig. 6.3 would be indifferent to the composition of that spending. Once it is recognized that people are not indifferent to the composition of spending, the use of aggregate magnitudes as providing a sufficient basis for theorizing about politics and macro variability must be rejected. Only people act, and the macro aggregates are just statistical recordings of such prior action. Something like Fig. 6.3 might be a useful summary of some observations, much as illustrated by that statement that a picture is worth a thousand words. But the action on which Fig. 6.3 is based is not captured by Fig. 6.3 but rather takes place below Fig. 6.3, so to speak.

The scene depicted by Fig. 6.3 emerges out of some microstructure of relationships that is not contained within Fig. 6.3. With respect to emergent-style theorizing, Fig. 6.3 *supervenes* on some underlying network of interaction. Beneath Fig. 6.3 should reside some micro model of political-economic interaction that under some circumstances might aggregate into Fig. 6.3, along the lines that Chapter 2 explored with reference to Fig. 1.3. Analytically speaking, it is impossible to infer the features of that microstructure from the macro portrait. It is, however, possible to generate a macro pattern out of some microstructure.

Consider the movement from a to b in Fig. 6.3. The incumbent party is facing a tough election, say as described by 50:50 odds of success, and can use its power of appropriation to spend some serious money, say $990 billion. According to Fig. 6.3, the incumbent should be indifferent as to how that money is spent. But anyone not blinded by such models will know better. For instance, suppose the parliament contains 99 seats. Further suppose that 33 of those seats are considered safe, 33 are considered impossible to win, and 33 are regarded as tightly contested. The neutral program would distribute the money equally among the districts, say $10 billion in each. This program would have less political gain than a discriminatory distribution that placed most of the money in the tightly contested districts. It is worth noting that this illustration is based on a parliamentary and not a presidential system. The illustration also leaves unstated how the additional expenditure is financed. It is simply asserted that the incumbent party can use its powers of office to provide the spending. At this point, the relationship between fiscal and monetary powers becomes relevant, as illustrated by Selgin and White (1999) and White (1999).

The macro-level portrait shown in Fig. 6.3 is erected on some micro-level structure of considerable complexity, and each such structure would play out in different fashion, and such structure would have to be incorporated into any exploration of the relation between politics and business cycles. Figure 1.3 illustrates what I have in mind. The top part of that Figure carries forward the macro framework of Fig. 6.3 in a standard AD–AS form. The bottom part, and the connection between the two parts, illustrates that the macro level supervenes on or emerges out of inter-action at the micro-level. Macro-level outcomes are not directly acces-sible through any causal relationship among macro variables, for macro-level variables emerge through interaction at the micro-level. With micro-level relationships construed in networked fashion, moreover, macro-level observations will vary with changes in the structure of network relation-ships.

For aggregate models, structure is irrelevant. By contrast, structure matters greatly for network-based models, as Potts (2000) and Barabási (2002) explain. A world that is generated in network-based fashion can always be characterized *ex post* in field-based fashion. This is what Fig. 6.3 does. But when the connection between the field-based summary and the network-based source of generation is removed, the field-based summary is left standing by itself, and it doesn't look so good when seen in this manner because there is no microstructure from which the macro por-trait is generated (Epstein 2006). Where partisan cycles seek to develop an alternative field-based statement that seems less embarrassing as com-pared with early PBC models, the path to sensible understanding surely resides in connecting the micro-level of action with the macro-level sum-marization, as illustrated by Dopfer et al. (2004) and Potts and Morrison (2007) in stressing a meso level of organization as residing between micro and macro levels.

The connection between micro and macro levels is not a sensible thing to deal with if one presumes that all observations pertain to equilibrium states. The significance of an effort at connection makes sense only if the analytical focus is placed on processes of motion and development and not on states of equilibrium, particularly once it is recognized that process is the natural home of knowledge that is both incomplete and asymmetric and of competition as a ceaseless activity by which people seek to thrive in the presence of entropy (Georgescu-Rogen 1971). This competitive process is naturally turbulent, as Wagner (2010) sketches.

Suppose we theorize about societal coordination in terms of the image of a crowd of pedestrians and not a parade. The coordination of a crowd is not as smooth as that of a parade. For a parade, all marchers are evenly spaced and march at the same pace. Hence a parade has none of the jostling and bumping that you experience in a crowd. When viewed from high enough above, the crowd would appear to be an imperfect example of a parade. Among other things, the crowd would exhibit turbulence, and in principle it would be possible to develop measures of this turbulence, or at least some features of it. These measures would all involve phenomena that would be absent from the parade. For instance, a person wanting to exit the moving mass from the middle of that mass would have to work to the edge before leaving. This could cause some jostling that would slow down other people; moreover, the person in question might not have made it to the edge in time to take the desired exit and so might have to traverse a longer route. Such things as I have just described are forms of capital losses where plans didn't work out as anticipated because the success of those plans depends also on actions taken by other participants in that nexus.

The standard literature on political business cycles reflects a presumption that polity and economy are separate entities, and with action inside each entity proceeding in sequential fashion wherein polity acts upon given data from economy. The analytical challenge is to develop alternative conceptualizations wherein economic and political action both occur simultaneously, and with each being sources for the generation of data. Here I refer to the notion of entangled political economy set forth in Wagner (2007, 2016) and applied to the recent financial crisis in Smith et al. (2011), in contrast to the orthodox notion of separated political economy as illustrated by Persson and Tabellini (2000) and Drazen (2000).

When we come to political economy, we need to bring political participants into that crowd and to do so in entangled fashion where there is interaction among the participants, as against the two types of participants comprising distinct crowds. Since the analytical challenge is to model an ecology of enterprises in a setting where there are constitutive differences among the enterprises, the analogy to a crowd would seem naturally to assimilate to a model where market-based pedestrians have somewhat different rules of motion than polity-based pedestrians. In any of several ways, these differences among entities would generate interactions that were detectably different from those among market-based entities. Much of the orderliness of ordinary pedestrian crowds comes about from the general dislike that people have in colliding with one another. The presence of political entities changes this setting by creating positions that gain utility by such collisions, as expressed by Jane Jacobs's (1992) treatment of how interaction between commercial and guardian syndromes can lead to "monstrous moral hybrids."

PROBING SOME ANALYTICAL POSSIBILITIES

I shall now consider briefly a few analytical possibilities that come into the analytical foreground once the hard core of a political economy centered on static equilibrium is replaced by a hard core centered on emergent dynamics. These possibilities are all variations on a common theme concerning the treatment of contract and coordination in the mixed-form catallaxy denoted by entangled political economy. Rather than coordination being postulated by presumption as a reflection of an equilibrium postulate, coordination is something that is generated in variable degree through interaction among participants who care little to nothing about global coordination but who care greatly about the success of their plans. Any explanation of the coordinated quality of pedestrian crowds would surely start with recognition that individual members of that crowd are seeking to be effective in action. They are not human variants of bumper cars; pedestrian crowds do not mirror demolition derbies.

An ecology of plans differs from a pedestrian crowd in that successful action within that societal ecology requires cooperative participation among other market participants. This cooperation we denote as contract (Fried 1981). Contract connects participants by coordinating their actions over some designated period covered by that contract, and with relational contracting extending beyond that explicit contractual period. Complete coordination would mean that all contractual promises proved to be mutually consistent. Such compete coordination doesn't prevail, but orderly procedures exist for repairing the breaches of contract that accompany inconsistent or incomplete expectations among contractual partners. Most breaches of contract occur without legal action and take the form of renegotiations of obligations and commitments previously made. In these activities, the desire for commercial success as calculated by profit and loss provides a common language through which coordination is secured within an inherently kaleidic world.

Contractual relationships with political entities don't work in the same manner, as Richard Epstein (1993) illustrates in explaining how bargaining with the state differs from bargaining with commercial enterprises. While political entities likewise recognize a language of gain, that language is of a different dialect from that of profit and loss. There are no positions of residual claimancy within political entities, at least not directly as against indirect positions of residual claimancy. Indeed, Epstein's description of bargaining with the state could well be modeled by treating the political members of that crowd of pedestrians as human equivalents of bumper cars.

One facet of the absence of residual claimancy is surely lowered contractual durability. One long-standing principle in this respect is that no legislature can commit its successors. Historically speaking, a subsequent legislature will typically continue with most of what has been inherited, in large part because most of the membership remains the same. Still, there are no contractual commitments in the sense that governs actions among market participants. Anyone who doubts this should place social security into contractual language, with one side of the contract being promises to recipients and the other side being promises to taxpayers: the unfunded liability of something on the order of $20 trillion (and with another $100 or so trillion for Medicare) represents the extent of the mutual misrepresentation of contractual promises. To be sure, nobody states the matter this way, but the failure to do so just reflects recognition that political entities import different operating precepts into society. A commitment made is not maintained just because it is a commitment, nor are breaches of commitment negotiated to a mutually satisfactory resolution due to an interest in future dealings. Public ordering entails different operating procedures than private ordering, even though both principles occupy the same social space, and with those different principles operating to tectonic effect.

One aspect of an entangled political economy concerns the pattern of connection among different types of enterprises. If political entities are analogized to the human equivalents of bumper cars, one question becomes whether those political entities are indifferent to the market entities onto which they connect or whether systematic patterns of connection seem likely to result. Connections don't just happen among enterprises, they are created. Connections between market-based firms are governed by a calculative language of anticipated profitability. But what is the language of connection between market-based and polity-based enterprises? Recurring to Fig. 3.1, compare two sets of market-based enterprises. One set contains enterprises that are new and small, recognizing that a number of these will become large over the coming years. The other set contains enterprises that are large and established, some of which have probably already seen their better days. The former set might be illustrated by biotech firms; the latter might be illustrated by automobile companies.

We can ask whether there is any good basis for thinking that political connections are more likely to form with the established and not the nascent set of firms. Nascent firms are unlikely to attract much political attention unless they seek it. In contrast, established firms almost surely will be unable to avoid attracting attention from political entities. It is surely also worth keeping in mind that nearly all taxes are collected by corporations, save for the tax on real estate, and even much of this tax revenue is collected by mortgage lenders through escrow accounts. While such taxes as those on personal income, earnings, and retail sales are nominally paid by individuals, nearly all of those taxes are collected by commercial enterprises and transmitted to political entities. It is easy to understand why tax collection agencies prefer obtaining revenues from large enterprises and not independent contractors. A nation of shopkeepers surely has less capacity for collecting revenues for political agencies than does a nation dominated by gigantic enterprises.

The PBC framework is really one of politically induced miscoordination and not cyclicity. Miscoordination might entail cyclicity, but it need not do so. There are many sources of disturbance to patterns of economic interaction, and these can vary greatly in their macro-level impact. Disturbances to money and credit are particularly noteworthy because they operate across all markets, in contrast to many other sources of disturbance that are narrower in scope. But it should not be thought that miscoordination implies cyclicity. Suppose we never observed fluctuations, at least of sufficient magnitude to be described as fluctuations as distinct from normal variability. Does this mean that miscoordination has vanished? This would be so only if miscoordination could manifest itself only through cycles. But miscoordination can manifest itself through other ways as well. Such activities as scrapping and renovating are surely examples of miscoordination. Any effort at plan revision points to some preceding point of miscoordination. There is no necessary reason why unemployment must accompany miscoordination, though as a practical matter the two would probably go together to some degree.

Consider a simple example of credit expansion within the framework of Austrian-style cycle theory as described by Garrison (2000). Credit expansion induces investment in projects that are relatively capital intensive. When that expansion comes not from saving but from credit creation, the initial expansion will be subsequently reversed because the investments will prove to be unprofitable. An investment-driven bust follows an investment-driven boom. This sequence of boom-and-bust is typically portrayed in terms of cyclical variability in employment. As a conceptual matter, however, it does not need to be this way. This process could conceivably work with continuous full employment, only with changes in the pattern of employment. For instance, more resources will be involved in revising and amending plans and in clearing away abandoned plans, than would have been the case that there been no ACT-type miscoordination. As a substantive illustration, the boom could entail the planting of hickory forests to exemplify the credit-induced shift into projects of longer maturity. The bust, however, need not entail unemployment, such as might have resulted had the young hickory forest been allowed to go to weed. Instead, people who would have been employed in maintaining the hickory forest could now be used to uproot and shred the young trees, and subsequently to plant the land with broccoli.

Our objects of scientific interest cannot be observed, for they are constructed theoretically. Those theoretical constructions might illuminate our object of interest, but they might also place it in the shadows as the Keynesianesque analytics have done for the mainline macro theory this book seeks to carry forward, though by adding new analytical concepts and tools. The reductionism of the new orthodoxy in political economy, whereby polities and economies are both reduced to point-mass entities, surely places the original concerns about the macro or systemic consequences of political-economic interaction into the analytical shadow land. What is required to escape that desolate place involves an extensive rethinking of political economy within an analytical setting that involves network-based conceptualizations grounded in notions of complexity and emergent dynamics. That analytical setting is one where macro-level observation supervenes on micro-level interaction, just as a traffic jam supervenes on interaction among the individual cars that constitute the jam (Resnick 1994).

SOME AGONISTICS OF RICARDIAN EQUIVALENCE

Contemporary macro theory is dominated by the Ricardian equivalence proposition that public debt is just future taxation, and, moreover, that the present value of those future taxes is equal to the amount borrowed. What appears to follow from this equivalence proposition is recognition that budget deficits cannot increase aggregate spending because deficits don't increase aggregate net worth (Barro 1974). Most of the controversy over Ricardian equivalence has centered on empirical magnitudes. The bulk of the post-Barro literature has found that budget deficits are associated with increased aggregate spending, but with that increase being less than the size of the deficit. Why this might be so, moreover, has generally been attributed to debt illusion where people do not take into full current account the future tax implications of budget deficits (Seater 1993). Ricardian equivalence is directly relevant for claims that budgetary politics promotes economic instability in the pursuit of political gain, in contrast to the Keynesianesque claims that budget deficits can close output gaps.

The simple empirics of Ricardian equivalence illustrate the ability of inaptly specified econometric estimations to generate illusory implications. This illusory quality holds both for New Classical claims on behalf of Ricardian equivalence and for New Keynesian claims that fiscal policy can influence aggregate spending. Both claims rest on the presumption that the statistical construction denoted as the aggregate economy can be acted on directly through politically implemented policy. This presumption forms the grounding for the econometric models, and with different constructions and interpretations of those models generating the competing answers about the effect of budget deficits on aggregate spending. As should be clear by now, this presumption is wrong because constructed aggregates are not direct objects of action, but rather are merely reflections of action, and of belief, ideology, and projection.

Once again, we recur to Fig. 1.3. The Ricardian proposition is a simple implication of double-entry accounting for a closed system of interaction. Public debt is no different from private debt in this respect. Private credit purchases enable the buyer to attain a different time profile of consumption, increasing current consumption while reducing future consumption to retire the debt. It is the same with public debt. By borrowing, a government can increase its present consumption, but that borrowing will require higher future taxation to retire the debt. This situation doesn't change if the government rolls over the debt rather than retires it. When debt is rolled over, as it typically is these days, public debt resembles an issue of perpetuities. Should public debt take the form of perpetuities, the Ricardian proposition remains in force, for now the borrowing is associated with a perpetual increase in tax extractions, the present value of which is equal to the amount borrowed. Whether bonds have maturity dates or are perpetuities is irrelevant for the validity of the Ricardian proposition.

The Ricardian proposition is valid with respect to the logic of double-entry accounting within a closed system of interaction. Taken alone, the upper part of Fig. 1.3 describes a closed system of interaction, as does the representative agent model. When the representative agent model is shattered into individual carriers of action in the bottom portion of Fig. 1.3, the closed system quality of social interaction disappears, and in several respects. Only if unanimity were required among all the entities in Fig. 1.3 would that Figure depict a closed system. Otherwise, the social system is open, and in multiple respects. It is open in the sense that dominant coalitions can impose costs on other people in society. It is also open in the sense that bonds might be sold to people who are outside the political system. Further openness is provided by recognition that the status of being a bondholder creates a specific interest group within the polity, in contrast to the generalized status of being a taxpayer. In other words, bondholders become an interest group with a preference for higher over lower taxation, in contrast to most taxpayers.

These various considerations mean that the orthodox discourse over fiscal policy and economic stimulation is a form of shell game. A shell game works by the organizer's seeking to divert the attention of the players, so they lose sight of the pea's location. It is the same with fiscal policy and budget deficits. Fiscal policy is not a source of wealth, so it can't be stimulatory as against being redistributive. Yet the associated budgetary actions are conveyed by a language of universal stimulation to an audience that has no good reason to pay attention anyway because they can't change the outcome when their consent is not necessary for political action to occur. With respect to Fig. 1.3, budget deficits pertain to some subset of nodes within the lower part of the Figure. There may well be no detectable effect at the aggregate level, and yet the budget deficit will have detectable economic consequences. To look for aggregate consequences is to look in the wrong place, as befits the playing of a shell game, as Eusepi and Wagner (2017) explain.

References

Akerman, J. 1947. Political Economic Cycles. *Kyklos* 1: 107–17.

Alesina, A., and N. Roubini. 1992. Political Cycles in OECD Economies. *Review of Economic Studies* 59: 663–88.

Barabási, A.L. 2002. *Linked: The New Science of Networks*. Cambridge, MA: Perseus Publishing.

Barro, R.J. 1974. Are Government Bonds Net Wealth? *Journal of Political Economy* 82: 1095–18.

Bergson, H. 1911. *Creative Evolution*. New York: Henry Holt.

Besley, T. 2006. *Principled Agents? The Political Economy of Good Government*. Oxford: Oxford University Press.

Bilo, S., and R.E. Wagner. 2015. Neutral Money: Historical Fact or Analytical Artifact? *Review of Austrian Economics* 28: 139–50.

Boettke, P.J. 2007. Liberty vs. Power in Economic Policy in the 20th and 21st Centuries. *Journal of Private Enterprise* 22: 7–36.

Bueno de Mesquita, B., et al. 2003. *The Logic of Political Survival*. Cambridge: MIT Press.

Burnham, J. 1943. *The Machiavellians*. New York: John Day.

Dekker, E. 2016. *The Viennese Students of Civilization*. Cambridge: Cambridge University Press.

Dopfer, K., J. Foster, and J. Potts. 2004. Micro-Meso-Macro. *Journal of Evolutionary Economics* 14: 263–279.

Drazen, A. 2000. *Political Economy in Macroeconomics*. Princeton, NJ: Princeton University Press.

Elias, N. 1939 [1991]. *The Society of Individuals*. Oxford: Basil Blackwell.

Epstein, R.A. 1993. *Bargaining with the State*. Princeton, NJ: Princeton University Press.

Epstein, J.M. (ed.). 2006. *Generative Social Science: Studies in Agent-Based Computational Modeling*. Princeton, NJ: Princeton University Press.

Eusepi, G., and R.E. Wagner. 2017. *Public Debt: An Illusion of Democratic Political Economy*. Cheltenham, UK: Edward Elgar.

Feiwel, G.R. 1974. Reflections on Kalecki's Theory of Political Business Cycle. *Kyklos* 27: 21–48.

Fried, C. 1981. *Contract as Promise: A Theory of Contractual Obligation*. Cambridge, MA: Harvard University Press.

Forte, F., and J.M. Buchanan. 1961. The Evaluation of Public Services. *Journal of Political Economy* 69: 107–21.

Garrison, R. 2000. *Time and Money: The Macroeconomics of Capital Structure*. London: Routledge.

Georgescu-Roegen, G. 1971. *The Entropy Law and the Economic Process*. Cambridge, MA: Harvard University Press.

Grice-Hutchinson, M. 1978. *Early Economic Thought in Spain, 1177–1749*. London: Allen & Unwin.

Grossman, H.I. 1975. Tobin on Macroeconomics: A Review Article. *Journal of Political Economy* 83: 829–48.

Hibbs, D.A. 1987. *The American Political Economy: Macroeconomics and Electoral Politics*. Cambridge, MA: Harvard University Press.

Jacobs, J. 1992. *Systems of Survival*. New York: Random House.

Kalecki, M. 1943. Political Aspects of Full Employment. *Political Quarterly* 14: 322–31.

Keech, W.R. 1995. *Economic Politics.* Cambridge: Cambridge University Press.

Lakatos, I. 1970. Falsification and the Methodology of Scientific Research Programs. In *Criticism and the Growth of Knowledge,* ed. I. Lakatos and A. Musgrave, 91–196. New York: Cambridge University Press.

Latsis, S. (ed.). 1976. *Method and Appraisal in Economics.* Cambridge: Cambridge University Press.

Leijonhufvud, A. 1981. *Information and Coordination.* New York: Oxford University Press.

Maine, H.S. 1861. *Ancient Law.* London: John Murray.

Mankiw, N.G. 2006. The Macroeconomist as Scientist and Engineer. *Journal of Economic Perspectives* 20: 29–46.

Newberg, A., E. D'Aquili, and V. Rause. 2001. *Why God Won't Go Away: Brain Science and the Biology of Belief.* New York: Ballantine.

Nordhaus, W.D. 1975. The Political Business Cycle. *Review of Economic Studies* 42: 169–90.

Ostrom, V. 1984. Why Governments Fail: An Inquiry into the Use of Instruments of Evil to Do Good. In *Theory of Public Choice II,* ed. J.M. Buchanan and R.D. Tollison, 422–35. Ann Arbor: University of Michigan Press.

Ostrom, V. 1996. Faustian Bargains. *Constitutional Political Economy* 7: 303–308.

Persson, T., and G. Tabellini. 2000. *Political Economics: Explaining Economic Policy.* Cambridge: MIT Press.

Potts, J. 2000. *The New Evolutionary Microeconomics.* Cheltenham, UK: Edward Elgar.

Potts, J., and K. Morrison. 2007. Meso Comes to Markets. *Journal of Economic Behavior & Organization* 63: 307–12.

Prigogine, I. 1997. *The End of Certainty: Time, Chaos, and the New Laws of Nature.* New York: Free Press.

Resnick, M. 1994. *Turtles, Termites, and Traffic Jams.* Cambridge: MIT Press.

Selgin, G., and L.H. White. 1999. A Fiscal Theory of Government's Role in Money. *Economic Inquiry* 37: 154–65.

Seater, J.J. 1993. Ricardian Equivalence. *Journal of Economic Literature* 31: 142–90.

Smith, A., R.E. Wagner, and B. Yandle. 2011. A Theory of Entangled Political Economy with Application to TARP and NRA. *Public Choice* 148: 45–66.

Stigler, G.J., and G.S. Becker. 1977. Die Gustibus non est Disputandum. *American Economic Review* 67: 76–90.

Wagner, R.E. 2001. Politics and the Macro Economy. In *The Elgar Companion to Public Choice,* ed. F.William Shughart II and Laura Razzolini, 422–39. Cheltenham, UK: Edward Elgar.

Wagner, R.E. 2007. *Fiscal Sociology and the Theory of Public Finance.* Cheltenham, UK: Edward Elgar.

Wagner, R.E. 2010. *Mind, Society, and Human Action: Time and Knowledge in a Theory of Social Economy*. London: Routledge.

Wagner, R.E. 2016. *Politics as a Peculiar Business: Insights from a Theory of Entangled Political Economy*. Cheltenham, UK: Edward Elgar.

White, L.H. 1999. *The Theory of Monetary Institutions*. Oxford: Blackwell.

Willett, T.D. 1988. *Political Business Cycles: The Political Economy of Money, Inflation, and Unemployment*. Durham, NC: Duke University Press.

CHAPTER 7

Public Policy as the Political Calculation of Economic Value

It is well recognized that societies are complex and not simple entities. In this respect, Warren Weaver (1948) distinguished between two types of complexity, organized and unorganized, with different analytical problems attendant to each type. The path of a single billiard ball struck by a cue ball is a simple phenomenon. In contrast, the path of the entire set of 15 balls illustrates unorganized complexity. The position of those balls after being struck can be examined by probability and statistics, as can such phenomena of even greater complexity as the diffusion of a contagious disease. In contrast, the pattern of economic activity illustrates organized complexity as observed patterns reflect intelligence at work inside the system. In the presence of intelligence and organization, intention to some degree replaces randomness as an analytical motif. Social organization is not random because it reflects intelligence at work. But whose intelligence is at work and how does it manifest is a vital question, as Weaver noted. Here again we come to one of those many forks in the analytical road. The original theorists from Salamanca and those who were later influenced by the Scottish Enlightenment treated societies as self-organized, meaning that organization emerged in consequence of each person's use of his or her intelligence. Interaction among those intelligences drove societal evolution.

Economic theory began with the efforts of theorists to understand and explain the perplexity of societal coordination. The economic activities of people throughout a society generally, though never totally, mesh together, giving the appearance of being coordinated, which they are,

© The Author(s) 2020

R. E. Wagner, *Macroeconomics as Systems Theory*,
https://doi.org/10.1007/978-3-030-44465-5_7

only without there being someone who plans and directs that coordination. By and large, people direct themselves, and yet each person's chosen pattern of activity meshes well with the similar activities of everyone else. It would be an instance of the "centralized mindset" (Resnick 1994) to attribute that coordination to some coordinating agent. Such coordination involves not only securing coordination among many people now but it also involves complicated issues of timing activities across years and even centuries. For the last few centuries, the mainline of economic theory has explored how human interaction within the framework of private property and freedom of contract enables the emergence of transactions and market prices that facilitate systemic coordination without a coordinating agent (Boettke 2012). These institutional arrangements economize on the gigantic stock of knowledge that otherwise would have to be assembled for some coordinating agent to produce that coordination. That stock of knowledge, however, would be so large that the decisions necessary to ensure coordination would become undecidable (Chaitin et al. 2011).

In contrast to the mainline of economic theory, the mainstream of economic theory has over the past century or so mostly ignored questions concerning the assembly of vast amounts of knowledge, much of it tacit (Polanyi 1958). Concomitant with the shift from what Boettke (2012) calls the mainline of economic theory to what he calls the mainstream has been an elevation in the presumed ability of politically organized power to secure economic coordination. This mainstream discourse on public or political policy entails a mix of reason and observation combined with a strong dose of mythology. The presence of reason and observation in the language of policymaking lends an aura of scientific deliberation to the formation of public policy, continuing a tradition that Jan Tinbergen (1952) set forth in articulating his scheme of matching goals and instruments in the selection of public policies. Tinbergen's scheme is carried forward in Acocella (1998), and with public policy cast as being a scientific as distinct from being an interest-dominated endeavor. One significant casualty of the mainstream predominance in economic theory is the effective abolition of tacit knowledge. By tacit knowledge, Polanyi (1958) recognized that societies worked in significant measure through kinds of knowledge that could not be transferred as formulas or precepts from person to person. People know much more than they can reduce to equations or rules, and with it being tacit knowledge and not explicit knowledge that led the mainline of economists to recognize that a flourishing social order entailed a societal architecture where the private ordering of social activity occupied the societal foreground while public ordering resided in the background. The past century has witnessed an incomplete though apparently continuing reversal of this societal architecture.

HUMAN NATURE AND THE STRUCTURE OF ECONOMIC ANALYSIS

Economists typically exclude themselves from the theories they develop, as Robert Tollison (1986) explains in treating economists as conforming to the principles of economics. This analytical posture of a theorist as being separate from the object the theorist examines is a common and even a necessary procedure for the natural sciences, especially when it comes to the inanimate objects of the physical sciences, and probably also for those biological sciences that treat insects, plants, and similar objects. When it comes to the higher mammals, the situation is perhaps not so obvious because humans are one of the higher mammals. Humans and their societies can surely be studied within the biological science of ethology. It would, of course, be fanciful to imagine gorillas, wolves, dogs, and such mammals as studying themselves. All the same, those mammals clearly exhibit patterns of action that show they are aware of one another and form beliefs and expectations about one another. It is perhaps a short step from recognizing such patterns in the higher mammals to engaging in anthropomorphic speculation by attributing desires, preferences, and similar mental states to those mammals. Despite such observations, we cannot interview those mammals, so statements we might advance about their mental states must necessarily be speculative. We do not and cannot truly know what it is like to be an orangutan or a dog, though we can always deploy our imaginations.

In contrast, we do have reasonable ideas about human mental states because we speak with one another continually. We have knowledge about human qualities that we cannot have about other mammals, at least at this stage in the development of scientific knowledge. Given the present state of knowledge, we can recognize through experience that people have the ability to speculate about counterfactual possibilities and potentialities. We can imagine ourselves in different situations and can look upon ourselves from a critic's point of view, which can lead to conscious change in patterns of action due to recognition that some previous pattern was heading in an undesired direction. Economists, as humans generally, possess a reflexive quality that enables them to look upon themselves as observers and not just as participants in the cosmic drama of society. We can observe our lives while at the same time we participate in our lives.

This duality of human nature leads Wagner (2007) to assert that both state and market are resident in human nature. States don't create markets, nor do markets induce the creation of states; to the contrary, both recognizable patterns of conduct are present within human nature. To be sure, this assertion concerns form and not substance. As substantive matters, both state and market are subject to enormous historical variability. Georg Simmel's (1900 [1990]) *Philosophy of Money* was concerned not with monetary theory but with the societal processes that undergirded the continual changes in the objects that could be subject to market transactions. Until the eighteenth century, owners of land could not sell their land but had to leave it to eldest sons. Only with the collapse of primogeniture could the modern notion of real estate markets develop. Yet there have always been transactions in real estate. Sometimes those transactions occurred through war. On other occasions they occurred through marriage, often as means of discharging debts. In the nineteenth century, married women could not own assets in their name but could own them only through their husbands. Only with the collapse of the practice of coverture could married women own assets and establish businesses. In these illustrations and countless others, the boundary between alienable and inalienable ownership has been subject to contestation and change.

Behind this ongoing variability in the reach of alienable ownership resides an enduring duality in the conception of ownership that points to ownership as being resident in human nature: individuality and sociality as both generic features of human nature. Individuality pertains to recognition of individual personhood, which even Siamese twins have, and which manifests in such phenomena as desires for recognition and accomplishment as well as recognition that pain and death are individual and not social experiences. As Hayek noted in his essay on true and false individualism (Hayek 1948), the true form of individualism leads to a theory of society and not a theory of rational individual action. In this respect, sociality does not entail any abnegation of individuality and its subsequent incorporation into some corporate body as befits many uses of the term solidarity. To the contrary, individuality and sociality are braided and entangled much as Norbert Elias (1939 [1991]) sets forth in his examination of *The Society of Individuals*.

This recognition about human nature maps directly into Richard Wagner's (2012a) inquiry into the social construction of economic theory. Economic theory has two facets as reflections of the duality resident within human nature. One facet reflects our natural curiosity. We sense that social reality operates in a regular and apprehensible manner. Societies clearly work, as the expression goes, and yet there is no puppet master in sight who directs our actions. To the contrary, there are many directors of parts of our actions. This plurality of directors has long been expressed by the image of an invisible hand to characterize the orderly quality of societies in the absence of a puppet master, with Aydinonat (2008) surveying some of the scientific history of the idea. With that idea, theorists formed the idea of self-ordered or inner-directed societies, with these ideas culminating in the heyday of liberal political economy that began to flourish late in the eighteenth century and reached its zenith around the middle of the nineteenth century. The efforts of theorists to explain the self-ordering properties of societies was largely a reflection of curiosity about how the visibly orderly qualities of human societies could be explained.

Arthur Lovejoy (1936) in his *Great Chain of Being* argues that our theories rest on presuppositions about which we typically are only vaguely aware. More explicitly, Lovejoy argues that social thinkers can be separated largely into two categories, which he describes as other-worldly and this-worldly. For other-worldly thinkers, thought should be animated by a desire to make a better world by participating in projects of societal elevation. In theological terms, the Social Gospel movement that emerged late in the nineteenth century is one illustration of Lovejoy's other-worldly category of presuppositions (Ealy 1889; Rauschenbusch 1917). In contrast, this-worldly thinkers were animated with a desire to understand the world we inhabit, and which might yield societal elevation as a by-product. By Lovejoy's formulation, this-worldly theorists would seek to explain the unseen reality (Kastner 2015) that lies beneath the surface of what is observable. One observable feature of reality is the presence of theorists and political figures who are engaged in what they describe as social reform. These activities, however, can be treated as ordinary facets of the ubiquity of economizing action (Tollison and Wagner 1991). Recognition that both curiosity and pragmatics are sources of demand for economic theories raises significant questions about the scientific status of economic theory and of the processes inside of which economic theories are created and validated, which Randall Collins (1998) treats in his examination of the social organization of scientific inquiry through competition among scholars for scarce attention space, and which Stephen DeCanio (2013) likewise treats in his examination on the limits of our ability to understand ourselves and the societies we generate.

LIMITED KNOWLEDGE AND THE MYTHS WE LIVE BY

The widespread presumption that what is commonly described as public policy represents some universal and hence neutral action corresponding to common notions of a rule of law founders on many rocks in the intellectual sea, some of which Rajagopalan and Wagner (2013) explore in their analysis of claims on behalf of rule of law as distinct from rule by people. For one thing, those notions founder on recognition that theories are constructed on beds of prior presumptions, and those prior presumptions are also subject to examination. There is no such thing as a pure and neutral reason; moreover, observation cannot be rendered sensible outside of some theoretical framework. As noted in earlier chapters, a theory that holds that observations pertain to states of equilibrium will not prove adequate for ordering observations when those observations pertain to processes that generate change through time. In this latter case, a different theoretical framework will be needed to order those observations.

Presumptions about knowledge lead one to conclude that public policy necessarily must entail a good deal of mythology to accompany any resort to reason and observation. Friedrich Hayek (1937, 1945) explained the inadequacy of any scheme of thought that postulates that social observations pertain to states of equilibrium, and with Hayek's mode of explanation extended and amplified in the essays that Joshua Epstein (2006) collected. Hayek explained that the knowledge necessary to create an equilibrium pattern of activity is distributed in bits and pieces throughout the society. For an equilibrium to be established, those bits and pieces must be assembled through the gamut of interactions within a society. Explaining how this might happen is an unfinished challenge for economic theory. It is easy enough to assume that Humpty Dumpty sits in assembled condition; it is an entirely different and presently unanswered theoretical endeavor to explain how Humpty Dumpty might be assembled after he has been shattered.

To assume a state of equilibrium necessarily entails the invocation of some mythology. One such invocation entails *assuming* that observations pertain to a state of *perfect competition*. In this case, reality is Pareto efficient, meaning that it will be impossible to improve one person's well-being without reducing the well-being of at least one other person in the society. An alternative invocation is to assume that observations pertain to states of *imperfect competition*. In this case, reality is Pareto inefficient, which means that it is possible to increase the well-being of at least one person without reducing the well-being of anyone else.

But is or is not reality Pareto efficient? People who start from perfect competition assert reality is Pareto efficient. People who start from imperfect competition assert reality is Pareto inefficient. It is, however, impossible to decide between these two possibilities without invoking mythological presuppositions. Those presuppositions engage a theorist in assuming to possess knowledge that no one can truly possess. To presume to possess such knowledge that would allow reality to be assembled in Pareto efficient fashion is to assume that a modern, complex society can be assembled without assistance from the knowledge that market transactions generate. This might be possible for a small tribe. To try to do this for societies of modern scale, however, would founded on the combinatorial arithmetic of the situation. Léon Walras (1874 [1954]) escaped this combinatorial arithmetic by invoking mythology to postulate the existence of an auctioneer who would continually cry out prices until equilibrium was established throughout the society. This was mysticism at work, and not plausible reasoning (Polya 1954). This myth enabled economists who wanted to embrace the theory of competitive equilibrium to do so despite its implausibility. This embrace had a remote tinge of plausibility because market processes bear some family resemblance to auctions. That resemblance, however, is remote, for coordination within a society is several orders of magnitude more complex than an auctioneer's distributing a small number of items among a small number of bidders. Economists who favored market processes and individual liberty could assert the reasonable quality of the Walrasian model. But economists who did not look so kindly on market processes could assert the implausibility of the Walrasian model and assert that reality was imperfectly competitive, even though a theory that is thought to be descriptively inaccurate can nonetheless provide a good fit with reality.

The contemporary theory of public policy creates a predisposition favorable to claims of imperfect competition and market failure. The situation was different during the classical period of mainline economics, which was dominated by plausible claims directed at specific situations.

In contrast, contemporary policy theory is formal and demonstrative. There is presumed to exist a disjunction between ordinary people and so-called "policy-makers." Policymakers initiate political action, and ordinary people both respond to policymakers and are the subjects that policymakers direct, presumably for their own good. We would, of course, never expect policymakers to announce they were acting to do anything other than to promote the public good. Most discourse on public policy, including macro policy, operates with two primary presumptions. First, it is presumed that policymakers operate independently of ordinary economic considerations; they are not part of the mundane and venal world of commerce and industry. Rather, they stand above and beyond that venal world, inhabiting a spiritual world devoted to the pursuit of public beneficence. Second, policymakers have superior insight and knowledge that allows them to perceive the relevant systems in their entirety, in contrast to ordinary people who have no option but to attend to their local concerns and interests, and who otherwise must rely on mythology.

To assert that a perfectly competitive equilibrium is a myth or that an imperfectly competitive equilibrium is a myth is not to denigrate these constructions. The same can be said for claims that the world works to everyone's advantage even though no one knows how truly to show how this outcome emerges in practice. Myths are fictions that nonetheless encapsulate mixtures of beliefs and knowledge that render the world of experience sensible and apprehensible to those who embrace those myths. The reality of social existence is far more complex than our understanding of it. The world obviously "works" even though our understanding of how it works is incomplete, so we complete that lack of understanding through the creation of myths that supply meaning regarding what we don't know; furthermore, we can't construct that missing knowledge starting from a situation where that knowledge is absent. All the same, scientific work proceeds under the presumption that we have the ability to push back our ignorance to uncover aspects of our unseen reality, to recall the title of Kastner's (2015) treatment of quantum physics.

Take such a simple concept as a plan which is the linchpin of any theory of human action. Does the concept of plan reside in the domain of science or is it a piece of mythology? James F. Allen, for instance, has worked extensively in articulating the concept of a plan, as illustrated by Allen's et al. (1991) *Reasoning About Plans*. Perusal of this and related works will quickly reveal two facets of reality about the ostensibly simple concept of a plan: (1) truly to sketch in substantive fashion what a plan entails can quickly become mired in complex patterns of interaction and (2) the knowledge required for the successful execution of a plan cannot be fully articulated because a good deal of tacit knowledge is also involved. We can theorize about such concepts as forming plans, an ecology of plans, and the like and develop models of these concepts. All the same, we should never forget that our knowledge always pertains to knowledge of the models we create and use, including implications that arise from manipulating those models. A good deal of the gap between the knowledge expressed by our models and what we think is knowledge of the external world is bridged by the knowledge contained inside our myths, including knowledge that is tacit. As scientists we can seek to uncover what is hidden within our myths. All the same the enormous complexity of our object of interest tells us that the knowledge we generate will always be of our models and not of what we perceive as reality. This is what Berger and Luckmann's (1966) meant by referring to the *Social Construction of Reality*.

THE MYTH OF SCIENTIFIC POLICYMAKING

To describe as mythical any presumption that policymaking is a neutral or scientific activity is not to denigrate such activity. It is rather to recognize that myriad questions remain unaddressed concerning the assembly from widely distributed bits and pieces of the knowledge that must be assembled to enable modern economic life to proceed. It is easy to buy pencils even though no one could assemble the detailed set of instructions extending over many years that would be necessary to produce the pencils that sit in stores. The ongoing project of mainline economics has always been to acquire insight into how such assembly occurs when no one possesses the array of knowledge necessary to do the assembly. In contrast, mainstream economic theory has significantly embraced what Hayek (1989) derided as a pretense of knowledge in his 1974 Nobel Prize lecture.

The standard economic theory of policymaking removes policymaking from the set of ordinary economic activity. This theory divides the world into two categories of people: policymakers and everyone else. Everyone else conforms to the laws and principles of economics, as expressed by recognition that people invariably seek to replace things and conditions they value less with things and conditions they value more. All choices among options entail a chooser selecting the option he or she values most highly (Buchanan 1969). It doesn't matter whether this is a consumer in a grocery store or the driver of a delivery truck bringing items to the store. All choices entail some selection among options, and with all choosers replacing what they value less with what they value more in making their choices. Furthermore, options are taken as data for the purpose of reasoning about people choosing among the options they face. But those options truly aren't data. They are constructed through someone else's preceding actions, illustrating yet again the enormous complexity of such a simple concept as a plan.

Policymakers are treated differently within this orthodox scheme of thought. Ordinary people think and act locally; they tend to their individual concerns; they are like sheep within the mainstream vision. Sheep need shepherds, and policymakers are the shepherds of society within the mainstream vision. Policymakers are not economizers in the normal sense of the term because the objects they value pertain not to them personally but to society as constructed mythically by invoking some concept of a social welfare function. An indefinitely large number of social welfare functions could be defined. One that is often employed is labeled an individualistic function, in that social welfare is an aggregate over individual states of welfare, as represented by $W = U_1 + U_2 + \ldots U_n$, where the society contains n individuals. This social welfare function has the look of being scientific and neutral, as does any social welfare function.

This look, however, is an illusion created by the successful playing of a shell game that leads observers away from questioning the epistemological basis of the analytical construction. To avoid that shell game requires recognition that the postulated welfare function has no substantive content and in no reasonable way can it acquire such content. Imperfect competition entails some marginal inequality within a model. There is no way, however, that inequalities are directly observable. Moreover, any such inequality also implies a profit opportunity as a matter of formal theory. Whether entrepreneurs will act on such inequalities is a substantive matter that is not addressable inside the theory. Playing the shell game by invoking imperfection and inequality promotes acquiescence by sheep in accepting the guidance of shepherds. The shell game can be avoided only by adopting a skeptical posture toward the claims of policymakers, recognizing that on occasion those policymakers might have made a valuable remark—though a remark that also identifies a potential source of entrepreneurial gain.

Avoiding the shell game requires recognition that meaningfulness in life cannot be reduced to some instant in historical time because it must be appraised over some interval of time. While economists sometimes hypothesize a functional relationship between welfare and income or wealth, they have never claimed to possess any instrument that would measure individual indicators of welfare, in contrast to the ability of instruments to measure weight, visual acuity, or blood glucose. Hence, welfare must remain a subjective matter, unlike weight, eyesight, or glucose. Any manipulation involving social welfare functions is necessarily a sleight of hand that seeks to induce observers into thinking they see what they can't possibly see. Furthermore, a person's life extends over some interval, and in large measure involves people in constructing their biographies. Hence, a reasonable welfare measure would probably be a measure of satisfaction with the biographies they are unavoidably in the process of constructing.

In short, scientifically neutral policy analysis is a myth that emerges out of competition among thinkers and policy advocates for limited attention space (Collins 1998). Gaetano Mosca (1947) asserted in his treatise on political science that people are more prone to accept formulations that assert some universal principle than formulations that promote particular people. Mosca's formulation does not deny that charismatic people have advantage in settings of political competition, perhaps particularly so in democracies with universal franchise. To the contrary, it reminds us that charisma can be particularly advantageous when enlisted in the service of what are portrayed as universal principles.

Policymaking as Quasi-profit Seeking

With respect to Fig. 1.3, policymaking is typically portrayed as shifting the configurations the upper part of Fig. 1.3 portrays. In typical macro-theoretic discussions, policy acts directly on such variables as aggregate demand, average interest rates, and similar variables that fall out of macro models. A major problem with this conventional treatment is that such variables as aggregate demand or average interest rate are not variables that are directly subject to some person's choice. The simple fact of the matter is that action at the macro level of Fig. 1.3 is impossible.

Action is confined to the micro-level, which is where all economizing entities operate. What is conventionally described as policymaking is treated as the province of political entities. Political entities, however, can no more act on the macro level than can private entities. In standard treatments of fiscal policy, a treasury department of a government is treated as acting directly on aggregate demand, as when it buys government bonds from the public. A treasury's sponsorship of buying bonds from the public will lead to an exchange of public debt for cash among those who sold debt to the treasury. This operation takes place, however, at the ground level of Fig. 1.3. So what, one might reasonably wonder, if the end result is an increase in aggregate demand? The issue here is whether the fiscal policy conforms to a neutrality proposition where the fiscal policy is reducible to a representative agent model. There is no way to answer this question without examining the process by which the treasury purchase of debt enters the society. The treasury will place an order with a brokerage house, with the broker buying bonds through market transactions. Will this lead to the increased spending envisioned by models of fiscal policy? Possibly, but not necessarily. It depends on what these people do who sell bonds.

More to the point, policy is not the sole province of politics. It is convention to treat "policy" as the exclusive domain of political action. In truth, however, policy can emerge anywhere from within an economic and social system. Some policy actions might exert large changes within society. Others might be barely detectable, or even undetectable. Politics might not even be the most significant source of social change. For instance, firms like Amazon and Walmart set in motion gigantic changes within retailing that have surely had greater impact on retailing than such political actions as mandatory labeling requirements.

For private enterprises, we have a reasonably clear notion of what would constitute a successful policy measure: the enterprise's net worth would be higher with the measure than without it. There is not much else that can be said about the matter. Some of those enterprise actions will spread throughout the economy, as illustrated by Amazon and Federal Express, spawning numerous changes in commercial operation throughout the society. Others will have local effects if they have any noticeable effects at all.

Setting aside the previously addressed issues regarding Ricardian equivalence, a treasury's sponsorship of buying bonds from the public will lead to an exchange of public debt for cash among those who sold debt to the treasury. This operation takes place, however, at the ground level of Fig. 1.3. All organizations, whether these are traditionally described as political or economic, are directed by goal seeking individuals. The operation of private property and freedom of exchange renders it reasonable to describe market-based organizations as being operated to maximize their net worth. It's not that market-based organizations possess a mentality that compels this type of conduct. Its rather that private property and free exchange operate to harmonize the interests of the owners and managers of firms (Alchian and Demsetz 1972; Meckling and Jensen 1976; Fama 1980). This tendency toward maximization is just a tendency, though a strong one. It is not a piece of demonstrable logic, unlike theorizing about proprietorships which are directed by a single person.

In contrast to proprietorships, corporations may operate with bureaucratic organizations within their borders. A corporation may have several divisions that sell different products and services. It is possible for those divisions to be operated in close contact with the generation of value to customers. For instance, division managers could be paid in good measure on the basis of division sales, and division managers might in turn compensate sales personnel similarly. Alternatively, the divisions could be operated as profit centers, and with managers paid on the basis of some profitability imputed to the division. These types of accounting devices are not identical to placing corporations on the same footing of personal responsibility as proprietorships. Among other things, corporations incur numerous forms of common and overhead costs for which any distribution among divisions will be arbitrary to some extent. Even here, one can claim following Alchian (1950) that firms that develop more accurate accounting schemes, and with accurate schemes being those that elicit the same actions as would be elicited from proprietors, would tend to have higher net worth because agency costs were lower.

Political enterprises will have higher agency costs, and for several reasons pertaining to the different institutional arrangements through which those enterprises are governed. For one thing, political enterprises lack value due to the absence of transferable ownership rights to the cash flows the enterprises generate. Those cash flows, moreover, are not generated through payments customers make for services received. They are generated instead through extractions from taxpayers that are apportioned among enterprises through some politically operated budgetary process (Wagner 2007). With enterprise value being absent, moreover, there is no way that executive compensation can be related to any measure of or proxy for firm value. Agency costs will be higher for political enterprises than for market enterprises. This difference in agency cost, moreover, is contrary to the standard macro-theoretic presumption that what matters is the amount of spending in the aggregate, and neither the organizational character of the spender nor the character of the plans out of which spending emerges. In other words, it is the bottom level of Fig. 1.3 that carries economically relevant action, and with different carriers of action yielding different macro-level projections of societal patterns and outcomes.

To treat governments as single entities that possess a coherent objective function is another instance of what Mitchel Resnick (1994) describes as the centralized mindset. Within the scheme of thought this book advances, what we denote as "government" is an order of politically created organizations, whose number is too large and whose activities are too complex to be directed by some single agent. Governmental entities, just like market entities, can act autonomously in reflection of Carl Schmitt's (1932 [1996]) claim on behalf of the autonomy of the political in society. To possess a range of autonomy in action is not to be free of constraints on the range of action. Each entity operates within an order of organizations, and the actions of other organizations channels and shapes the actions of individual organizations. Those organizations have scope for choosing their actions, and yet their options for choice are constrained by other organizations all the same.

Politically founded organizations operate within the same society as privately founded organizations. These different organizations are constituted through different institutional conventions and arrangements, and these differences matter for differences in conduct among the different forms of organization. The capital accounts of political organizations come typically from taxation imposed by a legislature and distributed among political enterprises through a budgetary process. In contrast, private enterprises secure capital by appealing directly to investors who in turn support the firm to the extent they anticipate they will receive a suitable share of the income the firm generates. Firms might not generate suitable returns to investors, who in turn might sell their ownership shares, driving down the price of ownership shares, which in turn might lead to a takeover of the firm by alternative management.

In contrast to private enterprises, political enterprises lack transferable ownership and so lack market value. Taxpayers are the de facto owners of political enterprises, but the use of their capital resides with the legislature and not with the individuals whose taxes provided the capital for the political enterprise. Political enterprises do not yield direct returns on their capital. All the same, we may be sure that a political enterprise would not have been created without those who controlled the relevant political decision thinking that this use of capital was superior to alternative uses of that capital. Those who control the creation of political enterprises and the allocation of capital to those enterprises are the *de jure* owners of those enterprises. It is this subset of legislators who can shrink or expand the capital base of different political enterprises through their budgetary decisions.

Any legislator, whether inside or outside a dominant set of legislators, faces options regarding the use of political power and the disposition of tax revenues. In all cases where options exist, the cost to a choosing individual of the option selected is that person's valuation of the next most valued option (Buchanan 1969). The accounting standards of profit and loss do not apply to political enterprises because those enterprises lack explicit capital accounts, and they also lack enterprise value. This difference between political and private enterprises is not some gigantic difference of principle, however, but is a matter of the different conventions associated with different institutional arrangements. For private enterprises, all investors are willing investors who have invested in the firm because they think such investment will yield superior returns to other investments. For political enterprises, many investors, possibly even a majority of them, will be forced investors who would rather have paid fewer taxes than have had those taxes invested in that political enterprise.

Political enterprises return gains, or quasi-profits, to those who control the relevant political decisions to support the enterprise. The point in this respect is simple. Capital that is directed to some political enterprise could have been directed to some alternative enterprise. That it is directed to the enterprise under examination and not some alternative enterprise must indicate that those political sponsors expected to receive higher returns from this investment than from some alternative investment.

All political enterprises operate on the ground level of Fig. 1.3, with macro-level consequences depending on how enterprise actions spread within the society. A central bank, for instance, is just one political enterprise within a societal catallaxy of enterprises. To be sure, a central bank is what Roger Koppl (2002) denotes as a Big Player. By this denotation, Koppl refers not just to size but to the absence of a budget constraint that renders the actions a central bank takes as less intelligible to other participants in the society than those actions would have been had the central bank been a profit-seeking firm. Many political enterprises are large, but most of them operate with budget constraints which means that to pursue one activity more fully requires them to pursue other activities less fully. Central banks are different due to their ability to create money.

Big Player or normal player, what is called public policy emerges at particular points within a society. The explanation of the pattern of public policy would follow the same formal analytical framework as explanation of the pattern of entrepreneurial action. This would be a logic of seeking higher over lower returns, recognizing the significant institutional differences between the governance of political and private entities. While the formal principle of seeking gain is universal, that principle plays out to different effect as between private and political enterprises. Private enterprises must be operated to the benefit of voluntary investors who can choose where to employ their capital. In contrast, political enterprises need only secure majority support within a legislative assembly, and in many cases even minority support will be sufficient. With political enterprises able to operate with forced investors, those enterprises have much scope for conferring advantages on some by imposing disadvantages on others.

Public Policy as Macro-theoretic Illusion

Economists repeatedly illustrate the power of economic analysis to illuminate questions pertaining to public policy. They do so, however, in a way that continues the centralized mindset by assuming away any coordinating process out of which policy actions emerge; in other words, policy is autonomous within society and does not lie at the end of some causal chain of action that resides inside society. With respect to that workhorse Fig. 1.3, economists assume that the upper part of that Figure is directly accessible to manipulation, as against that upper part emerging out of interactions inside the lower part. This distinction makes a huge difference, not least because it creates the illusion that manipulation through policy is a simple activity subject to direct action by policymakers.

Where Fig. 1.3 was constructed as a model of aggregate demand and supply to illustrate the macro theme this book explores, that Figure could easily be amended to incorporate any type of policy measure. Consider such a common textbook illustration as rent control. Those illustrations show some local market before-and-after rent control has been imposed. Those illustrations never bother with the lower part of the equivalent Figure, but if they did, they would illustrate numerous individuals interacting throughout the local housing market, some as buyers and others as sellers. The before-and-after scheme of analysis is a comparative static analysis of alternative equilibrium conditions. There is nothing wrong with such analysis, save that it gives no insight into the processes that might be generating the observations, a reductionist summary of which is presented in the Figure.

The order of movement in this conventional scheme of thought runs from macro to micro. The thought experiment starts with a free-market equilibrium that is subsequently disturbed by imposing a maximum limit on rents. How the individuals beneath the aggregate representation adjust to the change is their business and is insignificant for the macro-level analysis. Is this claim of insignificance really so obviously correct? In the standard theory, the rent control is a form of *deus ex machina*. It just happens because the theorist wants to illustrate a point. But what kind of point is being illustrated? It would seem to be the assertion that policy just happens as an insertion from outside the economic system, as befits an intervention from one of the gods. While such points of intervention might exist in dictatorial regimes, though even this is doubtful, they can't exist in democracies. Policy actions are not interventions but are emergences from within the social system.

Recognizing policy actions as emergences and not interventions surely leads directly into an inquiry into the conditions under which such emergences might manifest. Any policy action must mean that some people think they can attain more desirable states of existence than they think they will experience without the policy. Policy will emerge at specific locations within the societal space and will project onto the macro level relevant to that policy. Numerous are the detailed conditions under which a coalition can succeed in inserting a change into society. The most prominent textbook illustration concerns people with low income who secure rent reductions. This illustration is probably advanced because it enables supporters of such measures to feel good about themselves and their actions. It is by no means clear, however, that rent control operates to this effect. Some people with low income are likely to pay less for housing, but there will also be similarly situated people who get no housing in the locality. Other forms of response to the measure are also possible, and don't fit readily within the standard macro-theoretic presentation. For instance, an owner of a set of rental apartments might decide to abandon the business by not renting units as they become vacant, deciding instead to remodel the premise and convert it into a condominium.

The demand for a policy measure must arise because there are people who believe they will fare better after the measure than under the old situation. There is also a supply side to the creation of policy measures. Typically, these measures are attributed to legislatures, but they can also be created by bureaus and agencies. To say a legislature supports such a policy measure as a rent control does not mean that everyone within the relevant political unit supports the measure. It is quite possible for measures to be enacted within democratic legislatures even though most residents within that jurisdiction oppose the measure. Buchanan and Tullock (1962) give a simple illustration of this possibility. Suppose a city council has nine members, elected by district, and with policy motions acted on by simple majority vote within the council. Suppose that a modest majority of voters in five districts would favor rent control, while practically none would support it in the other four districts. Abstracting from logrolling by looking at this issue alone, a proposal for rent control could pass by a 5:4 vote. But if a referendum were held, the motion would fail by approximately a 3:1 margin. To clarify, suppose each of the districts had 100 voters. In five districts, 51 voters favored the rent control measure, and with no voters favoring the measure in the other four districts. In this instance, 255 voters would favor the measure and 645 would oppose it.

Eusepi and Wagner (2017) describe public debt as an illusion within a democratic system of government for the simple reason that democratic governments have no ability to be indebted. In contrast, monarchs of old could be indebted because they borrowed from subjects to whom they were indebted. Democracies, however, cannot truly be indebted. A set of politicians might approve a debt issue, but politicians come and go while debt remains. Public debt is a disguised set of lender–borrower "contracts" where many borrowers are forced borrowers. Democratic legislatures simply intermediate the complex of relationships whereby some people obtain public spending programs they desire while other people, who likely opposed the spending, become forced debtors who will see higher taxes in the coming years. To amplify this point, the future taxes associated with public borrowing could be assigned to taxpayers at the time the debt is created, whereas now those future taxes are left implicit until payments must be made to bondholders. In this manner, public debt would be handled in the same manner as mortgage debt, consumer, and corporate debt. We may be sure that less public debt would be created under this alternative set of institutional arrangements, and with less publicly organized spending following in the train of this alternative arrangement. Going beyond public debt, when public policy is presented in macro-theoretic terms it takes on illusory qualities. In this case, the macro-theoretic framework deflects attention away from the micro-level pattern of interactions out of which the policy measure emerges.

Two Environments for Action:
Logical and Non-logical

Policymaking is an ordinary economic activity, but this does not mean that all participants in the generation of policy, macro or otherwise, operate identically. When policymaking is described as an ordinary economic activity, it means only that all participants seek to replace circumstances and conditions they value less highly with circumstances and conditions they value more highly. This replacement is a universal quality of human action, for it says simply that people seek to be successful in the actions they undertake. Success in action is not assured in any human endeavor, but no one would construct a theory of action based on the presumption that people seek to fail at what they undertake. A person might well be observed to fail at some action, but behind this observation would surely lie some alternative desire that induced the apparent failure. For instance, a person's failure to perform well on a job may lead to being fired. However, if getting fired is accompanied by receiving welfare payments while quitting the job elicits no such payments, getting fired might not so much be a failure as a way of getting compensated for leisure.

To assert the ordinariness of economic policymaking is not to declare that private and public entities act identically because the two types of entity operate within different environments that push rational action in different directions, as Vilfredo Pareto (1935) recognized in distinguishing between logical and non-logical action. Pareto's distinction, however, is not the same as the common distinction between rational and irrational action that currently finds employment within behavioral economics (Patrick and Wagner 2015; Candela and Wagner 2016). For Pareto, all action is rational, only some is logical and other non-logical. Markets provide an environment that promotes what Pareto called logical action. In contrast, politics provides an environment that promotes non-logical action. To be sure, non-logical action is a form of rational action from a subjectivist orientation of personal probability.

Pareto's methodology centered on what he called the logico-experimental method. With respect to individual action, you can observe two things: what people do and the reasons people give for doing what they do. The former Pareto called actions, the latter he called derivations. Pareto also incorporated the concept of residues, by which he means the underlying motivations that truly drive the observed action. Subsequent to Pareto, Arthur Lovejoy (1936) explained that conscious ideas often rested on presuppositions of which the actor was partially if not totally unaware. These imperfectly or even completely unaware underpinnings of actions were equivalent to Pareto's concept of residues.

In market settings, people face choices that compel logical action in their actions both as consumers and as producers or entrepreneurs. As consumers, people face choices among options. Those options might pertain to the same type of product offered by different producers or to different types of product. In any case, the consumer must make a choice. The consumer is in the position of testing a scientific hypothesis. The consumer faces options and forms a hypothesis about which option offers higher value and chooses that option. The consumer tests the correctness of the hypothesis of relative value through experience. In making the choice, the consumer forms a conjecture about relative values of the options. Subsequent experience with the choice allows a form of test about the conjecture. In some cases, consumers might conclude they made a poor choice and take care not to repeat that choice.

It is also important to note that vendors are likewise in the position of facing consumers who are residual claimants over their choices. In selling products, vendors will need to attract attention from consumers who face numerous claims on their limited attention span. Advertising is one way of attracting attention from busy consumers, and with more elaborate and expensive advertising being often more successful in attracting attention. To say this is not to assert that advertising will *ipso facto* attract business. It might attract business once, but if the consumer's hypothesis about which vendor provides greater value is shown to be wrong by subsequent experience, the vendor will lose repeat sales. In other words, expensive advertising is likely to accompany products for which vendors have good reason to believe their offerings will be desired by consumers. In short, market transactions organized within the principles of private ordering will be characterized by a high degree of systemic or ecological rationality (Smith 2008). This high degree of rationality does not map into any notion of perfect competition. To do that would be to confound demonstrative and plausible reasoning (Polya 1954). Instances where consumers make choices they regret will always exist. So will instances where producers overestimate the attractiveness of their products for consumers, and thus lose money by producing too much and spending excessively on advertising. Plans will fail within a system based on private ordering, but the owners of those plans will have strong motivation to clear away the debris that those failures create (Wagner 2012b).

The situation differs with public ordering where we enter the realm of non-logical action. Voting in two-party systems offers a choice between two candidates. As a formal matter, it is reasonable to assert that voters choose the candidate they think will offer higher value along the dimensions they think relevant. The similarity with market choices and actions ends at this point. A voter cannot test the value of the option chosen against the expectation that led to that choice in the first place. The simple fact of the matter is that the value of that option never manifests in the world of experience. The market setting enables a comparison between a projected value from choosing an option and the subsequent experience with that option. This is not the case for political choice because the option a candidate offers is indefinite and not substantive.

Candidates in turn recognize that voters are not in the position of forming and testing hypotheses when they choose between vendors because a voter's vote does not make a choice between the candidates. An election results in a choice between candidates, but no individual voter makes such a choice. This environmental setting for political action changes the appeals that candidates make to voters. Candidates advertise, for sure, but voters are not residual claimants of the value consequences of their choices, because they do not truly make choices over the options they will experience. Electoral options will revolve around images (Boulding 1956). Voters will choose between images, selecting that image that enables them to feel better about themselves than the other image would have allowed. The electoral environment still incorporates rational action, for intelligence is still in play (Knight 1960). That intelligence, however, is deployed differently in political action than in market action. It is deployed in generating images that have durability, in contrast to market action where intelligence is deployed in developing products and services that will retain the allegiance of consumers against open competition from other vendors.

THE USE OF KNOWLEDGE WITHIN DEMOCRATIC POLITIES

Friedrich Hayek (1937, 1945) noted that a state of economic equilibrium required an assembly of knowledge that could not be possessed by any single person or office. The economic theory of markets and social organization seeks to explain how a socially coherent pattern of activity can arise even though no one can possess the knowledge necessary to create that coherence. To assume an equilibrium among people and their activities is to assume that sufficient knowledge has been transmitted among people to promote that pattern. Hayek claimed that economists neglected an important part of their obligation as scientists when they assumed such knowledge was present without explaining how this presence came about.

Subsequent theoretical work has done much to uncover the processes through which knowledge is transmitted in a manner that promotes societal coordination of economic activities, as illustrated by Devereaux and Wagner's (2020) effort to place game theory inside a synecological setting has knowledge of the entire game. A restauranteur offers a menu, initially by forming a judgment about what dishes people might like. The choices customers make among offerings provides information about what they like. The restauranteur might also elicit further information by periodically offering other items to gauge customer reaction. The restauranteur likewise contracts with suppliers to provide inputs, and those suppliers acquire knowledge of what kinds of items to stock from the buying patterns of their customers. The institutional arrangements of private property and freedom of contract generate a network of market prices that both adapt to myriad exchanges among market participants and provide information about the value to customers of different entrepreneurial choices. It would be impossible for some planning agency to organize production within modern societies, and yet such organization occurs readily within these liberal institutional arrangements.

How does political activity fit within this social division of labor and knowledge? Several times, Frank Knight asserted that it's not what we don't know that is harmful, but rather is what we know that isn't true (Knight 1947). This dichotomy about knowledge falls readily within Pareto's distinction between logical and non-logical action. When economists speak of democracy as a political system that operates through competition for office, they seem generally to think that electoral competition has similar properties to market competition (Wittman 1995). Without doubt, there are many similarities, for politics is a peculiar form of business practice (Wagner 2016). Much of significance depends on whether the peculiar features of political practice lead to small or large differences regarding the comparative qualities of competing for support from customers and competing for support from voters (Wagner and Yazigi 2014).

To address this question requires some consideration of the qualities for which any competitive process selects. It takes no great leap of faith to assert that open competition will select for superior qualities in performing well in any competitive endeavor. The identification of qualities, moreover, is not a simple task, though that identification typically is restricted to generic forms of competition, as illustrated by comparing market competition with electoral competition. For some purposes it is useful to stay with generic qualities, but for other purposes more detail might be required.

With respect to market competition, for instance, people who are good at selling consumer electronics to retailers might not be good at selling pharmaceuticals to physicians or insurance companies. There are probably some personality traits that are universal for effective salesmanship. But equally surely there is technical knowledge that differs among products and is not equally mastered by all possible candidates. It seems reasonable to speculate that similarities outweigh differences because technical knowledge can perhaps be mastered more fully than can the empathy and sympathy that are part of effective salesmanship. In other words, a market process will tend to produce through trial and error an allocation of people to positions that reflects their comparative advantages among the activities they might undertake. Sure, probably everyone has come across people who don't perform well in their present positions, for the claim that production occurs along the boundary between possible and impossible is but a tendency within the logic of private ordering. But private ordering does not operate exclusively even within private enterprises, and it operates far less so within political enterprises.

Within market environments, residual claimancy is present even if it is attenuated by public ordering. For instance, a sales manager might not be able to replace poorly performing sales representatives due to any of several forms of public ordering. Where once upon a time, poor performance could be accompanied by simple dismissal by the proverbial snap of a finger, now it must be accompanied by sometimes lengthy proceedings and gathering of testimony. Such requirements typically don't prevent dismissal, but they do create a type of mal-performance rent that someone can capture without being dismissed.

The performance properties of political enterprise typically differ significantly from those of private enterprise, even though the extension of public ordering norms to private enterprise can reduce the difference between the two types of enterprise. Most significantly, there are no positions of direct residual claimancy with respect to political enterprise. To be sure, there can be positions of indirect residual claimancy, many of them. A legislator might have a spouse, child, or even just a friend who receives advantage in business from the legislative connection, and this connection might open into lucrative post-legislative employment. What appears through one set of glasses as excess payments for services becomes an investment in future gain when viewed through another set.

This transformation comes about because political enterprises do not have directly to attract investors and customers. Instead, they can secure forced investment through taxation and they can compel patronage through regulation. To be sure, some modicum of consent is necessary within democratic polities, but short of the unanimity associated with market transactions this degree of consent is only partial. As Podemska-Mikluch and Wagner (2013) explain, the magic number for democratic transactions is three, in contrast to its being two for market transactions. This difference in magic numbers allows political enterprises to operate with an admixture of consent and force, whereby supporters of the political enterprise agree to impose liabilities on the remainder of the population.

Yes, political enterprises must attract supporters because any political enterprise must compete with other political enterprises for budgetary appropriations and regulatory authority. What must be noted, however, is the difference in conditions that govern the two forms of competition. Those differences promote different qualities between the different forms of enterprise. An enterprise that must attract investors and customers will act differently and select for different managerial characteristics than an enterprise that can survive and even thrive with the agreement of a subset of the population to impose burdens on those who don't support the enterprise. A clash of values is set in motion when private and public enterprises occupy the same societal space (Storr 2008, 2013). The intensity of that clash is variable and not fixed. Among other things, that intensity is weakened to the extent that democratic processes operate in consensual fashion, while being strengthened to the extent those processes operate in majoritarian fashion.

As an earlier chapter noted, moreover, that to describe a democratic process as majoritarian is not equivalent to saying that a majority of people expressly support a political enterprise. Acquiescence, for instance, is not the same as agreement. To the contrary, it is more like duress, as captured by the expression "going along to get along." This institutional setting can accommodate what Roger Koppl (2018) describes as a rule by experts, with the identity of the experts being certified by the relevant political enterprise. Within this setting, minority subsets of people with intensely held preferences can dominate relatively apathetic majorities of people, due to the fixed cost that must be borne in opposing political domination of private action and responsibility. A political enterprise might evoke modest opposition from a majority of people, but the intensity of that opposition might be less than the cost that would be entailed in opposing the political enterprise. Within a market setting, moreover, each person's opposition counts because they can withhold payment. Within a political setting, opposition amounts to nothing unless it is massed to overcome supporters of the enterprise. This enables political enterprises to operate in an all-or-nothing type of environment along the lines that William Niskanen (1971) set forth.

IMAGE, IDEOLOGY, AND COMPETITION OVER POLICY SPACE

Yes, competition is competition. And yes, any form of competition tends to select for excellence among the set of competitors. The social qualities of different competitive environments also raise reasonable and significant concerns. All social processes in societies of modern scale are polycentric and emergent, but there can be destructive as well as beneficial forms of emergent interaction. The familiar claim on behalf of undirected emergence is that social configurations can emerge that serve the general good even though no one planned or chose that configuration. It's also possible, however, for emergent processes to generate socially destructive outcomes. For instance, Warren Nutter (1962) explained that Russia was growing faster under the czars than it grew after the Russian Revolution. Nutter further explained that the post-revolutionary experience was disastrous for ordinary Russians even if it was beneficial for a few Communist Party officials, at least those who survived various purges that were an inherent part of the operating properties of that system of human governance. We should not forget, moreover, that Adolph Hitler was an ordinary person who secured democratic election, and then established his political program in opposition to other competing programs. Yes, competition is deeply rooted in human nature, sometimes working to the social betterment, but not always.

The theories of politics and political processes developed in the early twentieth century by Vilfredo Pareto (1935) and Gaetano Mosca (1947) go a long way toward explaining how democratic processes can generate more of a servile than liberal order (see Hilaire Belloc 1912; Alexis de Toqcueville 1835–1840 [1966]). Private enterprises continually make claims about their products through advertising and activities addressed at cultivating good public relations. Those claims are not terribly informative and are laden with puffery and not genuine information. They are aimed at evoking a favorable image in people's minds. In buying products, however, customers are working with their money in the presence of competing uses for their money. The competitive environment is filled with competitors in a system of free enterprise, and we should expect much puffery in advertising to secure a claim on the limited attention consumers have. Without doubt, products that buyers eventually find unsatisfactory will find first-time buyers all the same. This is inevitable within a system of free enterprise where people are free to pursue their commercial dreams. Still, the main force of a system of free enterprise will reside in the repeat dealings that arise through satisfactory experiences. At any instance, many enterprises will be formed, some subsequently to be revealed as good and others as bad. The bad ones die, and the good ones continue, and with a new cohort of enterprises to be formed the next period, and with the process continuing indefinitely.

The survival of political enterprises, however, does not depend on some aggregation of experiences over customers because there is no way such a customer can withhold payment and shift allegiance to another vendor. In the days when medical care was organized mostly through private ordering, people could choose among physicians based on their perceptions of the value of the service they received. Now, there is still a modicum of patient choice among physicians, but the environment in which services are supplied is largely collectively organized. What is now regarded as good medical care is registered through lobbying by interest groups in conjunction with the images created through advertising. No longer are systemic qualities generated through some market processes with respect to patient experiences and judgments.

At one time, the societal configurations regarding medical care were organized through the operation of logical action. Increasingly, however, except for perhaps the very rich, those societal configurations are organized through the operation of non-logical action. This shift in the source of societal configurations transforms those configurations from emerging out of the experiences of patients into emerging through the images (Boulding 1956) that are shaped by political advertising in conjunction with the interest-group machinations that help to generate that advertising.

Yes, competition is an ineradicable feature of human nature, but it can manifest in many ways and with variable social qualities. For instance, suppose a person wanted through some charitable sentiment to distribute one million dollars among one thousand people in $1000 increments. There are numerous ways this could be done. Some would qualify as private ordering and others would qualify as public ordering. The donor could solicit applications and provide details about how those selected could obtain their money. If the application were simple, entailing little more than a name and address, we may feel assured that many applications would be submitted. Alternatively, the donor could announce that the million dollars would be dropped from a helicopter as it passed over an open field at noon on the next Friday. This method would be characterized as private ordering. With a thousand $1000 bills to be dropped over the field, we may reasonably expect considerable mayhem to result as spectators fight for the money. The different distributional arrangements would have different social consequences even though the amounts distributed were identical.

GENERATIVE PROCESSES AND BRIDGING THE MICRO–MACRO GAP

The bulk of the economic literature forms relationships of the form $M = f(V)$, where M denotes some macro-level observation and V denotes a variable that is thought relevant. Hence, a rate of growth might be related to education spending as a share of GDP. Alternatively, aggregate public spending might be related to the form of government, perhaps with those forms distinguishing between presidential and parliamentary forms of democracy, as illustrated by Persson and Tabellini (2000) and Acemoglu and Robinson (2009). When faced with such relationships, one might reasonably wonder what instruction they offer. Might not a reasonable response to that wonderment be: nothing? Why nothing? Because macro variables can't act directly on one another because those variables are not carriers of action. To the contrary, they are emergent by-products of interaction among the relevant carriers.

To bridge the micro–macro gap that Fig. 1.3 sketches, it is necessary to specify some generative process represented by the thunderbolts that generates the macro-level observations from the micro-level interactions. There are numerous possible approaches to doing this, all of which would maintain the supervenience of macro observations on micro-level interactions. Within standard macro theory, the prevalent way of bridging this gap is to reduce the set of micro-level interactions to a single choice by a representative agent, under the assumption that representative agent carries all of the knowledge and values necessary to scale up to the macro-level observation. This approach to the micro foundations of macro proceeds by reducing away any process of micro interaction.

An alternative approach to constructing a generating process would recognize that macro outcomes emerge out of interaction among differently constituted enterprises. As noted in an earlier chapter, there is a good reason for thinking that genuine output gaps would hover around zero within a system based on private ordering. This can change with public ordering because public ordering opens into the possibility of subsidized leisure, thereby reducing the desire of subsidy recipients to supply labor. That restriction in the amount of labor supplied might also be supported by those who are employed, and whose labor would be competitive with those who are subsidized. For instance, an increase in the minimum wage will reduce the amount of employment in that wage range, leading to some increase in wage to those who remain employed. Those who become unemployed, moreover, may suffer no loss in welfare as earnings are replaced by the combination of welfare payments and leisure. Sure, the taxes that must be extracted to finance those welfare payments could have been returned to taxpayers, though most likely would have been appropriated instead for other uses. In any case, and to repeat the theme with which this book began: one cannot reasonably theorize about macro-level observations without theorizing about the micro-level institutions and interactions through which those macro-level observations emerge.

References

Acemoglu, D., and J.A. Robinson. 2009. *Economic Origins of Dictatorship and Democracy*. Cambridge: Cambridge University Press.

Acocella, N. 1998. *The Foundations of Economic Policy*. Cambridge: Cambridge University Press.

Alchian, A.A. 1950. Uncertainty, Evolution, and Economic Theory. *Journal of Political Economy* 58: 211–21.

Alchian, A.A., and H. Demsetz. 1972. Production, Information Costs, and Economic Organization. *American Economic Review* 62: 777–95.

Allen, J.F., Henry A. Kautz, Richard N. Pelavin, and Josh D. Tenenberg. 1991. *Reasoning About Plans*. San Mateo, CA: Morgan Kaufman.

Aydinonat, N.E. 2008. *The Invisible Hand in Economics*. London: Routledge.

Belloc, H. 1912. *The Servile State*. London: Foulis.

Berger, P., and T. Luckmann. 1966. *The Social Construction of Reality*. New York: Random House.

Boettke, P.J. 2012. *Living Economics*. Oakland, CA: Independent Institute.

Boulding, K.E. 1956. *The Image: Knowledge in Life and Society*. Ann Arbor: University of Michigan Press.

Buchanan, J.M. 1969. *Cost and Choice*. Chicago: Markham.

Buchanan, J.M., and G. Tullock. 1962. *The Calculus of Consent*. Ann Arbor: University of Michigan Press.

Candela, R., and R.E. Wagner. 2016. Vilfredo Pareto's Theory of Action: An Alternative to Behavioral Economics. *Il Pensiero Economico Italiano* 24: 15–29.

Chaitin, G., F.A. Doria, and N.C.A. de Costa. 2011. *Gödl's Way: Exploration into an Undecidable World*. Boca Raton, FL: CRC Press.

Collins, R. 1998. *The Sociology of Philosophies: A Global Theory of Intellectual Change*. Cambridge, MA: Harvard University Press.

DeCanio, S. 2013. *Limits of Economic and Social Knowledge*. Houndsmill, UK: Palgrave Macmillan.

de Tocqueville, A. 1835–1840 [1966]. *Democracy in America*, 2 vols. New Rochelle, NY: Arlington House.

Devereaux, A., and Wagner, R.E. 2020. Game Theory as Social Theory: Finding Spontaneous Order. Manuscript, George Mason University, Fairfax, VA.

Ealy, R.T. 1889. *Social Aspects of Christianity and Other Essays*. New York: Crowell.

Elias, N. 1939 [1991]. *The Society of Individuals*. Oxford: Basil Blackwell.

Epstein, J.M. (ed.). 2006. *Generative Social Science: Studies in Agent-based Computational Modeling*. Princeton, NJ: Princeton University Press.

Eusepi, G., and R.E. Wagner. 2017. *Public Debt: An Illusion of Democratic Political Economy*. Cheltenham, UK: Edward Elgar.

Fama, E. 1980. Agency Problems and the Theory of the Firm. *Journal of Political Economy* 88: 288–307.

Hayek, F.A. 1937. Economics and Knowledge. *Economica* 4: 33–54.

Hayek, F.A. 1945. The Use of Knowledge in Society. *American Economic Review* 35: 519–30.

Hayek, F.A. 1948. *Individualism and Economic Order*. Chicago: University of Chicago Press.

Hayek, F.A. 1989. The Pretense of Knowledge. *American Economic Review* 79: 3–7.

Kastner, R.E. 2015. *Understanding Our Unseen Reality: Solving Quantum Riddles*. London: Imperial College Press.

Knight, F.H. 1947. *Freedom and Reform*. New York: Harper.

Knight, F.H. 1960. *Intelligence and Democratic Action*. Cambridge, MA: Harvard University Press.

Koppl, R. 2002. *Big Players and the Economic Theory of Expectations*. New York: Palgrave Macmillan.

Koppl, R. 2018. *Expert Failure*. Cambridge: Cambridge University Press.

Lovejoy, A. 1936. *The Great Chain of Being*. Cambridge, MA: Harvard University Press.

Meckling, W.H., and M.C. Jensen. 1976. Theory of the Firm: Managerial Behavior, Agency Costs, and Ownership Structure. *Journal of Financial Economics* 3: 305–60.

Mosca, G. 1947. *Elementi di scienza politica*, 4th ed. Bari: G. Laterza.

Niskanen, W.A. 1971. *Bureaucracy and Representative Government*. Chicago: Aldine.

Nutter, G.W. 1962. *Growth of Industrial Production in the Soviet Union*. Princeton, NJ: Princeton University Press.

Pareto, V. 1935. *The Mind and Society*. New York: Harcourt Brace.

Patrick, M., and R.E. Wagner. 2015. From Mixed Economy to Entangled Political Economy: A Paretian Social-theoretic Orientation. *Public Choice* 164: 103–16.

Persson, T., and G. Tabellini. 2000. *Political Economics: Explaining Economic Policy*. Cambridge, MA: MIT Press.

Podemska-Mikluch, M., and R.E. Wagner. 2013. Dyads, Triads, and the Theory of Exchange: Between Liberty and Coercion. *Review of Austrian Economics* 26: 171–82.

Polanyi, M. 1958. *Personal Knowledge*. Chicago: University of Chicago Press.

Polya, G. 1954. *Mathematics and Plausible Reasoning*, 2 vols. Princeton, NJ: Princeton University Press.

Rajagopalan, S., and R.E. Wagner. 2013. Constitutional Craftsmanship and the Rule of Law. *Constitutional Political Economy* 24: 295–309.

Rauschenbusch, W. 1917. *Theology of the Social Gospel*. New York: Macmillan.

Resnick, M. 1994. *Turtles, Termites, and Traffic Jams*. Cambridge, MA: MIT Press.

Schmitt, C. 1932 [1996]. *The Concept of the Political*. Chicago: University of Chicago Press.

Simmel, G. 1900 [1990]. *The Philosophy of Money*, 2nd ed. London: Routledge.

Smith, V. 2008. *Rationality in Economics*. Cambridge: Cambridge University Press.

Storr, V. 2008. The Market as a Social Space. *Review of Austrian Economics* 21: 135–50.

Storr, V. 2013. *Understanding the Culture of Markets*. London: Routledge.

Tinbergen, J. 1952. *On the Theory of Economic Policy*. Amsterdam: North-Holland.

Tollison, R.D. 1986. Economists as the Subject of Economic Inquiry. *Southern Economic Journal* 52: 909–22.

Tollison, R.D., and R.E. Wagner. 1991. Romance, Realism, and Economic Reform. *Kyklos* 44: 57–70.

Wagner, R.E. 2007. *Fiscal Sociology and the Theory of Public Finance*. Cheltenham, UK: Edward Elgar.

Wagner, R.E. 2012a. The Social Construction of Theoretical Landscapes: Some Economics of Economic Theories. *American Journal of Economics and Sociology* 71: 1185–1204.

Wagner, R.E. 2012b. Viennese Kaleidics: Why It's Liberty More than Policy That Calms Turbulence. *Review of Austrian Economics* 25: 283–97.

Wagner, R.E. 2016. *Politics as a Peculiar Business*. Cheltenham, UK: Edward Elgar.

Wagner, R.E., and D. Yazigi. 2014. Form vs. Substance in Selection Through Competition: Elections, Markets, and Political Economy. *Public Choice* 159: 503–14.

Walras, L. 1874 [1954]. *Elements of Pure Economics*. Homewood, IL: Richard D. Irwin.

Weaver, W. 1948. Science and Complexity. *American Scientist* 36: 536–44.

Wittman, D. 1995. *The Myth of Democratic Failure*. Chicago: University of Chicago Press.

CHAPTER 8

Money, Credit, and Commanding the Societal Heights

Vladimir Lenin deployed the term "commanding height" in 1922 as a strategic template for the Communist Party to follow in its effort to communize the newly formed Soviet Union in the aftermath of the Russian Revolution of 1917. Lenin recognized that the Russian economy could not be communized at the proverbial stroke of a pen. Communism faced strenuous resistance and Lenin realized that he could achieve his objective of abolishing the economic organization of society through market exchange only in stepwise fashion. The first step in Lenin's effort was to gain control of what he regarded the commanding heights of what had been the Russian version of a market economy. For Lenin, the commanding heights referred to such industries as heavy manufacturing, public utilities, and transportation. Behind those particular industries and activities lies recognition that any program to expand the extent of collective control over what had been mainly a market economy has sequential character. A program of collectivizing an economy will proceed more rapidly if the right sequence is pursued because each act of collectivization reduces the resistance that subsequent acts of collectivization encounter.

Antonio Gramsci was an Italian communist who was a generation younger than Lenin, and who wanted to see Italian society communized but who thought that this Marxist objective would not be effective by starting with the collectivization of heavy industry and moving on from there. Contrary to Lenin who thought in terms of material categories and accepted Marx's belief that the material organization of production generated values and sentiments, Gramsci, who has streets and piazzas

© The Author(s) 2020

R. E. Wagner, *Macroeconomics as Systems Theory*,
https://doi.org/10.1007/978-3-030-44465-5_8

named after him in Italy, thought that the sentiments resident within a population led the material organization of production. For the communization of society to be successful, Gramsci (1971) thought that it would be necessary to take over the primary cultural institutions, a program that was later described as making a "long march through the institutions." The proponents of this program thought that the cultural hegemony of bourgeois society would require a cultural undermining of a variety of institutions and their practices before a bourgeois orientation would give way to the proletarian orientation that would support the communization of society. Rather than revolution, there would be a transformation of society as the long march continued to undermine bourgeois practices and institutions. At some point in this march, the population would have been converted into possessors of a proletarian mentality and socialism will have arrived.

Whether one works with the primacy of sentiment and value and so thinks in terms of the precedence of the cultural over the material or works with the primacy of the material, the desired end state is the same: the replacement of a bourgeois society where people largely govern themselves with a proletarian society where the few govern the many after the fashion of shepherds governing sheep. In either case, historical change is recognized to be a process where new emerges out of old, and most certainly not being some kind of choice among alternative arrangements for human governance. In this recognition of emergent historical processes, that famous question that Alexander Hamilton posed in Federalist No. 1 about whether people can choose their systems of governance or whether how they are governed must be left to the gods and to fate, must be recognized as being more rhetorical than meaningful. While conventionally we refer to 1787 in Philadelphia as a moment of constitutional choice that choice emerged through delegates who had different presuppositions regarding good government, as the subsequent controversy among Federalists and Antifederalists demonstrated. There was in force at that time a cultural hegemony that regarded government as a necessary evil more than a beneficent force within society. That hegemony has been disintegrating since the early days of the Republic, as Charles Warren (1932) explains pithily, and with that disintegration seeming to have intensified over the past century or so.

All the same, that disintegration or transformation proceeds in piecemeal fashion as befits a long march, in contrast to a transformative revolution. Typically in conventional thinking, political options are treated as reflecting a choice among options that reside within some given cultural system of human sentiment, as captured by such statements as we are all the same, we are all in this together, we owe this debt to ourselves, and similar assertions in support of various monstrous moral hybrid (Jacobs 1992). The alternative to this typical presupposition is that the options for political choice represent different forks in a long march through a vast array of institutionally governed practices. In this respect, Carolyn Webber and Aaron Wildavsky (1986) center their examination of the history of budgetary practice throughout the western world on the theme that budgeting entails continual conflict among people over how they will lead their lives when they must live in close geographical proximity to one another.

This chapter accepts Lenin's presumption that there exist commanding heights within a society while also accepting Gramsci's presumption of the precedence of sentiment and culture over the material as sources of non-logical action (Pareto 1935). While Gramsci's formulation does not locate commanding heights, it still enables recognition that transformation of some activities will generate larger future payoffs than would transformation of other activities. A long march through the institutions would doubtlessly look similar to an effort that looked first to occupying what were perceived to be commanding heights. Under either Lenin's materialist or Gramsci's cultural–sentimental formulation, the institutional arrangements governing money and credit would seem to be a primary objective to seize to destroy bourgeois practices. To be sure, I should note that the images of bourgeois and proletarian were taken from nineteenth-century practice, and don't have quite the same connotations today. Here again, we confront the distinction between eternal forms and particular practices. Practice has changed since the nineteenth century, but form is unchanged. Even into the early twentieth century, bourgeois referred to professional and white-collar occupations while proletarian referred to blue-collar occupations. These days, however, many professional occupations are staffed by people who dress-like many blue-collar workers dressed a century ago. Behind this changing substance lies a universal difference in social outlook between a presumption that people are capable of living well as they choose and a presumption that most people can't do that and so require the guidance of political-class shepherds. The institutional practices governing money and credit surely occupy a pivotal position under either the materialist or culturalist formulations of societal transformation.

Money and Credit in a Constitution of Liberty

Anthropologists have found numerous forms of money in use in early societies, as Paul Einzig (1966) surveys in his compendium on primitive money and as Jacques Melitz (1970, 1974) explores pithily in his theoretical examination of money in primitive societies, using that examination to show the weaknesses in Karl Polanyi's (1944) oft-cited claim that market exchange and its concepts were inapplicable until modern times. The anthropological record provides a luminous illustration of the theory of spontaneous ordering developed by such theorists of the Scottish Enlightenment as Adam Ferguson, Francis Hutchison, David Hume, and Adam Smith. Those theorists recognized and elaborated the insight that people through interactions with one another develop many practices and conventions that promote the general good of everyone without those practices and conventions having been established through legislation. The development of money was a major illustration of how the social good could be secured in this indirect manner.

The American Constitution established a government with limited as distinct from plenary or unlimited powers. Article 1, Section 8 enumerated 17 powers that defined and limited the activities that the federal Congress could undertake. Two of those 17 enumerated powers are especially relevant for this book. The fifth clause granted to Congress the power "to coin Money, regulate the Value thereof, and of foreign Coin, and fix the Standard of Weights and Measures." The sixth clause granted to Congress the power "to provide for the Punishment of counterfeiting the Securities and current Coin of the United States." These two enumerated powers incorporate insights from the Scottish Enlightenment into the constitution of liberty that had been articulated in 1776 and established in 1789.

The Constitution recognized that a uniform standard of weights and measures must be established throughout the land to attain the Founder's vision of a zone of free and open commerce. The significance of the fifth clause will be apparent to anyone who has visited a museum that displayed ancient coinage. That display will bring the viewer face to face with the royal practices of clipping, shaving, and sweating coins that passed through the royal mint to create material to issue new coins. Gresham's Law that low valued coins will drive high valued coins out of circulation reflects this feature of human self-interest. If a person holds two coins of equal exchange value, the lesser-valued coin will be used in exchange, with the result being the disappearance of the higher-valued coin from circulation. The sixth of those 17 enumerated powers sought to prevent the federal government from acting as a counterfeiter like the kings of old. This effort pretty much succeeded until the Federal Reserve Bank was established in 1913.

As part of its power to define a uniform set of weights and measures, the Constitution gave Congress the power to define a dollar. At the time of constitutional founding, a dollar was defined as 371.25 grains of pure silver. A dollar could also be defined as 232 grains of pure gold, recognizing as well that there are 480 grains in one troy ounce. Whether a dollar is defined in terms of gold or silver, and whether the unit of measurement is expressed in ounces, troy ounces, grams, or grains, the point of vital significance is that the dollar was defined as a *weight* of gold or silver. To promise to pay someone $10 this afternoon is to promise to pay that person 2320 grains of pure gold according to the conventions in play in 1787. This concept of a dollar as a weight of a precious metal differed radically from the concept that was embraced with creation of the Federal Reserve system in 1913. Within the American Constitution, the dollar was an invariant standard, just as a yard of cloth or an acre of land are invariant standards. An acre measures area; a dollar measures weight. Both measures are invariant across time and place. Healthy commerce, moreover, requires such invariance. This concept of a dollar as a weight of precious metal is altogether different from what people mean today when they bandy about such concepts as a gold standard. Today, a gold standard simply means that a government will exchange its currency for gold at a fixed price.

In 1933, for instance, President Franklin Roosevelt nationalized the ownership of gold, and declared its price to be $35 per ounce. Prior to nationalization, the price of gold had been fixed at $20.67 per troy ounce. It is perhaps worth noting that different terms are used for weighing precious metals than are used for ordinary items. Precious metals have 12 Troy ounces per pound, while there are 16 avoirdupois ounces per pound for other items. Prior to Roosevelt's nationalization of gold, people would have received $20.67 for each ounce of gold they held. After nationalization, they would have received $35, a near doubling of the price. Hence, the nationalization would have seemed to have nearly doubled the price of gold when a gold standard is treated as fixing the price of gold.

But this is not how gold and money were treated in the American Constitution. To say that American money was based on gold was not to say that the price of gold was fixed. The price of gold was not fixed, for it could rise and fall with economic conditions regarding the production of gold and the uses which people had for gold. A dollar denoted a weight of pure gold, actually silver at the time. A governmental entity could no more change the gold content of a dollar than it could change the weight of a cow. Governmental entities had to conform to standards of weights and measures just as did private citizens. In no way could governmental entities do with money what they chose to do. This situation changed with the advent of central banking, where what is now called monetary policy would have been recognized as counterfeiting at the time of the American constitutional founding.

To define a dollar as a weight is to incorporate government into the ambit of the *rule of law*. While many notions of the rule of law are in play, they all reflect the image that political officials are as much restricted by law as are private persons. It is an open question whether rule of law is an attainable object of constitutional construction or is a piece of ideology that democratic politicians invoke to feel good about their actions, as Rajagopalan and Wagner (2013) examine. Either way, defining a dollar as a weight places all entities in society on the same footing. Since 1913, however, the dollar has become what the Federal Reserve says it is, which in turn elevated the Federal Reserve to the Big Player status that Roger Koppl (2002) examines.

Money and the institutional arrangements surrounding its use surely constitutes a commanding height within society. Suppose after the fashion of Antonio Gramsci that someone wanted to set in motion a long march through the institutions to foment upheaval within the institutional order of what was a generally liberal society. Following Ludwig Lachmann's (1970) analysis of Max Weber's theory of institutional order, there is hierarchy among institutional arrangements, with some institutions being more foundational than others. For instance, institutional arrangements regarding the supply of day care services are surely less foundational than arrangements concerning wages and hours, for these latter arrangements would incorporate day care and numerous other activities. Arrangements concerning money and credit would be among the most foundational of institutional arrangements because money appears universally throughout the world of social practice. Likewise, most commercial transactions are credit and not spot transactions, so credit relationships are ubiquitous throughout society. Someone who wanted to promote the tearing down of the traditional liberal institutions of private property and freedom of enterprise would likely find no better place to start than with the arrangements and practices regarding money and credit.

THE SIGNIFICANCE OF GEORG
SIMMEL'S *PHILOSOPHY OF MONEY*

Georg Simmel's (1900) *Philosophy of Money* is now more than a century behind us. It would be natural for a reader to find archaic elements in this book, but the book also contains much of value for the systems-theoretic orientation toward macro phenomena this book pursues. It should, however, be noted that Simmel himself, in declaring that he was examining money from a philosophical and not an economic perspective, asserted that "not a single line of these investigations is meant to be a statement about economics" (p. 54). Regardless of what Simmel might have intended, his *Philosophy of Money* surely has much value to bring to contemporary monetary scholarship, as Laidler and Rowe (1980) offer from a monetarist perspective and as Wagner (2000) offers from more of a systems-theoretic perspective.

Simmel explores how a society's monetary arrangements form a commanding height within society. This recognition emerges out of Simmel's orientation toward economics as a science of exchange, along the lines of Buchanan (1964). This situation contrasts sharply with the choice-theoretic orientation that dominates contemporary economics. While Robinson Crusoe faces many problems, the uniquely economic problems arise only after Friday appears. What is the core model of economic science? Observing the textbooks and journals would surely lead one to say it is choice or rational action. A good deal of economic theory can be developed by traveling with Robinson Crusoe on his daily adventures. Crusoe would be construed as having a utility function which he maximizes as best he can as he wrestles with the various obstacles he confronts. This vision of economic theory adopts a representative agent (Kirman 1992) and presumes that one can learn about society by questioning the representative agent. In sharp contrast, James Buchanan (1964) argues that it is interaction and not choice that is the core model of economic activity. Robinson Crusoe might encounter an abundance of situations that call for choice among options, but economic theory comes into play only after Friday has entered Crusoe's life. Economics is a social science and not a science of rational action. Economics is a science of exchange and of the institutional arrangements that emerge through interaction among economizing actors. Simmel's *Philosophy of Money* precedes Buchanan in treating economics as a social science and not a science of rational action, recognizing, moreover, that Simmel was a sociologist by profession and not an economist.

The exchange or interactionist orientation toward money and credit clashes with much of contemporary macro-money discourse. Macro theory, the theory of the properties of the economic system in its entirety, is preponderantly written as if its phenomena were reflections of the choices of Robinson Crusoe, where deviations from expectations result from exogenous shocks. This kind of formulation might well be sensible as a description of Robinson Crusoe's mental state. After Crusoe acquired some experience, including meeting other Crusoes, he will surely have formed some belief about what he could reasonably expect from the people he meets. While Robinson Crusoe will clearly face problems of how to get along on his own, the uniquely economic phenomena will arise only after Crusoe meets Friday, and those phenomena will be numerous. Those phenomena emerge out of exchange-based relationships, and cover such things as property rights, contractual obligations, prices and their formation, and money and credit. None of these phenomena or institutions is relevant to Crusoe living on his own or as society reduced to a representative agent. These social phenomena all arise through the interaction among multiple Crusoes and Fridays. Crusonia-like economic modeling is simply not adequate for understanding the course of economic life in a society.

Most significantly, any effort to explain one macro variable in terms of another macro variable is to offer an explanation by invoking a mystery. Macro variables are emergent products of human interaction among micro entities. Without doubt, statistical regularities can be found among macro variables. But such regularities do not constitute a theory to connect those micro interactions to the macro data. Any such theory must contain a plausible generative process that yields the macro observations from the micro interactions. Crusonia-type modeling necessarily explains macro phenomena as arising out of the action of one macro-level variable upon another. It can be no other way. In a Crusonia framework, there is no scope for macro variables to emerge out of interaction among micro entities. Nonetheless, macro variables are not objects of direct choice. The objects of direct choice are the various contractual terms and forms of enterprise that people create and generate within a society. The rate of growth in aggregate output over some interval, for instance, emerges through the transaction-governed interactions among economic participants. To emerge, however, is not to be chosen. Those transactions, in turn, are mediated by an institutional framework, which suggests that the growth that emerges will depend on the quality of the governing institutional framework. The contribution of monetary expansions or contractions to growth would depend, in the first place, on how those monetary changes influence individual choices and, secondly, on the resultant implications regarding interactions among societal participants.

It is clearly reasonable to ask that macro theorizing be built upon some base of micro theorizing. After all, the macro economy is built up through transactional interactions among the constituent micro units. Such micro foundations should, however, be catallactical and not choice theoretic. In this manner, the movement from micro to macro would be a movement in the direction of increased complexity. This, of course, is not the direction of movement in contemporary macro theory, where textbooks on macroeconomics portray phenomena that are even simpler than those treated in microeconomics. This happens because macro phenomena are treated as if they resulted from Robinson Crusoe's choices in a setting where his plans were occasionally upset by exogenous shocks, and with macro theories diverging at this point between those that claim that Crusoe recovers quickly from shocks and those that claim that Crusoe has but weak ability to recover without outside assistance—and yet there is no place for an outside agent within the Representative agent construction.

In contrast, a catallactical orientation recognizes that people are substantively heterogeneous and most surely not homogeneous. Heterogeneous, moreover, refers not just to different preferences but also to such things as different cognitive beliefs about reality. There may well be a true model of a society, but, if so, this is known only to God. In society, many models are held among market participants, and many of those models are largely inchoate and tacit (Polanyi 1958). Observed economic data in a catallaxy would thus be generated within a setting where people acted on differing and inconsistent presumptions about the overall scheme of things. This scheme of economic theory would surely affirm the desirability of building macro theorizing upon a consistent base of micro theorizing. Those micro foundations, however, would be catallactical and not choice theoretic.

Money, Language, and Economic Calculation

The order of economic theory commonly proceeds from real to nominal values. The theory of economic equilibrium is presented in terms of real values. Contemporary economics treats real magnitudes as directly observable primitives. Microeconomic theory is portrayed wholly in terms of real variables, as expressed by relative prices. So too is monetary and macro theory, though with the additional step that it may be necessary to use price-level arithmetic to move from nominal to real magnitudes. But this move is a simple matter of multiplication that can be done almost instantly. Even monetary economics, in other words, proceeds as if it were the economics of a barter economy. Monetary economics adds nothing to the directly observable relationships of microeconomic theory, save for the notion that money is a kind of veil that may obscure a bit and impede a little the movement to the underlying real relationships.

We may doubt the plausibility of postulating that people can construct nominal to real conversions instantly in their heads. In *Philosophy of Money*, George Simmel accepted the primacy of nominal over real magnitudes. Simmel, however, did not treat money as a veil that obscured the real magnitudes that pertained to economic transactions. Money was too significant to be relegated to the status of veil. Money, along with language, are two primary tools of thought and communication within modern civilization. Without language and money and the cognitive activities that these facilitate, we would still be but food for lions and maggots. Economic calculation of any but the simplest, most primitive sort can take place only with the assistance of money and language.

To be sure, more than money and language are required for economic calculation. Such institutions as accounting practices and conventions are important as well. It is a simple and reasonable theoretical proposition that people move their capital from where the returns they anticipate receiving are relatively low to where their anticipated returns are relatively high. This movement, however, involves reasoning and economic calculation. In the complex transactions of modern enterprises, where current transactions have consequences that extend into the far future, and which could in principle be accounted for in any number of ways, profitability is a constructed and not a directly observable fact. Even for such a simple thing as depreciation, there is no truly correct method but only various conventions, along with tax requirements. Commercial communication and action take place within the domain of nominal values, or at least the process starts from nominal values. Real values must be derived and inferred from nominal observations. To call money merely a veil is to lose sight of its overwhelming significance for economical conduct.

This difference in orientation has significant implications for how one approaches a great number of economic phenomena. For instance, Simmel discusses (p. 264) some advice of Samuel Pufendorf that a prince would have a happier kingdom if he imposed many small taxes rather than one large tax. This proposition has long been present in the public finance literature as the theory of fiscal illusion (Amilcare Puviani 1903). While ideas and claims about fiscal illusion have been discussed for a long time, they have always occupied a kind of underworld position. In this, fiscal illusion is like its cousin, money illusion. If one starts from the direct accessibility of real variables and their values, fiscal illusion or money illusion seem to violate one of the foundations of the economist's canon, rationality. To be sure, there is an experimental literature on preference reversals (Loomes and Sugden 1983), though we all know that negative results by themselves never lead practitioners to abandon a theoretical construct without having a better theory in hand. So long as the theoretical edifice presumes that real values are directly accessible, what seem to be rationality-denying propositions, such as fiscal and monetary illusion, will remain stuck in the disciplinary underground.

It would be different with an orientation that started with nominal magnitudes, as by treating money and language as the two primary tools of economical reasoning and conduct. Still, it might be asked why people couldn't do that, and then simply do the necessary price-level calculations to derive the true real magnitudes? In a Robinson Crusoe world it could hardly be otherwise. For in that world real values are directly accessible. But in catallactic reality, the move from observed nominal values to inferred real values is difficult and problematic, and in several respects. To start, it is not a matter of some single, aggregate level computation. It is a matter for each individual to calculate. Moreover, that calculation is not a matter of one single, summary calculation, at the start of some imagined period based on some presumption of an appropriate deflator. It is rather a matter of continual calculation in response to the continuing parade of choice opportunities as time elapses. Furthermore, there is no single way of moving from nominal to real. An aggregate price index fits no one exactly, and probably fits many people quite poorly. And if this were not enough, calculation probably comes easier for some people and in some settings than in other cases. For instance, commercial enterprises will probably make greater effort to move from nominal to real than individuals as consumers will.

Returning to Simmel's discussion of Samuel Pufendorf for a moment, we might well expect greater use of excise taxes placed upon consumer goods than upon producer goods. At least this is plausible if the cost of organizing and conducting such calculation is lower for enterprises than it is for people. And this, it surely is. Enterprises keep accounts, and invariably those are computerized. While many households have computers these days, precious few seem to keep family accounts. For an enterprise, it would be a simple matter to calculate total taxes, whether paid through several small taxes or one large tax. An individual, however, would rarely have the calculative apparatus in place to do this. The only calculative apparatus would be some kind of sensory impression, and a comparison of those impressions under the two different tax regimes. If large taxes have an attention-arresting quality that small taxes lack, we might expect that political processes would favor taxes that were diffuse and indirect, at least to the extent they were directed at consumers (Wagner 1976).

Money is one of those examples of an institution that emerges through interaction among people, as against being selected *de novo* through some act of conscious choice. Some of the literature on Simmel's *Philosophy of Money* seems to draw a strong opposition between money as an institution that emerges through human interaction and money as the product of conscious choice, usually by a state. This opposition seems overstated, and in two respects. First, in such formulations as Georg Knapp's (1924) claim that money originated through political action, due primarily to rulers stipulating the means by which subject must discharge their tax obligations, Knapp actually acknowledges that money originates in custom, with the state coming later. Indeed, it is a common historical process of institutional development to see practices originate through individual initiative, with political officers entering the scene after the practice has proved successful. Indeed, Fig. 3.1's construction reflects this historical process. For instance, social insurance originated through private and sometimes charitable impulses, and with the state coming into play later. Whether the state's subsequent arrival adds positive or negative value to the overall economic process is something that can be debated indefinitely, in light of a historical record that seems to provide instances of each. In any event, this historical process surely illustrates the essentially bottom-up character of any march through the institutions, regardless of the direction of march.

When Knapp says that the "soul of currency" resides in "legal ordinances," it is surely not reasonable to draw an opposition to the "custom" to which he attributed the emergence of money. It is possible to acknowledge that money, like language, is an emergent institution, while at the same time acknowledging that political officers and their allies can seek to circumscribe custom through politically articulated ordinances. This it might do for any of several reasons, ranging from claims about needs of macro stabilization to claims about seigniorage as a source of revenue (for instance, Frankel [1977] and Selgin and White [1999]). Whatever the rationale advanced for political involvement in money, there is surely some limit to the extent to which the substance of legal ordinance can diverge from what custom would have generated. The proliferation of financial instruments is one illustration of this. The growth of Internet commerce is another. And the presence of black markets and underground economies is yet a third. Legal ordinances work best when they channel people in directions they pretty much want to go anyway; the more they seek to move people in other directions the more resistance they meet and the less successful they become. To be sure, while such ordinances may come increasingly to encounter resistance, they can nonetheless be sources for the generation of rents in the short run. And never forget that if the suitable rate of discount is ten percent, rent for seven years is half as good as rent that lasts forever.

Neutral Money: Historical Process Vs. Comparative Statics

Within the process-oriented mode of exposition with which this book works, society is not so much a structural entity as it is an ongoing process of spontaneously generated ordering. Any program that seeks to incorporate a process orientation into economic theory requires adoption of some form of historical or evolutionary frame of reference. In this respect, an evolutionary orientation applied to monetary phenomena would clash severely with the dominant orientation found in contemporary economic analysis. This dominant orientation applies the method of comparative statics in a framework of presumed systemic equilibrium. In this approach to generating hypotheses and explaining observations, the focus centers on the existence of a set of market-clearing prices. The method of comparative statics compares two sets of presumed initial data to compare their equilibrium properties. The presumption is that this exercise of pure logic

independent of any movement through the calendar is nonetheless sufficient to capture historical movement in response to new data. It would
be a very curious history if this were truly the case. Even though time
would be moving forward, people would remain stagnant, holding hard-
and-fast to their old ideas, beliefs, preferences, and all such other features
that together would constitute a stagnant society.

One notable feature of this comparative static orientation is the very
difficulty in finding a place for money and monetary phenomena. If the
real economy is directly accessible and if all economic plans are presumed
reconciled in advance of actual economizing action, there is no place for
money. Indeed, the literature on real business cycles, which represents a
vigorous application of this orientation, seeks to explain economic cycles
without money. A significant claim, going back at least to Richard Cantillon (1755 [1931]), is that the process of monetary injection influences
the real pattern of economic activity. This would seem to suggest that
money influences price relationships, in contradiction to common neutrality propositions. In contrast, in most contemporary formulations changes
in aggregate money supply exert only transitory effects on real variables.
In the long run the effect is restricted to the realm of the purely nominal,
where expansions or contractions in the stock of money affect only the
price level.

This neutrality proposition seems largely to be an artifact of the
method of comparative statics. In a stagnant world where nothing moves,
it is hardly surprising that monetary change exerts no real effects. How
could it? Real effects are possible only as time passes and knowledge
changes, but these are precluded by comparative statics. What happens
if money is injected in a world of movement? There are, of course, many
conceivable means and processes by which money may enter or leave an
economy. With the social process as one of continual movement, the very
process of monetary injection through one channel rather than another
will surely stimulate certain kinds of activities over others. In the stagnant
world of comparative statics, this stimulation affects nothing. In historical
reality, however, learning responds to activity, and different processes of
monetary injection involve different nodes of stimulation within a society. Hence, different patterns of learning are set in motion, depending on
the process of monetary injection. Once we recognize that activities set
in motion processes of learning by doing, changes in preference, and the
like, we must also recognize that the pattern of economic activities in a
society, as observed at some point after a monetary injection, will differ

depending on the point of monetary injection, along the lines that Bilo and Wagner (2015) explore.

To be sure, this does not imply that there would be observable differences in conventional macro variables, depending on the points of initial injection. Rather it says that the process of monetary injection will influence the concrete pattern of activities within a society by changing the entrepreneurial experiments that receive initial support. Such a possibility cannot be brought to the analytical foreground by comparative statics because time is frozen, and that logic is focused on an equilibrium structure of relationships. In much of the monetary literature, what has just been characterized would be dismissed as representing "mere distributional effects." This dismissal arises out of a frame of reference where all that matters is the state of some aggregate economic variables. Yet the dynamic forces that are at work at shaping societies precisely work their way through those micro channels; the aggregate resultants are objects neither of choice nor of desire.

Reclaiming the Ex Ante-Ex Post Distinction

Perhaps nowhere is the agenda-limiting character of the absence of transactional micro foundations more on display than in the predominance given to price-level or money-supply expectations as the source of monetary-induced disturbance in economic relationships. A transactional orientation would surely have a strikingly different character. Someone who incorporated a transactional orientation could never be content with an analytical construction that placed all the weight regarding monetary-induced disturbance on errors in forecasting changes in some measured price level. There would be multiple objects of expectation within a society, and not one universal object of expectation. While it would surely be reasonable to characterize people as trying to construct their commercial plans in a reasoned and rational manner, this would be conducted in a setting where people were concerned with diverse objects of expectation.

It is surely an evasion of the problem to postulate a mutual consistency among those diverse plans. To be sure, this consistency is postulated only as a hypothesis, and is subject to disturbance through exogenous shocks. To do this, however, is to render all the action in society as taking place outside the economic process. Yet such actions can never truly be outside the economic process, for that process is nothing but the entirety of people and their interactions. How might elementary requirements of rationality in the formation of expectations operate within the purview of a transactional orientation toward macro phenomena? The use of the faculty of reason to form expectations would surely have to occupy a prominent position in any analytical effort. That those expectations are products of reason and imagination is surely noncontroversial at the level of general principle. It is a different matter, however, when it comes to methods for implementing that principle. For one thing, it should not be thought that transactional micro foundations must seek somehow to explain how diverse people can form reasonably consistent plans, if that explanation is thought to mean that those plans are all formulated independently of each other. As Butos and Koppl (1993) explain, plans are not simply expressions of thought. Rather, they are expressions of disciplined and structured thought, where the discipline and structure are provided to a large extent by such things as professional conventions and institutional rules.

In significant degree, coherence among individual commercial plans is generated through the disciplining and structuring framework that is provided by market-generated institutions. Not all institutions within a society are generated through market processes, which, in turn, raises the possibility that some incongruency may exist among the institutions within a society, as Ludwig Lachmann (1970) explains. One possible source of such incongruency would seem to arise from Big Players, because their absence of residual claimancy renders them less predictable and dependable than ordinary market participants. Butos and Koppl also note that by not being governed by residual claimancy, Big Players can counteract the institutionalized discipline and order that would otherwise be present.

Crusonia-like macro modeling destroys any meaningful distinction between *ex ante* and *ex post*. Variability in growth rates through time is claimed to depend merely on inaccuracies in forecasting inflation. Indeed, forecasted inflation is the only variable of relevance for the explanation of why macro variables do not follow some steady-state path. A de-trended flat line is the norm, with variability due either to exogenous shocks to the natural rate of growth or to error in forecasted inflation. Nowhere in this formulation does room exist for macro variability to result from processes of interaction among people. There is simply no room inside that conceptual framework for coordination to proceed with some variable degree of smoothness that, in turn, influences observed macro outcomes. Yet the degree of coordination, as well as such things as rates of growth, is surely an emergent property of an economic system, and it is hardly sensible to treat it as an exogenous shock to that system. Further, it is hardly sensible to claim that the only object of future interest to market participants is a forecast of future inflation. Yet entrepreneurs who made their choices based only on information about probable inflation would be acting foolishly in the extreme. In most instances, a rate of inflation has but limited relevance for economical conduct. Of much greater importance would be forecasts that pertain to the various markets in which an entrepreneur is engaged. There would be different objects of expectation, depending on the activities about which expectations are being formed.

If the course of the economy is built up out of dispersed individual decisions, and with a rate of inflation rarely being a consideration in those decisions, how do expectations about inflation come to command such strong interest in the macro literature? It comes back to the presumption of postulated order. It may be granted that people form expectations over specific variables that are of interest considering their commercial niches. So long as a consistent array of equilibrium prices is assumed to exist, individual expectations must be consistent with one another, and with all being consistent with some aggregate price level. The postulated order framework thus presumes a consistency and sustainability among plans and prices that make it seem plausible to resort to aggregate measures in place of individually relevant variables. It does so, however, at the price of eliminating any semblance of transactional micro foundations via the neutering of economically significant differences among people. Also neutered is any distinction between *ex ante* and *ex post* orientations toward economic phenomena by relegating the distinction to a simple error term. Yet that distinction is central to any transactional treatment of the economic process, as is the distinction between frequentist and subjectivist approaches to probability.

CREDIT CONTRACTS AND PROCESSES FOR CRAFTING THE FUTURE

The world of experience is one where tomorrow will differ from yesterday, and in numerous ways. Some familiar firms will disappear, and new ones will appear. Some new products and services will be provided, and some familiar ones will disappear. Credit markets are the site where the future is mostly made. It is within credit markets where new entrepreneurial plans mostly receive their support. Sure, many entrepreneurs finance their undertakings with their own capital, but so too are many of those under-takings supported by investors, either through buying equity shares in the enterprise or in becoming creditors to the enterprise. Setting aside self-financed projects, most entrepreneurial undertakings are financed through credit transactions of some type. Some of those transactions are explicit, as illustrated by lending contracts. Others are implicit, as illustrated by investors buying into an enterprise. Either way, a *quid pro quo* relation-ship is established whereby each party anticipates gaining from the trans-action. These transactions denote what economists typically describe as a credit market. When expressed in equilibrium terms, a credit market would entail demanders of credit who are seeking sources of capital and suppliers who have money balances they would like to use to earn a return.

Equilibrium in the market for credit has often been described by the loanable funds theory of interest. This formulation is convenient because it can be described by amending modestly the upper part of Fig. 1.3 by making only slight changes in nomenclature. Rather than denoting aggre-gate supply and demand, this reconstructed figure would denote the sup-ply and demand of loanable funds. The nominal rate of interest would clear the market. To be sure, the rate of interest is stipulated as part of a lending transaction though this leaves out transactions in equity instru-ments. Still, beliefs that investors have about their prospective returns will influence the entire credit market. For instance, should investors generally become more optimistic about the prospects for their investments, they will become more eager to buy shares in enterprises and less eager to buy bonds. At this point we bump into information that would be contained within the bottom equivalent to the lower part of Fig. 1.3. The loanable funds market is constituted through numerous individual transactions that generate the macro summary that the upper part projects. Macro-level theories mostly focus on aggregate formulations, and yet the action that generates the macro-level portraits derives from the micro-level interac-tions. The macro level of the loanable funds market cannot be accessed directly, for it can be accessed only through engaging in micro-level trans-actions. Macro-level summaries provide meaningful information, provided only that it is recognized that they can't offer a direct guide to action because action can enter the catallaxy only at the action or micro level of analysis.

In his *Theory of Economic Development*, Joseph Schumpeter (1934) noted that "entrepreneurship is the source of leadership in a capitalist society." Schumpeter's claim has much value to it, as well as much ambiguity. The value lies in recognition that entrepreneurship lies at the core of the efforts that bring about societal transformation. These days, a language that speaks of societal transformation seems to refer to something revolutionary and dramatic and stands in contrast to what we might mean by ordinary life. This is perhaps a consequence of the expansion in public ordering within societies, for public ordering brings tectonic politics into action. Yet at its most basic level, all entrepreneurship is transformational by injecting novelty into society. Most of that novelty is relatively minor, but some of it can be major. The replacement of horses with internal combustion engines was certainly a major transformation, in contrast to developing nondairy alternatives for milk.

All successful entrepreneurial action transforms the patterns of activities in which some people engage, mostly to small and barely noticeable effect but sometimes in a large way, as when automobiles replaced horse-drawn carriages. Schumpeter wrote at the time when the dominance of private ordering in society was coming to an end. Half a century before Schumpeter, Henry Maine (1861) issued his pithy summary of western civilization in explaining that the "direction of movement in the advanced societies has been a movement from status to contract." Maine himself wondered whether that direction of movement was being reversed as he wrote. And by Schumpeter's time, any era of High Capitalism, real or imagined, had ended. Regardless of the relative positions of private and public ordering in societies, entrepreneurial action will occupy a leading edge in bringing about social change. Without entrepreneurial action, tomorrow will be a repeat of yesterday, with random events being the only possible source of social change. Entrepreneurship brings change into the foreground of economic activity, as people seek to develop new products, new forms of commercial organization, and articulate new political slogans, all of which and many more like them, would lead people to hold different expectations tomorrow than they held yesterday. In whatever manner that tomorrow's societal configurations differ from yesterday's, entrepreneurial action will be the situs of bringing those differences about.

It is, however, misleading to use the theory of private ordering and a market economy to make inferences regarding the properties of contemporary systems of entangled political economy, as Wagner (2016) explains. This would be a reasonable procedure if economics were reasonably approached in linear fashion, for then actual forms could be reasonably described as convex combinations of pure forms. In Schumpeter's time, a reasonable private–public mix was on the order of 90:10. Today, it is probably on the order of 60:40. Such comparisons, moreover, are more speculative now than they were a century ago because budgetary magnitudes have become less meaningful. Measures of tax revenue relative to aggregate output can be highly misleading once it is recognized that whatever a political entity can accomplish through taxation can be accomplished through regulation. For instance, a city could eliminate its budgetary appropriation for public schools simply by requiring parents to send their children to approved schools. Schools would now be operated under private ordering through contractual relations between schools and parents. Public ordering would disappear. Or would it? Instead of public schools, there would now exist politically established bureaus devoted to certification and inspection of schools, and approval of schools, curriculum, and the like.

A Political Economy of Public Property

As noted earlier, an entangled scheme of political economy envisions a society as operating with two sets of institutional arrangements that entail incongruous operating features that generate regions of societal tectonics along the lines that Wagner (2007) sketches in noting that private property can operate only in the presence of common property and that Wagner (2016) elaborates in setting forth a vision of entangled political economy. In its central features, moreover, that vision reflects an updated classical political economy prior to the reduction of economics to a theory of rational choice during the neoclassical period of economic theory, representing a continuation of the argument Wagner (2010) pursued.

Chapter 3 elaborated an insight from Maffeo Pantaleoni (1911), who characterized societies as operating with two pricing systems: one a system of market prices and the other a system of political prices. Pantaleoni's insight has much potential value for contemporary theorizing in political economy, starting from its recognition that all processes governing social interaction are polycentric, as Vincent Ostrom (1997) set forth with especial cogency. The object of a theory of political economy is to explain observed patterns of societal interaction when those patterns entail local domains of planning taking place within a society that is not itself an object of planning because systemic planning is overwhelmed by the complexity of the task. All entities act through time and so engage in planning; there is, however, no entity that plans the entirety of social interaction because social ecologies are too complex for this to be possible.

Yet what gets produced, both where private ordering and where public ordering prevail, generally accords with what people would like to see happen, on average but not in exact detail. The theory of private ordering sets forth a good explanatory mechanism grounded in private property and freedom of contract to explain this systemic property. It is the willingness of entrepreneurs to chase fame and fortune that generates patterns of economic activity that can be reasonably described as generating the activities that people would generally like to see undertaken, and to do so in an economizing or least-cost manner. What doesn't exist, though, is a genuine theory of public ordering that arrives at the same analytical destination. What exist instead are various theories of market failure and welfare economics, all of which operate by explaining how planning by the right-minded political officers can correct the defects of private ordering.

Wagner (2016) recognizes that Pantaleoni (1911) offered important clues for the construction of a theory of public ordering. That theory starts with Pantaleoni's recognition that political activity bears a parasitical relation to market activity. It is the offerings of market entrepreneurs that shed insight into patterns of consumer valuation. In social territory that market entrepreneurs don't seek to occupy, you won't see political entrepreneurs setting up shop. Market entrepreneurs send out soundings to locate where consumer demand lies. Political entrepreneurs then determine how to package political programs that will appeal to a successful political coalition. Doing this is tricky business because it resides within the domain of non-logical action which is dominated by competition among ideologically created images because there can be no direct experience with the claims advanced by political entrepreneurs. To be sure, the inability to experience such claims doesn't prevent such claims from being made, but it does call our attention to uncharted analytical territory regarding construction of theories of public ordering, along the lines that Munger and Munger (2015) explore.

WHAT IS MONETARY POLICY
IF NOT THE ENFORCEMENT OF CONTRACTS?

Nowhere within the two clauses of enumerated powers to which money pertains does there appear a reference to monetary policy. To coin money and regulate its value refers to the power of Congress to determine the denominational structure into which coinage may be divided, always being consistent with the standard of weights and measures. Congress can determine whether coins would come in $1, $5, and $20 increments or in $2, $8, and $40 increments. Or any other pattern. Likewise, it can determine coins beneath a dollar will come in three, five, or any other number of increments. Whatever the number of those increments might be, all would be rendered consistent with the standard of weights and measures. Congress, moreover, is obligated to punish counterfeiting. Doing this will obviously require some police and investigatory power and some budgetary appropriation, but neither of these would seem to require any distinct form of activity described as monetary policy.

Since creation of the Federal Reserve in 1913, however, monetary policy has become a major activity of the federal reserve and has become a major subject of public debate, mostly concerning whether the Fed should expand or contract the rate of monetary expansion in some fashion. Yet there is clearly no constitutional authority for what is now described as monetary policy. All the same, there is no nucleus of people who note the lack of Constitutional authority for monetary policy. This situation appears to be another instance of Charles Warren's (1932) recognition that what passes constitutional muster in the world of practice need bear little to no relation to what would pass muster under a plain reading of the text, a point that Runst and Wagner (2011) amplify. Whether the United States should have a central bank was a point of controversy during the nineteenth century, but there is now little controversy over the use by the Fed of its powers to manipulate the supply of money and credit.

Claims on behalf of monetary policy bring us back to the state theory of money. That theory wrongly claimed that money was created by political action, as against emerging through custom. One could, following Knapp (1924), assert that state intervention into the production of money enabled a refinement and expansion in monetary arrangements. This version of the theory would accept that money emerged spontaneously through usage in relatively primitive states of social existence. It was, however, state intervention into the organization of money that enabled the spread of monetary calculation throughout society, bringing about modern conditions of material standards of living.

As a scientific proposition, the state theory of money does not have much going for it. Even Knapp recognized this when he claimed not that politicians invented money, but only that they perfected money to unleash its potential for promoting flourishing societies. It is surely worth noting that the state theory of money was articulated in 1924, as the dramatic expansion in the relative size of government throughout the western world was getting underway. Suppose you were to ask what is it that government could not support under the enumerated powers formulation of monetary powers and what they are able to support now. When you ask a similar question about Charles Warren's (1932) treatment of the growing divergence between what a plain reading of the general welfare clause of the Constitution required and what the politicians and their allies wanted to interpret it as saying, you will surely see a family resemblance between the two cases. A plain reading of the text restricts strongly the range of governmental action articulated in an age when people treasured freedom from political control. As support for freedom weakened and waned relative to desires for security, new readings were constructed through intellectual articulation. The general welfare no longer meant a project must benefit everyone, for it can be reinterpreted to mean that Congress has determined that it provides enough benefit to enough people to pass Constitutional muster. The state theory of money says that strict limits on monetary manipulation by governments might have been important at an earlier period, but in our modern age we can capture the advantages that modernity offers us only if we allow our monetary arrangements to help us capture those advantages. As for what those advantages might be and whether they are real or imagined, that brings us into the domain of continuing political contestation over how the cosmic drama in which we all inescapably participate will unfold when that drama is improvisational and not scripted, at least in so far as anyone truly knows even though many people act as if they have such knowledge, which is a posture that is also part of that drama.

MONEY AND CREDIT AS OBJECTS OF CONTINUING SOCIETAL CONTESTATION

Suppose we reconsider the loanable funds theory of the nominal rate of interest but do so from the ground or transactional level of Fig. 1.3 and not from the top level where this theory is typically lodged and presented. At the transactional level, there would be large numbers of suppliers seeking to offer credit to numerous demanders. We could imagine a system of completely private ordering. Within this system, all decisions about who receives credit, and how much on what terms, would be determined through agreements among the participants. A borrower who was rejected by one lender could always try another lender. That rejected borrower could also offer to renegotiate the rejected deal. In any case, an equilibrium allocation of credit would lead to selection among potential borrowers according to the prospective profits the lenders thought they could obtain from those loans. While loans would be made that turned out *ex post* to be failures, from an *ex ante* perspective all loans would have positive expected value to the lenders.

Credit markets, however, are not privately ordered. For one thing, many political agencies are directly engaged in the supply of credit, as when political agencies supply loans for students who are attending college. In other instances, political credit is offered indirectly as when political agencies guarantee loans that private vendors make, thereby increasing the willingness of those vendors to offer loans to that category of borrower. Loans for real estate are often accompanied by political guarantees. When guarantees are offered, moreover, private vendors lose the ability to determine their loan portfolios because guarantees are accompanied by requirements. Those loan portfolios become subject to political auditing to ensure that those portfolios meet politically determined standards. Those standards include such specifications as requiring a minimal share of loans to be made to borrowers whose income or asset level is at least 40% below the average level for that zip code or county. There also exist categories by age, gender, and race.

The practical import of all such regulatory categories is to modify the pattern of credit allocation from what would result under wholly private ordering. There would, after all, be no point to a regulation that had no effect on the allocation of credit. We may imagine a set of suppliers who have lines of credit they would like to place with borrowers. We may similarly imagine a set of demanders who would like to obtain loans. A credit market generates some matching between suppliers and demanders, and with various institutional arrangements possibly governing those markets, recognizing that the concept of equilibrium does not apply to public ordering in the same way it applies to private ordering. For private ordering, a set of preferences and prices can exist that is consistent with a market equilibrium. For public ordering no equilibrium exists based on preferences. Prices are set politically by ruling coalitions through their control over the power to tax, to borrow, and to create money. Electoral outcomes that change the committee structure within legislative assemblies can change the choices that ruling coalitions might make even though preferences remain unchanged.

Control over money and credit forms a commanding height in society, for monetary arrangements provide a pivotal bastion for exerting domination over the entrepreneurial choices among projects that will shape future societal configurations. There are two prime avenues for gaining dominion over future configurations of economic activity. One avenue is to dominate real values. Someone who supports a political program of eliminating internal combustion engines from society would have to make alternative sources of engine power sufficiently cheaper that such engines would be selected through ordinary market channels over internal combustion engines. To accomplish this outcome would doubtless require high subsidies for the production and use of such engines. This *subsidy-first strategy* would have to be applied to all instances where ruling coalitions supported alternative technologies. Proponents of such subsidies would doubtless have much explaining to do with their willingness to offer massive subsidies when alternative technologies are working well and are clearly cheaper.

An alternative, *finance-first strategy* might offer what might be regarded a cheaper option through enlisting private vendors apparently in support of the strategy. With this strategy, political enterprises would impose regulatory requirements on the investment portfolios of different engine manufacturers. This scheme would not represent a heavy-handed push to compel politically favored technologies. Rather, it could be cast as an effort to provide some balanced test among different technologies. The political agencies would appear in the background of these efforts to promote alternative technologies, in contrast to their prominent position under the subsidy-first strategy. With this strategy, it would be the vendors of the different products that dominate the foreground of the effort to gain acquiescence in the alternative technologies. However the future unfolds, public ordering will generate continual controversy over new technologies, and with those technologies always bring orchestrated to the same music.

That orchestration begins with recognition public and private ordering are entangled within democratic systems of political economy. This institutional arrangement generates societal tectonics much as Fig. 3.1 and the accompanying text illustrates. Enterprises that operate with their own capital will operate differently than enterprises that operate with politically provided capital. Within a society where economic activity emerges within an admixture of private and public ordering, money and credit will provide arenas of continuing societal contestation because those institutional arrangements can differ in the image they generate regarding the costliness of alternative policy measures.

Hyman Minsky (1980, 1986) argued that capitalist economies are inherently unstable due to the workings of financial institutions and arrangements. One could always posit an equilibrium pattern of financial arrangements. Minsky's point, though, is that any such arrangement would be fragile, resembling a pyramid resting on its apex. The stability of that arrangement depends heavily on perceptions people hold of what other people are likely to do. In Minsky's judgment, such fragility required more public ordering to promote resiliency. At this point we encounter one of those recurring questions of how to incorporate democratic processes into economic arrangements. For Minsky, democracy resembled Fig. 6.1 more than Fig. 6.2. Should Fig. 6.2 be more apt, the remedy for financial instability would seem to lie in the direction of greater prominence for private ordering. Either way, we are doubtlessly living in a second-best type of world where instability will be part of the human predicament in any case (Wagner 2015).

MISES, HAYEK, AND AUSTRIAN CYCLE THEORY: A BEAUTIFUL DIAMOND TERRIBLY SET

In his masterful treatise on the history of thought on business fluctuations *Prosperity and Depression*, Gottfried Haberler (1937) listed what he called the monetary-overinvestment theory as the leading candidate in a crowded field. That moment was probably the heyday of the Mises–Hayek theory of economic fluctuations, as the gathering Keynesian avalanche swept away all competitors. By describing the Mises–Hayek approach as a monetary-overinvestment theory, Haberler was pointing to the ability of the Mises–Hayek theory to overcome the dichotomy between nominal and real disturbances as sources of fluctuation. Mises (1912) and Hayek (1931, 1933) both start from an economic system in a state of general equilibrium, as nearly all serious theorists did at that time. To be sure, the Mises–Hayek theory recurred to late-nineteenth century works by Knut Wicksell (1898) and Eugen von Böhm-Bawerk (1884), giving the theory an Austro-Swedish flair.

That theory started by asking how it was possible for an economic equilibrium to turn into an economic slump while economic participants continued to engage in rational action as described by marginal cost pricing and utility maximization. One simple and perhaps canonical illustration of the Mises–Hayek approach starts by asking us to imagine a central bank that exogenously increases the supply of money. By the long-used quantity-theoretic logic, there would be a proportionate increase in prices with output unchanged. But Mises and Hayek were not quantity theorists, in that they recognized that to derive aggregative consequences of monetary change it was necessary to work through the micro changes that were set in motion by the monetary expansion. Mises and Hayek reasoned in terms of a macro–micro entanglement similar to that which Fig. 1.3 illustrates.

Yet the theoretical tools that were in play at the time Mises and Hayek wrote were not crafted for network-based interactions. These tools imposed a form of analytical homogeneity on their analyses that gave it its distinctive character and at the same time neutered most of its potential as a useful line of theoretical inquiry. In accord with Fig. 1.3, new money would enter the economy through specific transactional nexuses. Only the tools for thinking this way weren't in play, though it was conventional to distinguish between consumers and investors as categories. At that historical moment, new money typically entered the economy through bank lending to support commercial enterprises. For Mises and Hayek, it thus followed that the monetary expansion would find its way mostly to entrepreneurs and investors.

But entrepreneurs constitute a large number of people distributed among disparate commercial ventures. Mises and Hayek distinguished between investment projects that would mature quickly and those that would mature slowly, for they recognized that monetary expansion would affect these different entrepreneurial projects differently. In particular, a reduction in the nominal rate of interest would prove more advantageous to projects that matured slowly than to projects that matured quickly. Following this conceptualization, it is but a short step to conclude that booms and busts would mostly plague the capital goods industries, especially those dominated by longer-lived projects.

The Mises–Hayek theory did not require that the boom–bust sequence be driven by political money creation. It could also be driven from within a banking system where bankers became more exuberant about the prospects for repayment of their outstanding loans, and thus reduce the reserves they hold against adverse clearings, and in this respect makes contact with the Minsky-inspired literature on financial instability. It is elasticity in the supply of money and credit and not politically created money *per se* that triggers the boom-best sequence. The Mises–Hayek theory rested on a diamond-quality intuition; however, that intuition was set within a theoretical setting that hid the brilliance of that intuition.

The intuition was that there was no fixed point on which all economic transactions are anchored. General equilibrium theory uses fixed point theorems, but this is a stratagem to enable proof of the existence of general equilibrium. There is no presumption that such a fixed point to which all economic activity can be reconciled is a feature of reality. The classical economists had searched for an invariant standard of value but failed. The Mises–Hayek theory accepts that failure and goes forward from there. But the complexity-based scholarly tools required to carry forward and amplify the Mises–Hayek intuitions were not yet in sight, and still aren't in any great measure. This situation illustrates the dependence of our ability to think about topics on the tools for thinking that a theorist has. The contemporary home of the Mises–Hayek intuitions about economic processes surely resides in some form of network-based theorizing without some universal basin of attraction, and with those intuitions counseling theorists to get comfortable with living on the edge of chaos, but only on the edge because human nature will rebel against chaos just as it is attracted to chaos. Heraclitus was right about not being able to step twice into that same river, even as Ecclesiastes was also right about there being nothing truly new under the sun.

REFERENCES

Bilo, S., and R.E. Wagner. 2015. Neutral Money: Historical Fact or Analytical Artifact? *Review of Austrian Economics* 28: 139–50.

Böhm-Bawerk, E. 1884. *Capital and Interest*. London: Macmillan.

Buchanan, J.M. 1964. What Should Economists Do? *Southern Economic Journal* 30: 213–22.

Butos, W., and R. Koppl. 1993. Hayekian Expectations: Theory and Empirical Applications. *Constitutional Political Economy* 4: 303–29.

Cantillon, R. 1755 [1931]. *An Essay on the Nature of Commerce in General*. London: Macmillan.

Einzig, P. 1966. *Primitive Money*. London: Pergamon Press.

Frankel, S.H. 1977. *Two Philosophies of Money*. Oxford: Basil Blackwell.

Gramsci, A. 1971. *Selection from the Prison Notebooks*. New York: International Publishers.

Haberler, G. 1937. *Prosperity and Depression*. London: George Allen & Unwin.

Hayek, F.A. 1931. *Prices and Production*. London: Routledge.

Hayek, F.A. 1933. *Monetary Theory and the Trade Cycle*. New York: Harcourt Brace.

Jacobs, J. 1992. *Systems of Survival*. New York: Random House.

Kirman, A.P. 1992. Whom or What Does the Representative Individual Represent? *Journal of Economic Perspectives* 6: 117–36.

Knapp, G.F. 1924. *The State Theory of Money*. London: Macmillan.

Koppl, R. 2002. *Big Players and the Economic Theory of Expectations*. New York: Palgrave Macmillan.

Lachmann, L. 1970. *The Legacy of Max Weber*. Berkeley, CA: Glendessary Press.

Laidler, D., and N. Rowe. 1980. Georg Simmel's *Philosophy of Money*: A Review Article for Economists. *Journal of Economic Literature* 18: 97–105.

Loomes, G., and R. Sugden. 1983. A Rationale for Preference Reversal. *American Economic Review* 73: 428–32.

Maine, H.S. 1861. *Ancient Law*. London: John Murray.

Melitz, J. 1970. The Polanyi School of Anthropology on Money: An Economist's View. *American Anthropologist* 72: 1020–40.

Melitz, J. 1974. *Primitive and Modern Money*. Reading, MA: Addison-Wesley.

Minsky, H.P. 1980. Capitalist Financial Process and the Instability of Capitalism. *Journal of Economic Issues* 14: 505–24.

Minsky, H.P. 1986. *Stabilizing an Unstable Economy*. New Haven, CT: Yale University Press.

Mises, L. 1912. *The Theory of Money and Credit*. London: Jonathan Cape.

Munger, M.C., and K.M. Munger. 2015. *Choosing in Groups: Analytical Politics Revisited*. Cambridge: Cambridge University Press.

Ostrom, V. 1997. *The Meaning of Democracy and the Vulnerability of Democracies*. Ann Arbor: University of Michigan Press.

Pantaleoni, M. 1911. Considerazioni sulle proprieta di un Sistema di prezzi politici. *Giornale Degli Economisti* 42 (9–29): 114–33.

Pareto, V. 1935. *The Mind and Society*. New York: Harcourt Brace.

Polanyi, K. 1944. *The Great Transformation: The Political and Economic Origins of Our Time*. New York: Farrar & Rinehart.

Polanyi, M. 1958. *Personal Knowledge*. Chicago: University of Chicago Press.

Puviani, A. 1903. *Teoria della illusione finaziaria*. Palermo: Sandron.

Rajagopalan, S., and R.E. Wagner. 2013. Constitutional Craftsmanship and the Rule of Law. *Constitutional Political Economy* 24: 295–309.

Runst, P., and R.E. Wagner. 2011. Choice, Emergence, and Constitutional Process. *Journal of Institutional Economics* 7: 131–45.

Schumpeter, J.A. 1934. *Theory of Economic Development*, 2nd ed. Cambridge, MA: Harvard University Press.

Selgin, G., and L.H. White. 1999. A Fiscal Theory of Government's Role in Money. *Economic Inquiry* 37: 154–65.

Simmel, G. 1900. *The Philosophy of Money*, 2nd ed. London: Routledge.

Wagner, R.E. 1976. Revenue Structure, Fiscal Illusion, and Budgetary Choice. *Public Choice* 25: 45–61.

Wagner, R.E. 2000. Georg Simmel's *Philosophy of Money*: Some Points of Relevance for Contemporary Monetary Scholarship. In *Georg Simmel's Philosophy of Money: A Centenary Appraisal*, ed. J.G. Backhaus and H.J. Stadermann, 13–32. Marburg: Metropolis.

Wagner, R.E. 2007. *Fiscal Sociology and the Theory of Public Finance*. Cheltenham, UK: Edward Elgar.

Wagner, R.E. 2010. *Mind, Society, and Human Action: Time and Knowledge in a Theory of Social Economy*. London: Routledge.

Wagner, R.E. 2015. Welfare Economics and Second-Best Theory: Filling Imaginary Economic Boxes. *Cato Journal* 35 (2015): 133–46.

Wagner, R.E. 2016. *Politics as a Peculiar Business: Insights from a Theory of Entangled Political Economy*. Cheltenham, UK: Edward Elgar.

Warren, C.O. 1932. *Congress as Santa Claus*. Charlottesville, VA: Michie.

Webber, C., and A. Wildavsky. 1986. *A History of Taxation and Public Expenditure in the Western World*. New York: Simon & Schuster.

Wicksell, K. 1898. *Interest and Prices*. London: Macmillan.

CHAPTER 9

Reason, Sentiment, and Democratic Action

In *Democracy in America*, Alexis de Tocqueville (1835) offered a chapter titled "What Sort of Despotism do Democratic Nations have to Fear?" Tocqueville explained that democratic despotism was more likely to be accompanied by velvet gloves than by mailed fists. Around a century later, Friedrich Wieser (1926) and Bertrand de Jouvenel (1948) offered similar treatments of how despotism manifests within democratically organized societies. It is common to treat despotism as some external insertion into an otherwise peaceful society, as illustrated by the image of peaceful townspeople terrified by bandits. This situation violates the presumption that democracies are self-governed through consensus. As Wieser and Jouvenel explain, however, the sentiments reflected in public opinion can also be despotic as those sentiments are marshaled into political programs. Dictators and autocrats often have a narrow range of interests, which can lead in some instances to relatively liberal regimes. In contrast, there is no practical limit to the reach of democratic regimes because democratic actions depend on popular sentiment and the articulation of political programs. The concept of the enlightened despot is not a fiction. Nor is the equation of freedom with democracy a tautology.

Democracy is a system of government where candidates compete for office by seeking votes. Yet voting belongs to the realm of non-logical action, which is to say that voters mainly embrace images in casting votes because they can't call on experience for guidance (Pareto 1935). Within the precincts of private ordering where social organization proceeds through logical action, reason and sentiment are complementary. In

© The Author(s) 2020
R. E. Wagner, *Macroeconomics as Systems Theory*,
https://doi.org/10.1007/978-3-030-44465-5_9

this setting, sentiment nominates possible courses of action with reason then evaluating those courses. With public ordering where non-logical action predominates, sentiment in conjunction with rationalization dominates democratic action. The application of reason in these situations will typically entail an effort to rationalize actions that the speaker desires when those actions place the speaker in an advantageous position before some cohort of listeners. In her *Systems of Survival*, Jane Jacobs (1992) coined the term "monstrous moral hybrids" which can fit the relation between reason and sentiment within settings dominated by non-logical impulses to action where the "test" to the value of action resides in opinion and not in market-generated results of action.

The Misguided Lure of the Intuitively Obvious

Both market competition and political competition are actuated by the creation of images that the competitors hope will resonate more strongly with the relevant selectorate than the images articulated by other competitors. This creation of images is the domain of advertising and public relations and is an activity that is pursued by political competitors as well as by market competitors. One significant difference between the two forms of advertising is that market competitors mostly pay vendors to carry their advertisements while political competitors often obtain free placement of their advertisements. Also, political advertising is often disguised through such activities as political agencies sponsoring speakers' bureaus as a vehicle for broadcasting some of the agency's activities. Beyond these differences between the two forms of advertising lies the divergence between environments that elicit logical action and those that elicit non-logical action.

In either case, advertising is a necessary element in the competitive process. The old folk wisdom summarized by the adage "build a better mousetrap and the world will beat a path to your door" is wrong, and its wrongfulness illustrates the ways in which particular theoretical frameworks channel analytical attention. Within a theory centered on competitive equilibrium, relevant knowledge is assumed to be possessed by market participants. As a theory that seeks to elaborate the properties of a set of equilibrium conditions, this orthodox framework is useful; however, if the analytical concern resides with explaining the operation of the hidden ordering processes that undergird experienced observations, a suitable theoretical framework requires some ability to probe those processes. Building a better mousetrap won't do you any good unless you can convey that knowledge to interested persons. To do this, some form of advertising will be necessary. Rarely will that advertising convey technical information about the product, for doing this would impose a tax on the attention span of potential buyers. Advertising is mostly puffery, designed to deliver an appealing image to busy potential buyers. Rare would be a buyer who would truly want to read technical information.

The generally uninformative quality of market advertising is irrelevant because buyers can experience the product and test it against their anticipations. Vendors, moreover, know that buyers can test their claims on behalf of their products, and this environment will tend to be one where initial puffery maps onto customer satisfaction. It is different with political advertising where the puffery of image creation cannot be tested against the experience of voters. For this reason, fraud is surely more prevalent in advancing political claims than in advancing market claims. To be sure, the preceding statement adopts as a standard of fraud the principles of logical action and private ordering. The very meaning of fraud is questionable in the presence of non-logical action and public ordering because the statements advanced pertain more to associations and images than to experiences that result from action. Invisible hand principles warn us to be wary of initial impressions or what appears to be intuitively obvious because interactions set in motion by actions at one point in the societal catallaxy can exert influences throughout that catallaxy.

Perhaps most significant for political competition is the intuitively obvious identifications of output with expenditure. If voters have become more concerned with crime, the obvious programmatic response is to increase spending on crime-related activities. There are, to be sure, different programs that candidates could puff, all of which would have an intuitively obvious connection to crime. One candidate might tout the merits of increasing the police force. Another might tout the merits of increasing the stringency of sentencing while lowering cost through privatizing jails and prisons. There could be plenty of controversy among candidates, but that controversy would be limited to what seems intuitively obvious, for anything else is unlikely to have salience with voters. Yet other measures might be more effective for invisible hand reasons. For instance, moving away from public schooling and embracing more vocational-type education might have superior implications for crime in present value terms although not immediately.

Political discourse abounds with intuitively obvious dichotomies when reality entails vastly more nuance and complexity. In this regard, Frank Knight's (1960) treatment of *Intelligence and Democratic Action* distinguishes between debate and discussion. While those two terms are often treated as synonyms, they are hardly that. They are more opposites than synonyms. The only similarity is that both involve talk. For debate, the talk is between holders of opposing positions, and occurs before an audience that judges a winner. Debate is closed-ended and mirrors a setting where shepherds duel before a set of sheep who will judge which of the shepherds will guide the sheep.

In contrast, discussion is open-ended and can involve multiple participants who recognize the need to arrive at what would at least qualify as some *modus operandi* that allows the participants to continue to live together reasonably well within the geographical space they necessarily must share. Discussion ends not by taking a vote but by observing the emergence of some element or degree of consensus. Discussion is open-ended and entails recognition among the participants that they potentially can learn from one another. While people often refer to "democratic discussion," this language is either mistaken or deceitful when such talk occurs before an audience who will vote on the presenters in a setting of non-logical action.

Consider current controversy over abortion in light of the debate–discussion dichotomy. Present public discourse is centered on a debate between two options; an unlimited ability to abort and no ability to abort. These options entail a polarity that can be mapped as the endpoints of a some east–west spectrum. Once that polarity is established, it becomes possible to think of compromises that fall somewhere along that spectrum. All the same, the presence of that spectrum controls any outcome. For instance, that spectrum leads naturally to selecting different locations along that spectrum, such as unlimited abortion only in the first trimester. This simple dichotomy mirrors a debate between opponents. It does not, however, reflect genuine discussion among people who are seeking to probe and explore options in an environment where there are deep and substantive differences among the participants. Without doubt, genuine discussion, in contrast to the eristic discourse that is paraded as discussion, would doubtlessly unfold as a complex manifold in place of an east–west spectrum. For instance, institutional arrangements regarding adoption would become relevant to any such discussion.

The same can be said about current disputation about immigration. Within the context of debating teams who are trying to secure favorable judgment from an audience, the issues must be framed rigidly as entailing polar options. One option entails open borders; the other entails politically controlled limitation on immigration. This framing of the options is a feature of contestation over the deployment of democratic power guided by non-logical appeals to sentiment. Unavoidably, we live inside environments that require us to live in groups in close proximity to one another. These groupings will provide opportunities for mutual gain while also generating conflict, and with there being a variable mix of cooperation and conflict. The ideology of self-governance calls for discussion among participants, but the reality of democratically deployed power reduces the setting to debate between holders of fixed positions. For instance, nowhere in present debate do considerations of assimilation versus separation arise to any significant degree. Within the context of discussion, those considerations would arise, and their entrance into those discussions would surely lead into an examination of diversity and identity politics, and all of this in an open-ended framework.

Robert Michels (1912 [1962]) noted that democratic systems tend to operate in oligarchic fashion because of limitations on time and attention. Michels's theme was echoed in Bertrand de Jouvenel's (1961) treatment of the problem of a disinterested chairman. Suppose you postulate the presence of a disinterested chairman who wants to ensure that a complex topic receives thorough discussion. To do this requires granting all interested parties the opportunity to set forth their thoughts. It also requires the granting to all parties the opportunity to offer reflections and further thoughts in light of what other participants have set forth. This process should continue, moreover, until some semblance of consensus is attained, recognizing that complete agreement is probably impossible to attain in human affairs where the issues involved are of even moderate complexity and subtlety. Throughout this discussion, moreover, it will be necessary to maintain an audience of listeners who pay attention to other people's presentations. Recognition that such open discussion is impossible to maintain leads to oligarchical arrangements where some people are able to set the agenda by which the group moves toward making some choice. That agenda will include limits on who can speak and how long they can speak, leading to recognition that democratic processes unavoidably become oligarchic beyond small scales of interaction.

PARETO'S THEORY OF ACTION AND DEMOCRATIC COMPETITION FOR POLITICAL OFFICE

The theory of public choice could have gotten underway with Joseph Schumpeter's (1944) set of chapters on two different theories of democracy, which would have been similar to James Burnham's (1943) *The Machiavellians* whose opening two chapters contrasted Dante's idealistic theory where politicians were other-worldly and other-regarding, with Machiavelli's theory that was grounded in sober realism. But public choice didn't start there, though its subsequent initiators were aware of Schumpeter.

Public choice took shape over a dozen or so years starting in 1948, with interaction among several types of contribution leading to the emergence of what later became recognized as public choice. First in point of time was Duncan Black's (1948) paper on the economic theory of group decision-making. In 1951, Kenneth Arrow published *Social Choice and Individual Values*, which argued that it was generally impossible to move from information about individual preference orderings to determination of some coherent social choice. In 1957, Anthony Downs published *An Economic Theory of Democracy*, which was closer in analytical spirit to Schumpeter than the preceding two books. Also, to be mentioned as a fourth pillar is a set of papers James Buchanan wrote starting in 1949, culminating in a collection of essays (Buchanan 1960), which sought to reconstruct the theory of public finance on an individualistic foundation, as Wagner (2017) explains in his intellectual reconstruction of Buchanan's body of work. It was from these works that the theory of public choice acquired scholarly momentum.

While I date the formation of public choice with the appearance of a body of literature in English, I have on several occasions (Wagner 2007, 2016) located the origin of public choice in an Italian tradition within the theory of public finance whose prime initiator was Antonio de Viti de Marco (1888). Before this flourishing of Italian scholarship, public finance had almost universally been approached as offering maxims for statecraft. Public finance sought to develop maxims regarding such matters as how progressive an income tax should be, when should narrow excise taxes be used in place of broad income taxes, and how should the benefits of public spending projects be measured. Answers to these types of questions were envisioned as providing useful information for the practical conduct of statecraft—and with it taken for granted that the holders of political power would invariably use their offices to promote the public good, provided only that fiscal scholars were able to supply apt guidance. In sharp contrast, the Italian theorists starting with de Viti (1888), and with a later version translated into English (de Viti 1936), sought to construct an explanatory theory of public finance. The central presupposition was that political actors were as much economizing agents as were market actors. Politics operated inside a society and with economizing action being a universal principle of human nature, though it manifested differently across institutional environments. Where Francis Edgeworth (1897) sought to articulate a good tax system as one that minimized the sacrifices of utility that taxes imposed on subjects, Amilcare Puviani (1903) sought to explain how actual tax institutions and practices reflected an underlying logic of economizing action that played out inside some political-institutional setting. Puviani sought to explain the configurations he observed, regardless of how the theorist might appraise those configurations. While Puviani (1903) has not been translated into English, he has been translated into German (Puviani 1960). That translation contained a Foreword written by Gunter Schmölders, whose work on fiscal psychology (Schmölders 1959, 1960) is a precursor to the contemporary interest in behavioral economics. In his Foreword to the German translation, Schmölders explains that "over the last century *Italian public finance has had an essentially political science character*. The political character of fiscal activity stands always in the foreground.... This work [Puviani's book] is a *typical product of Italian public finance*, especially a typical product at the end of the nineteenth century. Above all, it is the *science of public finance combined with fiscal politics*, in many cases giving a good fit with reality" (Puviani 1960: 7–8, my translation and italics).

Three points are notable about Schmölders's Foreword and his assessment of the Italian orientation toward public finance, and for which he had chosen Puviani to represent, with de Viti having already been previously translated into German in 1932. One is that Puviani's book was not some outlier within the literature of public finance but was a typical work within the Italian orientation that had been taking shape since 1888. A second point is that the Italian theorists were concerned with *explaining* the institutional configurations that comprised the material of public finance; they wanted to pursue public finance in a scientific manner, as contrasted with advancing maxims for practical statecraft. Third, public finance called for a blending of economics and politics, creating a genuine political economy; the Italian theorists treated politics and politicians as residing inside the economic system and not as governors who stood apart from and outside that system.

There is no necessary antagonism between pubic finance as explanation and public finance as statecraft. A theorist can set forth maxims of what he or she thought would comprise a good tax system while also describing and explaining the processes through which the material of public finance actually emerges. The same theoretical formulation can't do both, but a theorist can work with both types of formulation, only not at the same instant. A theorist can populate a theoretical foreground with concerns of fiscal justice while recognizing that fiscal processes might not operate with a single-minded devotion to pursuing that notion of justice. Likewise, one can place scientific explanation of observed fiscal configurations in the analytical foreground while recognizing that the normative appraisal of those configurations is also a normal human sentiment.

It is also notable that Schmölders's Foreword was published in 1960. This was eight years before the term "public choice" received explicit articulation. In 1966, Gordon Tullock started the Journal that he titled *Papers on Non-Market Decision-Making*. In 1968, this title was changed to *Public Choice*, in conjunction with establishment of the Public Choice Society. In 1969, the Center for Study of Public Choice was established at Virginia Tech. It would be even a few more years before the blending of economics and politics that public choice represented would achieve a modicum of scholarly recognition beyond the founding circle of scholars. Yet as Schmölders recognized in 1960, Italian theorists of public finance had long been pursuing a blending of economics and politics. If, such noted contributors to the Italian tradition as de Viti, Pantaleoni, Borgotta, or Puviani had fallen asleep for a long duration, to awaken in Rip Van Winkle fashion in 1968 when the originating meeting of the Public Choice Society was held, it is easy to see that they would have felt comfortable with the topics being discussed under the rubric "public choice." While the Italians would have advanced some different analytical insights, it would have been clear to all participants, both Italian and American, that they were exploring a subject of common interest. Public choice represented an interrupted continuation of what the Italian theorists a generation earlier had started, with James Buchanan (1960, 1967, 1968) being the figure who bridged these periods more fully than anyone.

Within that short-lived Italian tradition of explanatory public finance, substantial controversy arose over how closely political and individual action could be brought under the same analytical framework, and with Michael McLure (2007) examining carefully the controversies between such theorists as de Viti and Maffeo Pantaleoni, who thought it unproblematic to merge the two, and Vilfredo Pareto and Gino Borgatta, who found difficulties in bridging between fiscal and market processes due to the cleavage between logical and non-logical action. For Pareto, non-logical action occurred within an environment that led rational action to play out differently than it would within environments suitable to logical action. The participants were fundamentally the same across both environments, but their actions manifested differently due to those differences in environment.

Within the Anglo-Saxon conception of fiscal politics, a taxpayer-voter choosing among candidates is no different from a customer choosing among competing products or vendors. The analysis starts with individuals having well-ordered utility functions defined over what they regard as goods, some of which are supplied through private transactions and the remainder supplied through politics. Just as private vendors compete for patronage, so do political candidates. It's easy to envision individual preferences for politically supplied activities arrayed in commodity space. Candidates are construed as offering programs to voters, with the winning candidate being the one who receives the largest number of votes.

This analytical scheme matches the form of the theory of markets. But does substance accompany form? Pareto answered negatively, invoking the distinction between logical and non-logical action in doing so. It is clear how closely the substance of market action matches the form of logical action. It is only through metaphor or high abstraction that political campaigns can be said to have the same or even similar substantive properties as market action. For substance to match form, it would be necessary for candidates to make specific promises in detail. Nothing like that happens in politics. What are offered instead are vague generalities along such lines as improving education or protecting the environment, without offering any detail that would truly enable individual voters to know what exactly would be done and how much they would pay. Pareto recognized that a gulf divided markets and politics, just as a gulf divided logical and non-logical action.

All the same, both types of action occur within the same society comprised of the same people. If we were to assume that everyone had identical utility functions, it would be possible to bridge the gap between markets and politics because that gap would not exist. What creates that gap is differences among people in their desires or values. In market settings, these differences are reflected in different patterns of purchase. In political settings, these differences are reflected in some people being pleased and others not, and the existence of displeasure indicating that political activity has not yet ended, contrary to the treatment of political action as just a different form of market action.

Put differently, political competition generates tectonic relationships between political and market entities within society, as Fig. 3.1 sketched, and as Buchanan (1954) set out in his critique of Kenneth Arrow's (1951) general possibility theorem. The political process creates winners and losers for the most part, though it is possible to imagine circumstances, more local than national, where political action reflects relatively high degrees of consensus. Market action, however, conforms to the principles of contract and the obligations of promise (Fried 1982). Political action is unfettered by such principles. Theorists who want to avoid dealing with the gap between logical and non-logical action create a commodity out of reputation, thus claiming that politicians who don't keep promises loose reputational value. To argue this way, however, is to engage in magical thinking where something is explained by invoking a mystery. The alternative is to dig into the material to uncover the processes at work, as best this can be done. This brings us to recognition of the work done by the gulf between reason and sentiment in human affairs.

REASON AND SENTIMENT IN HUMAN AFFAIRS

Wagner (2010) explains that economic theory underwent a transformation starting late in the nineteenth century. Prior to that time, economics, or what was then identified as political economy, was thought to be a theory of society approached through the theoretical lens of economizing action as a universal principle. To adopt economizing action as a universal principle is in no way to adopt homogeneity as a postulate. People can universally be treated as economizers while recognizing that the objects over which they seek to economize are both variable and often antagonistic with the objects over which other people economize. As for what objects people might seek, this is the province of thymology as distinct from praxeology (Mises 1957). When economics is conceived as a theory of society, moreover, the objects of action can include the actions of other people, creating interaction between praxeology and thymology.

With the transformation of economic theory that began late in the nineteenth century, economics came increasingly to become a science of rational action. With economies treated as entities where individuals bore an equilibrium relationship to one another, it appeared sensible to reduce a plurality of individuals to a representative individual who was treated as a miniaturization of society. Within this transformation, reason became rationality and rational action. This transformation was momentous for economic theory. Prior to the transformation, reason and sentiment were two central human faculties which provided points of entry into constructing social theories.

Reason pertained to conscious mental activity, as conveyed by the idea of thinking and reasoning about something. But what are the objects about which Reason reasons? These come from sentiment or emotion and can lead to people acting without thinking about that action. Reason cannot nominate objects upon which to act because that is the domain of sentiment. As the equilibrium treatment of economics took shape, individuality among the members of a society gave way to some formal and universal model of a representative individual as portrayed by a well-ordered utility function. Reason was no longer a faculty that someone could exercise to greater or lesser extent, nor was it a faculty that people could exercise with higher or lower quality. Society had become universalized to render sensible and tractable the model of general equilibrium. Sentiment was left with no work to do, becoming the domain of irrationality until it was partly brought to life through the development of behavioral economics.

Vilfredo Pareto stood apart from this trend in economic theory. He was mathematically sophisticated and worked with the theory of economic equilibrium, seeking to improve on Léon Walras's economic theory. Pareto's distinction between logical and non-logical action fit well the classical distinction between reason and sentiment. Logical action pertained to environments in which people would generally fare better the more effective they were in thinking through the consequences of different actions.

Pareto's category of non-logical action carried forward the category of sentiment, and it was this category that was particularly significant for understanding matters of political economy as distinct from market action. Non-logical action pertains to sentiment and not to reason. Elections are the realm of popularity contests and not the realm where experience is tested against expectations. On the surface, political competition mirrors advertising by market competitors. No one thinks advertising does much by way of conveying information about the attributes of products. Advertising is mostly about trying to get potential customers to take a look by leaving those customers with favorable images of the products. Whether those products would deliver experiences commensurate with the image is something that can be determined only as the customer tries the product.

Political campaigns are advertising without voters having any ability subsequently to try the product. While many economists try to maintain the presumption that candidates make promises about programs, examination of campaign literature reveals not specific programs but generalities. What is reason within a context of market action becomes rationalization within a context of political action. With market action, people can give reasoned explanations for why they prefer one brand or restaurant over another. Or why they were willing to invest in someone's business undertaking while not investing in someone else's. They can give reasoned responses to such questions because it is they who make the choices and it is they who bear the consequences of those choices. The market environment forces logical action upon people, and with those people faring better because they are better able to make those choices.

With political choice, all that exists are the images created by the candidates. Candidates project images that will appeal to some voters and not to others. It is still possible to place candidates within some abstract model of candidate location within X–Y space. The dimensions of that space, however, are not the hedonic dimensions used within spatial models of political competition. Within those models, candidates announce programs in terms of such variables as amounts to spend on education, parks, and police. Sure, things are never this simple, but models are to be judged more by the insights they offer than by some sense of descriptive accuracy.

Within spatial competition, voters have predetermined desires with respect to the issues, and candidates seek to position themselves to appeal to more voters than other candidates. This formulation fits the standard approach to markets where people have utility functions and vendors seek to appeal to those preferences. Political competition, however, is all about images because there can be no recourse to experience grounded in choice. Candidates still try to appeal to voters and voters still choose among candidates. But the environment inside of which this happens is not conducive to logical action. That environment is one of non-logical action. Candidates project themselves onto a set of voters, and voters respond by voting for the one whose projection they prefer. To be sure, candidates project images that have objective referents. Political campaigns and voting are processes of social interaction. Candidates must give voters reasons they can give their associates for supporting a candidate. In these interactions, it is never sufficient for a person to say he or she supports one candidate just because that's the way it is. To maintain good social relationships, it is necessary to advance some reasonable-sounding basis for supporting one's candidate. To enable voters to do this, it is necessary that candidates provide objective points of reference. This is the realm of rationalization and not reason, which is the only realm possible in environments of non-logical action. It is worth noting in this regard that David Hume (1748 [1973]) claimed that a vital function of human reason was to check the expressions of sentiment masquerading as reason in human affairs.

COMBINATION, PERSISTENCE, AND SOCIETAL TECTONICS

In *The Great Chain of Being*, Arthur Lovejoy (1936) advanced and elaborated the thesis that our consciously held ideas rest upon a bedding ground of presuppositions of which we may be at best only vaguely aware. Vilfredo Pareto's (1916 [1935]) concept of residues bears a family resemblance to Lovejoy. Action is directly observable, as are the reasons or justifications for those actions people might give if asked. Those justifications will put the speaker in a favorable light but need not identify the motivations that truly generated the actions. While Pareto identified several categories of residue, two were of especial significance for theorizing about political economy. These, Pareto identified as combination and persistence, both of which generated predispositions in support of particular forms of action, though these residues can reside within individuals in variable mixture and intensity.

Combination pertains to a predilection for adventure or exploration. Creativity, for instance, can be represented as a combinatorial activity where a creator selects n elements among m possible elements. When m is much larger than n, the number of possible combinations is staggeringly large. This is perhaps the person who when told not to do something will do it to see what will happen. The residue of combination maps onto entrepreneurial action and animal spirits. It is a residue, moreover, that a liberal order releases so long as the actions do not violate prior obligations of property or contract.

Persistence pertains to a predilection for stability or conservation. It is reflected in habit and leads to a preference for what is familiar over peering into what is unfamiliar. Both types of residue can reside in the same person, for a residue is not some observable action but is some precognitive predisposition that is at work in generating the actions a person takes in a situation. Residues give order to preferences. Faced with the same prices and incomes, different residues will lead people to make different choices despite those common prices and incomes. The justifications or rationalizations they might give for taking those actions may have nothing to do with the identification of residues and may instead depend on the effect the rationalization has in the situation where it was advanced. A boy comes home after his father's curfew. He might say he forgot to wear his watch, or that he had a flat tire—and show his dirty hands which he had wiped on his tire. To the contrary, he had met some new people who had excited his residue of combination but knew it would be bad to tell this to his father.

Suppose the types of residues vary among people. Do some activities and occupations tend to select for carriers of some residues over others? For instance, might not people heavily endowed with the residue of combination be attracted to entrepreneurship, adventure, and experimentation, while people heavily endowed with persistence are attracted to various conserving occupations, including law and politics? Pareto's characterization of residues is meant to be scientifically descriptive and not normatively evaluative. It is not a matter of either combination or persistence being superior, but rather it is that interaction among carriers of those residues has significant analytical work to do in constructing social theories. The relation between combination and persistence is one of dialectical tension, which is necessary for theories that seek to explain change as something that is internally generated rather than some exogenous shock. Liberty, for instance, is a condition that can erode through a failure to practice it (Ostrom 1997). People seized by combination might undermine liberty in their rush for experimentation, whereas maintenance of liberty requires a good deal of persistence in maintaining the permanent things.

The dialectical tension created by interaction among carriers of different residues creates societal tectonics and not social equilibrium. To speak in terms of equilibrium is to convey placidity. What is here today will be here tomorrow, and the day after. To speak in terms of tectonics is to speak of the societal equivalent of earthquakes. In the physical world, earthquakes occur when sliding plates rub against one another. Most earthquakes are unnoticeable unless they are detected by seismic instruments. By contrast, some earthquakes are catastrophic in their local regions, and can even extend far away through tsunamis. In the social world, the equivalent of earthquakes occurs when carriers of combination collide with carriers of persistence. Consider how the free-market institutions of private property and freedom of contract give vent to the residue of combination, which leads in turn to the experimental search for new products, new ideas, and new forms of business enterprise.

To illustrate a point, suppose five entrepreneurs start new businesses, and hire other people in the society as employees. As time passes, two of those businesses become successful as judged by the willingness of the owners to keep them going. In contrast, the owners of the other three businesses decide their businesses have failed, and so liquidate them. Within the rhetoric of a free economy, the owners of those three businesses move into other activities, including possibly starting new businesses. The institutional framework of property and contract accommodates equally well the expansion of successful businesses and the liquidation of failed businesses. But is democracy necessarily congruent with the institutional framework of a free economy?

Consider a simple model of majority voting, and suppose the people associated with the failed firms outnumber the people associated with the successful firms. Might this hypothetical situation bring us to one of those analytical forks in the road? Down one branch of that fork, the failed firms liquidate, and the people associated with those firms move into other activities. Down the other branch, a legislative motion is enacted to create an Agency of Business Promotion. That agency is financed by taxes on successful firms, and the funds are used to help other business compete successfully in the commercial world. For instance, the Agency might make interest free loans to keep in operation those business that otherwise would have been liquidated.

As presented, this operation would be a simple tax-transfer scheme where the successful support the unsuccessful. No supporter of this program would justify it by claiming that successful firms owe a duty to support firms that fail. Supporters need to feel good about the objects they support, so will couch their support in terms of what Pareto described as derivations. For instance, they might couch their support for the Agency for Business Promotion on grounds of providing equal opportunity. In this respect, claims might have been advanced that the successful firms had better connections within the society than the firms that failed, and the point of ABP was to promote equal opportunity and most certainly not to tax success to reward failure.

How this situation might play out is anyone's guess. We know that humans have immense ability to convince themselves that they and their programs are socially beneficial. Joseph Stalin and Adolph Hitler most assuredly never thought of themselves as evil, but surely thought of themselves as promoting good in the world. Contestation is everywhere in society, as Carl Schmitt (1932 [1996]) illustrates lucidly. The human imagination, moreover, can be fertile in generating reasonable-sounding derivations in support of the causes for which a person is seeking support. Politics, moreover, is not the prime source of entrepreneurship in society, although the term political entrepreneurship enjoys wide currency today.

Societal tectonics there will always be, for living in society is to live inside an earthquake zone where what has become familiar is not guaranteed to persist, nor is what appears to be a good idea sure to be accepted into society. It is the process of continual contestation and not some end state that resides in the foreground of our worlds of experience. For instance, one can easily imagine a constitutional amendment that read "Congress shall pass no law in restraint of trade." On its face, this Amendment would seem to preclude an Agency for Business Promotion. But would it? Supporters of the ABP are not seeking to restrain trade, they would surely say, but are seeking to promote fairness or equal opportunity. Any restraint that might result is incidental to the ABP's objectives. In an open-ended and creative universe, constitutional provisions have little scope for bringing closure independently of the contested processes in play within a society. And those processes, moreover, surely respond more strongly to the resonance of sentiment than to the logic of reason, for reason can reinforce sentiment but it can't set sentiment in motion.

COMPLEXITY AND THE CONFOUNDING OF CAUSATION WITH SYSTEMIC PROPERTIES

The theory of economic equilibrium treats its objects as simple and subject to causal analysis through the method of comparative statics. The method of comparative statics addresses "what if" types of questions where all but one variable is assumed fixed, and the analytical challenge is to examine how a postulated change will affect the model's equilibrium. Causation is a simple concept when applied to such simple systems as a parade. A parade is scheduled to start crossing a certain boulevard at 10:15. Yet by 10:20 the parade is not yet visible. It is reasonable to ask what has caused the delay, and it is also reasonable to expect a sensible answer. Investigation might show that a rider fell off an equestrian unit due to an apparent heart attack, causing a ten-minute delay in the parade.

Any simple system for which notions of systemic equilibrium are reasonable is one for which deviations from what had been expected must have some cause for the deviation, provided the theory that posited systemic equilibrium was correct. The Great Depression of the 1930s and the Great Recession that began in 2008 are both major changes in economic conditions that have led numerous scholars to inquire into their sources or causes. Those inquiries map nicely into the standard dichotomy that has characterized macro theory throughout the postwar period. One pole of this dichotomy, associated these days with new Keynesianism, asserts that markets are plagued by instabilities that require appropriate policy action to prevent, or to mitigate. In this vein, the Great Depression and the Great Recession were significant failures of market processes. The other pole of this dichotomy claims that excessive regulation is, by injecting rigidity into an economy, the source of the experienced recession.

Once again, we butt up against recognition that our models not only focus our thinking but influence what it is we think we see. Any DSGE-type model will have to explain failures of economic coordination as due to some failure to satisfy the necessary conditions for systemic equilibrium. One source of failure can result through market interaction, as illustrated by exogenous increases in the demand for money. The other source can result from governmental disturbances to the equilibrium conditions, as when a government's tax extractions discourage capital spending. The written record shows numerous instances of each type of explanation, both for the Great Depression and for the Great Recession. If a recession is equivalent to a delay in the arrival of a parade, the analytical challenge is to determine the cause of the delay. Contemporary macro theories treat societies as if they were parades. The difference among those theories is only how they imagine parades failing to conform to the image of a well-working parade. The systemic approach to causation pursued in this book seeks to locate the ebbs and flows of economic activity as properties of a system of economic interaction as Friedrich Pryor (2008) explains and which Armen Alchian (1950) advanced about survival among experiments.

Complex social systems have properties that emerge out of interaction among participants within that system. The western institutions of liberal democracy were accompanied by a western moral imagination rooted in sportsmanship and fair play, which meant, among other things, that losers in competitions for office would congratulate winners and would be able to work together going forward. To be sure, western-style liberal democracy has moved in a collectivist direction with public ordering moving more into the foreground of economic life. Even within western-style liberalism, different systems for ordering human interaction will have different systemic properties. A credit market with total private ordering will have different properties than a credit market where public ordering appears throughout the market. With wholly private ordering, negotiations between individual borrowers and lenders are conclusive. This situation changes when public ordering appears because political conditions can be forced onto what otherwise would have been private transactions. In consequence, public ordering will modify the pattern of loans from what would have resulted under private ordering. Among other things, public ordering will force lenders to lend to politically favored clients, leading to an expected increase in the amount of bad debt, and perhaps also bailouts to cover over those negative consequences. Rather than trying to force an answer as to whether the Great Depression or the Great Recession illustrated market failure or government failure, a coherent analytical alternative would seek to explain systemic variability as properties that vary in intensity among different systems of human ordering.

FROM LIBERAL DEMOCRACY TO NEO-FEUDALISM: AN EVOLUTIONARY UNFOLDING

This book carries forward the theme that societies are continually evolving through interaction among an ever-changing cast of members who do *not* have a hard core of common belief outside our common biologies. In the absence of that hard core, societies will feature continuing contestation over position and status. This contestation will generate evolutionary movement through time. The United States began as what can reasonably be described as a system of liberal democracy where liberty held the foreground and democracy the background in people's moral imaginations. The liberal orientation held that people were responsible for conducting their lives within the institutional framework provided by private property and freedom of contract, with some modest accommodation made for a small amount of political action. Within this framework, social organization emerged largely through free markets, as modified by modest government action. Such government action as there was, moreover, was carried out mostly by state and local governments rather than by the federal government, as Jonathan Hughes (1979) explained in *The Governmental Habit*, which explored governmentally imposed economic controls in Colonial America.

The liberal republicanism of early America contrasted with the feudal arrangements that dominated Europe at the time. Feudal arrangements were hierarchical and were arrangements into which people were born. If well-bred, you would be a lord who had some contribution to make to governance of the realm. If you were not well-bred, you would tend to your station in life, and not concern yourself with what was not yours to be concerned about. In contrast to these feudal arrangements, the American Declaration of Independence asserted that "governments derive their just powers from the consent of the governed." In contrast to the feudal pattern of a multiplicity of intersecting duties and obligations, liberal republicanism began with individual liberty, with governments deriving their just powers from consent among the people to be governed. Writing in the mid-nineteenth century, Henry Maine (1861) summarized the pattern of social evolution up to that point by declaring that "the direction of movement of the progressive societies has been one from status to contract." Over the past century or so throughout the west, this direction of societal movement has reversed, though the extent of that reversal is subject to impressionistic judgments.

Contract is the realm of private ordering; status is the realm of public ordering. It is possible to imagine credit being allocated wholly through private ordering. Credit contracts are rental contracts. They entail an owner of an asset ceding temporary control of that asset to a borrower under mutually agreeable terms. Whether or not a borrower obtains credit is for the owner of the asset to decide. A person whose application for credit is denied is always free to approach another lender, but the asset owner's decision on granting credit is always final.

Those lenders operated mostly inside a corporate shell that contained procedures and categories. For instance, lenders could not be utterly confident that their outstanding loans would be repaid in timely fashion. To maintain solvency in the presence of uncertainty, lenders would maintain reserves rather than lending out all their assets. The level of those reserves and the form they would take would be for the lenders to determine under a system of private ordering. In any case, determination of how to handle reserves was the bailiwick of the lenders within a system of private ordering.

Mid-nineteenth century America has often been mischaracterized as a period of free banking, sometimes called wildcat banking. This characterization reflects a terrible misunderstanding both of banking arrangements and of the difference between public and private ordering. What were called free or wildcat banks were regulated in many ways by states, so public ordering intruded heavily into the organization and operation of banks. For instance, banks were not free to determine such organizational features as the use of branches or peering arrangements. These matters were governed by state governments. Banks could not determine the level of their reserves or the form they would take. These, too, were governed by state regulation (White 1999).

It is but a short step from state regulation of banking in the nineteenth century to federal regulation in the 20th since the creation of the Federal Reserve in 1913. Federal regulation reaches more deeply into banking practices than did state regulation in the nineteenth century. In either case, however, credit markets are governed significantly by public ordering. There are still regions of private ordering, but these are shaped and limited by the requirements of public ordering. Indeed, it is somewhat ironical that economists still refer to a credit market in terms of the demand and supply of loanable funds, for this model conjures up notions of free exchange. But free exchange does not characterize credit markets as against characterizing it along some margins of action. With private ordering, there is open competition for access to credit. In contrast, public ordering creates sheltered positions of status. For instance, lenders must have portfolios that reserve certain volumes of loans by such status positions as income, wealth, gender, race, and zip code.

This ongoing transformation from contract back to status that has been underway for a good century is a product of the search for support within democratic processes. It should not be thought that this transformation reflects some move from inferior to superior, as is often thought to be the outcome of competitive processes. This might be a reasonable conclusion to reach in environments that are driven by logical action. This quality doesn't follow, however, for environments driven by the sentimentality of non-logical action. With respect to sentimentality, it is often thought that sentiment works for the public good through approbation. There are certainly circumstances where this is possible, but this is surely not a universal outcome.

Approbation entails creating rank orders with respect to relative deservedness. As Arthur Lovejoy (1936) explains, approbation is cousin to envy. If scales of valuation differ among people, what is approbation for some can become envy for others. Is commercial success an object of worthiness that elicits approbation? Within some precincts of society, it surely is. But there are surely other precincts where commercial success is not an object of worthiness, but rather elicits envy. At this point we enter some treacherous territory regarding the relationship between private and public ordering and the place of sentiment within an environment of non-logical action.

In *Capitalism, Socialism, and Democracy*, Joseph Schumpeter (1944) argued that liberalism was destined to give way to socialism. Schumpeter seems to be right with respect to the general direction of movement within societies since late in the nineteenth century, with one possible caveat. Public ordering is responsive and reactive, it is not creative. It is difficult to see how creative action could originate in politics, at least within democratic regimes where some modicum of agreement is necessary for action to take place. So, we have a process, like what Chapter 3 sketched, where entrepreneurs locate profit opportunities, after which political operators move into claim some of the low-hanging fruit, so to speak.

Within this setting, there is always a form of cat-and-mouse game in play. Entrepreneurs locate sources of wealth, and after some period of operation politicians identify those entrepreneurs and their activities. Thereafter, entrepreneurs must operate differently because they operate inside the shadow of the state. While this is happening, however, new entrepreneurs are identifying new opportunities outside the state's shadow. Entrepreneurial gains are thus short-lived and not permanent. But how much does this short-lived character really matter? At a 10% rate of discount, a rent that lasts seven years is about half as valuable as one that lasts forever.

References

Alchian, A.A. 1950. Uncertainty, Evolution, and Economic Theory. *Journal of Political Economy* 58: 211–21.

Arrow, K.J. 1951. *Social Choice and Individual Values*. New York: Wiley.

Black, D. 1948. On the Rationale of Group Decision-Making. *Journal of Political Economy* 56: 23–34.

Buchanan, J.M. 1954. Social Choice, Democracy, and Free Markets. *Journal of Political Economy* 62: 114–23.

Buchanan, J.M. 1960. *Fiscal Theory and Political Economy*. Chapel Hill: University of North Carolina Press.

Buchanan, J.M. 1967. *Public Finance in Democratic Process*. Chapel Hill: University of North Carolina Press.

Buchanan, J.M. 1968. *Demand and Supply of Public Goods*. Chicago: Rand McNally.

Burnham, J. 1943. *The Machiavellians*. New York: John Day.

De Jouvenel, B. 1948. *On Power: Its Nature and the History of its Growth*. London: Hutchinson.

De Jouvenel, B. 1961. The chairman's Problem. *American Political Science Review* 55: 368–72.

De Tocqueville, A. 1835 [2002]. *Democracy in America*. Chicago: University of Chicago Press.

Downs, A. 1957. *An Economic Theory of Democracy*. New York: Harper & Row.

Edgeworth, F.Y. 1897. The Pure Theory of Taxation. *Economic Journal* 7: 46–70.

Fried, C. 1982. *Contract as Promise: A Theory of Contractual Obligation*. Cambridge, MA: Harvard University Press.

Hughes, J.R.T. 1979. *The Governmental Habit*. New York: Basic Books.

Hume, D. 1748 [1973]. *An Enquiry Concerning Human Understanding*. Indianapolis: Hackett.

Jacobs, J. 1992. *Systems of Survival*. New York: Random House.

Knight, F.H. 1960. *Intelligence and Democratic Action*. Cambridge, MA: Harvard University Press.

Lovejoy, A. 1936. *The Great Chain of Being*. Cambridge, MA: Harvard University Press.

Maine, H. 1861. *Ancient Law*. London: John Murray.

McLure, M. 2007. *The Paretian School and Italian Fiscal Sociology*. Houndmills: Palgrave Macmillan.

Michels, R. 1912 [1962]. *Political Parties: A Sociological Study of the Oligarchical Tendencies of Modern Democracy*. New York: Collier Books.

Mises, L. 1957. *Theory and History*. New Haven, CT: Yale University Press.

Ostrom, V. 1997. *The Meaning of Democracy and the Vulnerability of Democracies*. Ann Arbor: University of Michigan Press.

Pareto, V. 1935. *The Mind and Society*. New York: Harcourt Brace.

Pryor, F. 2008. System as a Causal Force. *Journal of Economic Behavior & Organization* 67: 545–59.

Puviani, A. 1903. *Teoria della illusione finaziaria*. Palermo: Sandron.

Puviani, A. 1960. *Die Illusionen in der öffentlichen Finanzwirtschaft.* Berlin: Dunker & Humblot.

Schmitt, C. 1932 [1996]. *The Concept of the Political.* Chicago: University of Chicago Press.

Schmölders, G. 1959. Fiscal Psychology: A New Branch of Public Finance. *National Tax Journal* 12: 340–45.

Schmölders, G. 1960. *Das Irrationale in der öffentlichen Finanzwirtschaft: Probleme der Finanzpsychologie.* Hamburg: Rowahlt.

Schumpeter, J.A. 1944. *Capitalism, Socialism, and Democracy.* New York: Harper & Row.

Viti, De, and A. de Marco. 1888. *Il carattere teorico dell'economia finanziaria.* Rome: Pasqualucci.

Viti, De, and A. de Marco. 1936. *First Principles of Public Finance.* London: Jonathan Cape.

Wagner, R.E. 2007. *Fiscal Sociology and the Theory of Public Finance.* Cheltenham, UK: Edward Elgar.

Wagner, R.E. 2010. *Mind, Society, and Human Action: Time and Knowledge in a Theory of Social Economy.* London: Routledge.

Wagner, R.E. 2016. *Politics as a Peculiar Business: Insights from a Theory of Entangled Political Economy.* Cheltenham, UK: Edward Elgar.

Wagner, R.E. 2017. *James M. Buchanan and Liberal Political Economy: A Rational Reconstruction.* Lanham, MD: Lexington Books.

White, L.H. 1999. *The Theory of Monetary Institutions.* Oxford: Blackwell.

Wieser, F. 1926. *Das Gesetz der Macht.* Vienna: Julius Springer.

CHAPTER 10

Liberalism, Collectivism, and Democracy

Are there some ways for people to live together in close geographical proximity that are superior to other ways? This question may have no clear and obvious answer. All the same, it is doubtful that there are many people who would like to lead their lives residing in war zones or in concentration camps. Yet, the historical record shows that war zones continually erupt within human societies, so there cannot be any universal abhorrence to combat zones. Liberalism and collectivism are commonly portrayed as two antipodal forms by which people can live together. These forms, moreover, map onto the common distinction between market and state, with market denoting liberalism and state denoting collectivism. To be sure, Wagner (2007, 2016) claims that this denotation is analytically incoherent because desires for both individuality and community are resident in human nature, which means that all historical options entail both market and political entities in some fashion.

This is the world of entangled political economy which Fig. 10.1 summarizes in three stages, despite all stages being collapsed onto the same figure. The first stage is an ordinary production possibility function where the output bundle (G, M) distinguishes between political and market output. If the Figure were to stop there, it would give the impression that some social planner chooses the allocation of resources denoted by R. Subtended to the allocations G and M are the institutional designations "public law" and "private law." These designations convey recognition that complex societies cannot operate through hierarchical planning but must operate in some polycentric fashion where allocations

R. E. Wagner, *Macroeconomics as Systems Theory*,
https://doi.org/10.1007/978-3-030-44465-5_10

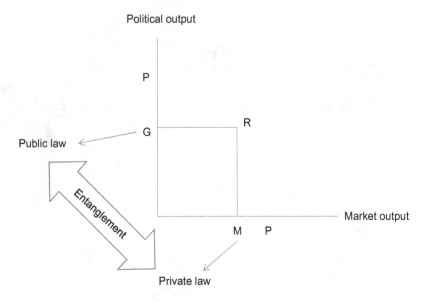

Fig. 10.1   Entangled political economy trumps private vs. public ordering

emerge through interaction among participants inside some set of institutional arrangements. In this respect, Walter Eucken (1952) explained that what we denote as market allocations are the emergent products of human interaction guided by the private law principles of private property and freedom of contract. No such comparable explanatory theory yet exists with respect to public law, and yet the explanatory principle is the same: what we denote as public outcomes are likewise emergent products of interactions among participants inside the institutional arrangements denoted as public law.

Those arrangements denoted as public law and private law are not, however, independent of one another. Market participants exercise influence over political action just as political participants exercise influence over market action. This is the world of entangled political economy portrayed by the double arrow connecting public law and private law in Fig. 10.1. While it is conventional to work with rigid distinctions between market and state, the idea of entanglement holds that societies contain only one institutional order, and an extraordinarily complex one that cannot even be apprehended in full without resort to mythology. It is still meaningful to distinguish between those enterprises that are established through people using their rights of private property and those enterprises that are established through political processes denoted by public law. But the operation of political processes will be influenced by private citizens just as the operation of market processes will be influenced by political entities. We can distinguish private from public conceptually, and yet there can be only one institutional arrangement in play in society at any one time.

Within the precincts of private law, people can do such things to establish enterprises and supply labor to enterprises, earning income to make purchases from those products in the process. These actions fall within the domain of private law, though not completely. Income derived from market transactions is typically taxed. How heavily it is taxed is determined through processes established by public law, and with many of the participants in those processes simultaneously engaging in transactions organized within private law. Even more, the spheres of private and public law are not independent of one another, for societies really operate with a complex manifold of institutional arrangements along the lines that Ludwig Lachmann (1970) sets forth. An enterprise might hire people to work for it within contractual terms governed by private law. Yet those terms are not the sole province of private law because public law can set limits on terms of private contract. Likewise, private citizens can establish enterprises through private law to create associations to lobby for changes in public law. Societies operate with a complex manifold of entangled institutional arrangements, though for many analytical purposes it is helpful to distinguish private from public even though this distinction operates with permeable boundaries.

MAILED FISTS, VELVET GLOVES, AND DEMOCRATIC DESPOTISM

When Tocqueville commented on democratic despotism, he did not analogize that form of life to living in a war zone. He had something milder in mind, though a form of despotism all the same. Whether one embraces a brutal or mild form of despotism, despotism is not liberalism. Whatever the form of despotism, it clashes with the classical liberal orientation toward the place of politics within a good society and clashes as well with the liberal political philosophy on which the United States was founded, aside from slavery. Whatever system of governance a nation has, it will have systemic qualities that are the object of a theory of the macro entirety of the society, as distinct from theories pertaining to micro-level interactions inside that society. For a political philosophy to have relevance for the human problems of living together, it must be trans-latable into organizational, institutional, and constitutional arrangements, and also moral imaginations alive within the population. These different arrangements have different social qualities and properties, and the dis-cernment of these qualities is the task of a macro theory as it manifests in a society's constitutive arrangements. Care must be taken, however, not to claim too much for our theoretical claims (DeCanio 2013). No one can truly see the entirety of a society because no one possesses a god's-eye vantage point. We each see parts of phenomena of interest within our field of vision and competence, and it takes assembly in some fashion to even approach the societal entirety inside of which we live. In doing this, we must take recourse to mythology or political philosophy.

Liberalism and collectivism are the two generic political philosophies that map directly onto the market-state dichotomy. Within the contours of that dichotomy, a liberal society operates largely through private order-ing, with public ordering serving mostly to reinforce private ordering. This vision of society reflects the American constitutional founding, bear-ing in mind Jonathan Hughes's (1977) portrayal of widespread local reg-ulation in Colonial America. Despite such regulation, people mostly bore first-order responsibility for making their way in life, recognizing that peo-ple who grow up in family situations that offer succor and support also learn to call upon various organizations inside the precincts of civil society to support that first-order responsibility. Politics is present within the lib-eral spirit, but only in a background role as befits the image of politicians and bureaucratic officials as "public servants." To be sure, modern prac-tice and experience has elevated politicians and bureaucrats beyond the status of "public servants." Still, and keeping with Tocqueville's vision of democratic despotism, those politicians and bureaucrats mostly wear velvet gloves.

The collectivist or progressivist vision of society inverts liberalism's sense of foreground and background. The progressivist version of collec-tivism recurs to feudal times with its status-grounded relationships. With velvet-gloved progressivism there are two categories of objects of action, some of which are open to everyone and some of which are open only to a few. Those objects open only to a few are the province of the contemporary equivalents of lords of the manor, mostly politicians and bureaucratic experts who construe themselves as protecting individuals who lack the cognitive ability to care for themselves (Koppl 2018). In this respect, the growth of behavioral economics, with its research program of illustrating how individual actions fall short of theoretical standards of rational action, is a natural emergence out of the progressivist vision. Indeed, it would surely be reasonable to regard the research program of behavioral economics as the theoretical arm of the progressive movement.

To be sure, liberalism and progressivism do not exhaust the range of possibilities regarding how people can live together in close geographical proximity. Other possibilities abound, but these entail use of mailed fists in place of velvet gloves, creating a divorce from any ideology of democratic self-governance. In contrast, liberalism is expressly a theory of self-governing people. Indeed, James Buchanan's massive body of scholarship started with Buchanan (1949) where he set forth contours of a democratic theory of public finance where it could be plausibly claimed that political outcomes reflect genuine self-governance, as distinct from tautological statements that identify democracy *ipso facto* as a system of self-governance. As Wagner (2017) explains, Buchanan's entire body of work can be derived from his initial interest in exploring the organizational requisites for genuinely self-governing republics.

Whether people truly want to be self-governing is a different matter. Self-governance imposes obligations on people, as Vincent Ostrom (1997) explores with great care. Living well requires attention and effort, and it's imaginable that a good number of people might prefer not to bear that cost, at least so long as the alternative entails bureaucrats wearing velvet gloves, though it might be different if they wore mailed fists. In this respect, Buchanan (2005) advanced the possibility that many people might be afraid to live as free persons. Living as a free person is costly, and in several ways. There is the cost of acquiring information and making choices. Hillary Clinton (1996) claimed that it takes a village to raise a child. In this, she was surely right. A mother and father don't have all the tools they need to raise a child. They will have to call on other people in the village to help them out. But doing this will be costly both in time and in money. Clinton's answer was to turn over the raising of children to a Health and Human Services bureaucracy. Doing this wouldn't save any time, once you consider the queuing that would inhabit this arrangement when prices don't ration supply. And it surely wouldn't be any cheaper once you consider the taxes that would be extracted, many of them hidden from sight. Still, there seems to be a widespread though far from universal sentiment that such activities as raising children, seeking medical care, and buying suitably nutritious food are better produced by some rule of experts (Koppl 2018).

IDENTIFYING DESPOTISM: OBJECTIVIST AND SUBJECTIVIST ORIENTATIONS

In conventional and popular discourse, despotism is defined or identified by objective conditions as illustrated by the distinction between mailed fists and velvet gloves. If political officials are able to act arbitrarily, the associated regime is considered despotic. But if those officials are constrained to adhere to the principles of a rule of law, despotism is vanquished. Within this objectivist orientation toward the presence or absence of despotic governance, some set of external standards or conditions can tell whether despotism is present or absent. This objectivist standard, however, requires an observer to render judgments, which introduces subjectivity into the identification.

Consider Rajagopalan and Wagner's (2013) examination of the rule of law. As a formal and abstract matter, the opposite of rule of law is rule of men. Rule of law seems to abolish arbitrary action from all political precincts by virtue of the term standing in opposition to rule of men. Rule of law thinking is often illustrated by a set of people agreeing in advance to play some game by some agreed-upon set of rules, and subsequently to monitor play and enforce the rules through consensus among the players. This not only is a pleasant image but also it conforms to the experiences nearly everyone has in such common activities as people meeting to play poker or bridge or to play basketball at a nearby court.

To go from a few people playing poker or basketball to the modern world of organized political activity is to travel a long and winding road, as Robert Michels (1912) recognized in his treatment of democratic oligarchy. Most significantly, the object denoted as "law" can never rule because it is inanimate and incapable of making or enforcing rules. Only people can make and enforce rules. Rule of law is an abstract concept and perhaps mostly a statement of aspiration. The only reality possible, at least given the present state of knowledge, is rule of men. Whether the reality of rule of men conforms to some idealized standard of rule of law is a topic to be explored and not something to be asserted through a judicious selection of assumptions.

Consider the organization of commercial corporations. Within economic theory, corporations are governed by a form of rule of law, not because law truly rules but because the institutional arrangements regarding corporate governance mostly operate to render this claim plausible. Corporate executives who fail to maximize corporate value are susceptible to expulsion through the efforts of other people seeking to secure capital gains through running the failing corporation more efficiently. While nominal corporate governance is controlled by corporate executives, those executives who fail to act in accordance with principles of wealth maximization are candidates for replacement through competition among executives for position. Corporations nominally are governed by executives, but the actions of executives are induced to conform to wealth maximization by virtue of the institutional arrangements of private property and freedom of contract, though public ordering also operates to restrict the operation of such corporate takeovers.

Political entities have corporate form just as do commercial enterprises. Can we extrapolate from commercial entities to political entities and conclude that political and bureaucratic executives likewise must conform to rule of law properties? This extrapolation is surely dubious. First of all, a significant number of commercial corporations no longer operate inside the precincts of a truly free economy. The very presence of political regulation of commercial activity often impedes rule of law principles. Consider a financial firm that faces a simple rate-of-return regulation where the allowed return is less than what the firm potentially could earn. Should that firm maximize its operating profit, any profit in excess of what the regulation allows will be confiscated, either by the regulating agency or by the treasury. In this situation, any expenditure by the corporation that reduces profit will impose no loss on corporate shareholders. Corporate executives will manage their firms differently in the face of a regulatory limit on their net incomes. They will likewise manage their firms differently when they face regulatory requirements regarding distribution of their lending portfolios by such status-based features as age, race, gender, and income. No longer can it be reasonably claimed that corporations are governed by rule of law principles.

Even more, some corporate enterprises in their fiduciary duties to maximize the value of the enterprise might be well advised to incorporate political enterprises into their enterprise plans. There is probably no human activity that can be totally specified in advance by rules. If this is the case, opportunities will always exist to act with some degree of discretion. Some firms might seek to increase their net worth not by producing products in higher demand but by convincing regulatory agencies to impose rules that work to the relative detriment of competitors. In short, for many purposes it is useful to distinguish between political enterprises and market enterprises, and yet we should always remember that societies are governed by a single institutional order, though one that is exceedingly complex and which undoubtedly contains incongruencies among its numerous elements, as Ludwig Lachmann (1970) explored in his examination of the legacy of Max Weber's thinking on social organization.

At this point we return to the problem of scale in democratic political economy. In particular, are democratic networks scalable or are they scale-free? In the former case, expansion of a network from one thousand participants to one million participants would reflect a multiplication of the same pattern of attachment. The formation of connections within that graph would be random. The opposite of random attachment is preferential attachment. In this case, new nodes find some existing nodes especially attractive. In this instance, a graph of a network with a million nodes will not resemble a graph with a thousand nodes. To the contrary, some of the nodes become especially attractive and the graph comes to resemble a monocentric network, blurring the dichotomy between polycentricity and monocentricity.

For the last century or so, western democracies have been morphing from largely polycentric systems governed largely by principles of private property and freedom of contract into hybrid forms of polycentricity where polycentric principles are amended through the insertion of monocentric islands into the society. Hence, the generality norms associated with rule of law principles are never rejected. All the same, the operation of those principles is constricted by insertion of those monocentric islands where status-based orders of precedence are inserted by politically supported power into society.

SCIENCE, ART, AND POLITICAL ECONOMY

This book treats economics as social theory approached through interactions among economizing individuals. In contrast, when economics is pursued as a science of rational action, other people are effectively eliminated from any individual's field of vision because an equilibrated society is reducible to a representative agent. A representative agent is necessarily solipsistic because there is no one with whom the agent can interact. Once economics is treated as social theory, it is easy to recognize that people care about the environments in which they live, which means in turn that people effectively have preferences toward other people and their actions. Personal actions are no longer limited to choosing one's strategies for acting with respect to the individual as an organism but extend to seeking to shape the societal environment.

Political economy can be approached as science and as art, and there is tension between the two (Wagner 2018). Political economy as science holds that there is a rhyme and reason to the patterns that emerge through our interactions with one another. To be reasonable objects of explanation, these patterns must belong to the realm of necessity because explained objects cannot have volition. Economics as a theory of society recognizes that societies have law-like properties, while also recognizing that the members of society have some ability to influence their environments. There is a tension between recognizing that societies are subject to law and recognizing that people in various ways can shape their futures. Inside this tension resides the lure of the "intuitively obvious." There may be nothing more intuitively obvious than the assertion that the sun rises in the east and sets in the west.

Being intuitively obvious does not guarantee the aptness of a scientific explanation. A deeper and more challenging problem resides in stepping away from the intuitively obvious and the superficially apparent and entering the realm of spontaneous ordering and emergent phenomena. Any such policy action as a rent control or a minimum wage will enter the society at some of the nodes within a society's network of transactions. Participants in those transactions will seek to rearrange their transactions in response to the policy actions. For minimum wages, employers will hire fewer people. For rent control, owners will lease fewer units. But these changes at the point of transaction are just the proverbial tip of the iceberg. Adjustments at one point in the societal catallaxy will reverberate throughout the society, depending on the pattern of connection among nodes within the society. How those changes reverberate depends on the opportunities people see and seize as well as on their imaginations. Either way, policy actions cannot be apprehended simply by looking at the transactional node where they were inserted. For instance, rent control increases competition among potential recipients of subsidized rents due to a reduction in the supply of units. Some of those people will be lower-cost tenants than others and so will be favored by rent control over the other potential tenants. Alternatively, minimum wages might well increase wages for some, but others will go without obtaining jobs. And what will they do to secure the means to support themselves which they had hoped to secure by working? People left unemployed might turn to panhandling or to fencing stolen merchandise. They might turn to petty theft. They might escape the regulation by turning to self-employment. There is no way to know in detail, though we can know that disturbance at the policy-affected node will reverberate elsewhere within the societal network.

In his insightful treatment of *The Viennese Students of Civilization*, Erwin Dekker (2016) explained that the prominent Austrian economists between 1870 and 1930 were economic theorists only secondarily, for primarily they were students of civilization. This position as students of civilization gave a different tenor to their economic theories than was common at the time. For one thing, art and science commingled. Those theorists recognized that forces were at work in shaping civilization, along with recognizing that those forces had law-like character. Those forces, however, did not operate independently of the people who were subject to those forces. To the contrary, those forces were complex products of interaction among the people subject to those forces. People participated in the generation of civilization even as they were governed and shaped by it. Economic theory had both explanatory and normative aspects, and the two types of concern were commingled in their thinking.

Civilization is an encompassing object. It is not constructed. It cannot be engineered. It can, however, be influenced and modified along various dimensions, but this is all. It is civilization that gives tone and meaning to life and which shapes personal character and values. Sure, humans are biological organisms whose nature compels various forms of action to enable survival. But as civilization grows out of rudimentary states of existence, people come to sense new opportunities and acquire new wants and desires. What economists recognize as preferences are not autonomous beyond the level of basic survival, but rather these are artifacts we generate through our interactions inside the civilization in which we are encased (Emmett 2006). Human action is only incompletely determined, as people also have scope for volition to shape and choose their actions inside their civilization's environment.

Polycentricity: Distinguishing Form from Substance

Michael Polanyi (1958) is the theorist most fully associated with asserting the knowledge-generating features of polycentric arrangements of inter-actions within societies. Vincent Ostrom has occupied the foreground among contemporary theorists in elaborating the significance of poly-centricity for self-governing forms of democracy. Ostrom (1971 [2007]) explains that the American republic was established as a compound and not a simple republic, which means that governmental power was orga-nized in polycentric fashion. Ostrom (1974) set forth American public administration within a polycentric setting. Ostrom (1997) meditated on the significance of Alexis de Tocqueville for political economy, explaining that the avoidance of democratic tyranny requires not only a polycentric arrangement of the offices of government but also complementary moral imaginations among the citizenry.

It should be noted, however, that many forms of polycentricity are possible. Polycentricity means only that there is no single node to which all other nodes are subservient. A system can be polycentric and yet have one or a few nodes that exercise predominant influence within a system. In this respect, Paul Craig Roberts (1971) explains that the Soviet Union was a peculiar form of polycentric governance. To say a polity has poly-centric character is only to say only that it is not at the beck-and-call of some master puppeteer. Polycentric orders can feature widely dispersed zones of autonomous action, as illustrated by the theory of free mar-kets. They can also feature strongly concentrated zones of autonomy as in Soviet-style economies where Party officials are sheltered from compe-tition from most of the society, so are able to reserve the best cars and houses for themselves while the rest of the society is pretty much free to compete for the remaining scraps.

The debate between liberalism and collectivism is really a debate over the character of a polycentric order. There can be a liberal style of poly-centricity and a progressivist or collectivist style, though there are some grounds for thinking that the progressivist style is a waystation on the road to what Tocqueville described as democratic despotism. Within the liberal style, social organization forms and changes largely through private action. While political organization will be present, those political orga-nizations will be small in size and limited in scope. Public law will take its bearings from private law. This relationship between private and public law is illustrated nicely by Richard Epstein's (1985) analysis of the taking clause of the 5th Amendment of the American Constitution. The Constitution allows government to take private property, but it imposes two major obstacles to such taking. First, that taking must be for a genuine public use, meaning that it must be of general benefit within the society as distinct from being of benefit to a small number of people. Second, that taking must be accompanied by just compensation, which means something like the market value of the taken property. This, anyway, is what the language says, though we should also recognize that language cannot interpret itself, for only people can do that.

Any parcel of private property that a government could acquire through taking could also be acquired through the government's buying it. It is obviously cheaper to take something than to buy it. To require government to buy and to preclude taking could possibly preclude some generally beneficial takings from occurring, though it would also preclude some redistributive takings from occurring. Taking is not a feature of private law. It belongs to public law. What the 5th Amendment was probably thought to accomplish was to render public law subservient to private law. Yet law can't enforce itself, and attitudes can change markedly as Charles Warren (1932) illustrates. Fifth Amendment jurisprudence is controversial, both because it inescapably touches upon ambiguities as to what is a genuine public use and because the United States has increasingly slid from a liberal regime where public law mirrors private law to a progressivist regime where public law is autonomous and with private law conforming in significant respects to public law.

FROM GENERAL WILL TO STRUCTURES OF POWER: DEMYTHOLOGIZING DEMOCRACY

In referring to the "general will" of a people, the French philosopher Jean Jacques Rousseau (1762 [1978]) initiated a pattern of thought whereby democracy was transformed in the mind from a method for deciding about undertaking action on behalf of groups to a product of sorcery and magical thinking denoted as the general will. To speak of democracy as reflecting some general will is clearly an archaic and magical pattern of expression. The concept gives no guidance as to how actual democratic processes relate to the general will. Is it that any and all democratic processes will find the general will, rendering the construction tautological? Or is it that some processes will do better at finding this general will than other processes? If so, which processes. And how can one tell? In other words, notions of democracy as reflecting a general will are reminiscent of pre-scientific modes of thought when what soothed the mind was accepted as gospel because of its soothing quality independently of any analytical coherence. To be sure, one can and must recognize that what we sense as reality is beyond our capacity to know in full, which means that myth will always be part of the stories we tell ourselves as we pursue our paths in life. Nonetheless, the faculty of reason will be helpful in distinguishing between such plausible myths as the idea of competitive equilibrium and such fantasies as there being a general will.

This book treats democracy as a method for selecting the people who will staff political offices and for arranging patterns of relationship among political offices. Elections provide the method for staffing political offices while eligibility to vote is pre-democratic. At one time in the United States, the electorate was limited to white males who owned property. These days, there are few limits, and some people support further extensions of the franchise by opening it to felons and non-citizens. In any event, democracy pertains to the use of elections to staff political offices. A second and surely more significant facet of democracy concerns the organizational arrangement among political offices. It is here where the distinction between monocentricity and polycentricity comes into play as well as recognition that an indefinitely large number of polycentric arrangements of offices are possible. Any such arrangement will entail a networked pattern of connections among offices. The simplest possible arrangement is hierarchical, with a head of state at the apex, and with the head of state being the only elected official who in turn appoints all other office holders.

American constitutional arrangements are polycentric, starting with its federal system where a federal political apparatus has independent constitutional standing from the individual states with their independent offices. To be sure, the degree of independence between federal and state offices is unclear and subject to contestation. Within the initial Constitution, the Supremacy Clause gave priority to the federal government in any dispute with states. At the same time, however, the federal Senate was appointed by state legislatures, creating a form of council of states within the federal legislature. This council-like character was abolished by Constitutional amendment in 1913. Furthermore, the federal government acquired the power to tax personal incomes in 1913, which led to the use of federal grants to states as a means of creating conformity of state actions with federal legislation, converting a system of competitive federalism into one of cartel federalism, which Michael Greve (2012) describes as an upside-down constitution.

In any case, any democratic arrangement of offices will have a network character of nodes staffed by elected officials and patterns of connection among those offices. For instance, a city might be governed by a five-member council, with the members elected by district. This arrangement would illustrate one specific instance of the democratic form. The city might have a mayor, with that position rotating regularly among the council members. Alternatively, the mayor might be a separate office and filled through an at-large election. This situation would constitute an alternative system of democratic organization. Yet a different pattern of organization would form if city officials could seek reelection than if they could not.

True to the principles of combinatorial arithmetic, the number of possible democratic arrangements of offices and relationships among offices is indefinitely large. Those arrangements, moreover, pertain to the micro level of action, recurring again to Fig. 1.3. With respect to the macro level of democratic outcomes, these are emergent products of interaction at the action level. In this regard, there is a literature that compares political outcomes across presidential and parliamentary forms of democracy, illustrated and summarized by Persson and Tabellini (2000). These comparisons are terribly generic because they make no effort to explain how outcomes emerge from structured patterns of relationship and interaction. With respect to Fig. 1.3, the empirics pertain to the upper part, and the lower part doesn't exist other than a division between presidential and parliamentary forms. This literature conforms to orthodox macro theory, with the different democratic forms associated with differences in rates of economic growth and inflation, without making any effort to explain how these observations might come about. If the information provided by analyses of this type is of any use, it is useful to hypothesized societal planners who are imagined to be able to choose which form of democracy to obtain to promote one outcome over the other.

Specialized Knowledge and the Social Organization of Expertise

To speak of societal planners is, of course, to take resort to some non-democratic process to generate democratic outcomes. This is how it is with the progressivist vision of democracy where the levers of governance reside with a set of experts who act as contemporary lords of the manor. Nearly all human endeavor is led by experts, as a simple corollary of the division of knowledge in society whereby each of us knows a lot about a small share of the activities that matter to us while knowing nearly nothing about most of them. Market economies are riven by expertise, and it couldn't be any other way. What is of central significance is the process by which experts are selected and certified. This can be accomplished through market or through political processes. A few such exceptions as Roger Koppl (2018) aside, it seems to be generally presumed that markets often generate inferior options for choice, and that political oversight can improve the situation.

It is intuitively obvious that consumers often cannot discern significant qualitative attributes of the products they buy. Will a hair dryer electrocute a user who uses it while contacting water? There is no way to tell by simple inspection, which in some eyes might warrant the setting of standards by a governmental agency. Setting a standard fits the image of a political agency providing consumer protection. But is this image accurate? Is it accurate with respect to consumers being unable to secure protection through private ordering? Is it accurate with respect to public ordering's ability to offer superior protection? For both questions, a reasonable answer is no, both because private ordering can produce such protection and public ordering is unlikely to do so.

It is fully consistent with the principles of private ordering for a set of producers, whether of hair dryers or any other product, to form a cooperative association to certify standards for the products offered. Such certification would speak to potential consumer concerns that otherwise would impede sales. If those concerns included the possibility that a dryer might cause electrocution upon incidental contact with water, the certification process would include examination for such a possibility. To be sure, there could be producers that did not participate in the cooperative, and thereby were able to offer cheaper products. There is no way that private ordering could eliminate the production of such products. Private ordering cannot offer some utopian scheme of a harmless world. Doing this is beyond human capacity. But the concern of vendors with the net worth of their businesses will create strong tendencies for vendors to manage their businesses to avoid dissipating their net worth.

It is different with public ordering where political agencies have no capital value they can lose. A political agency that has the power to impose standards will certainly do so. But by what logic is that agency likely to operate in the absence of market guidance? That logic will entail two aspects that conforms to Bruce Yandle's (1983) analysis of interaction between Baptists and bootleggers. With respect to Baptists, the political agency will cultivate an image of an agency dedicated to protecting consumers and erring on the side of caution in what the agency portrays as an inherently dangerous world. With respect to bootleggers, the agency will act on behalf of the major producers who can amass more political influence than the other producers. What will result are cost-increasing regulations that drive cheaper products out of the market even if they are safe, in the process forcing consumers to pay higher prices than they would have paid under private ordering.

HANDSHAKES AND GUNS
IN SECURING HUMAN FLOURISHING

Of what is organized humanity capable? The historical record would seem to show that we are capable of nearly anything ranging from the sublimely beautiful to incredibly atrocious nastiness and brutality toward one another. In opening *Federalist #1*, Alexander Hamilton asked whether the qualities of the governments we experience are things we can control or at least influence, or whether we are fated to live with whatever the muses of history throw our way. Vincent Ostrom repeatedly cited this passage from Hamilton as posing the challenge of bringing intelligence to the challenge of living well together. Frank Knight's (1960) *Intelligence and Democratic Action* raised a similar conundrum, though perhaps voicing even less optimism, or perhaps recognizing more difficulty, than did Ostrom.

It is a very simple act of ordinary intelligence to understand the principle of comparative advantage and its fundamental lesson that through specialization and trade we can all attain higher material standards of living than we could ever attain living in isolation. In this respect, the fundamental normative lesson of economic theory is that we should celebrate each other's existence because this enables us to secure higher standards of living, and with the theory of comparative advantage being the theoretical insight that warrants this normative claim. It is easy, even perhaps natural, for economists to focus on gains from trade and to rail against actions that appear to retard the exploitation of gains from trade. We should not forget, however, that actors don't circumscribe possible gains from trade because they possess some masochistic gene. To the contrary, a failure to pursue fully some gains from trade must reside in recognition that people can also pursue values that require them to refrain from full pursuit of possible gains from trade.

We don't live by bread alone, even if we might use bread as an image to stand for all the material goods in the world. If anything, we can have a surfeit of goods. But what else besides bread is there? Here, the answers are myriad and perplexing. A place in the sun. A sense of accomplishment. Respect from others. Self-respect. Almost endless are the descriptions that poets, philosophers, and others have given as to the non-bread objects after which people strive. Many of these objects, moreover, have a zero-sum character in that more of it for one person is less for someone else.

Throughout his *oeuvre*, Frank Knight deemphasized the material component of life per se, stressing instead the game-like component. Free societies promote advances in material standards of living, but this promotion is to a large extent a by-product of the playfulness that is unleashed within an enterprise economy where people are free to deploy their imaginations in inventing new technologies, products, and forms of business organization. The energetic and inquisitive few are in the forefront of improving our material standards of living because they can't help themselves because liberalism unleashes the spirit of human playfulness along the lines that Johan Huizinga (1938) explores.

This quality of liberalism does not, however, work universally to the good. Playfulness maps into treating life as a game, following Bernard Suits's (1967) examination of life's being a game. Games require the overcoming of challenges. Those challenges can be against nature, but most commonly people compete against themselves and also against other people. Even competition that often appears to be against nature is often against other people. For instance, someone can pose a challenge of scaling free solo a thousand-foot granite cliff. This appears to be a game against nature. It can also be a game against oneself. A second person might try to do the same thing, and the game can become one against another player in seeing who can do it more quickly. Once we are in this social setting, the game creates winners and losers. So long as games occur inside an ethics of sportsmanship, winners and losers can enjoy the competition and enjoy one another's company after the play has ended. But from where comes an ethic of sportsmanship? What sustains it? Once again, we recur to the perplexities of moral imaginations, their generation and their erosion.

It is customary within the political economy of liberalism to think of government as maintaining the rules of just conduct. As it stands, this is just exhortation. We must ask to whom this exhortation is addressed. There is no effective option to its being addressed to some political entity. Is it reasonable to think that a political entity would maintain just rules of open competition when the alternative is to skew the rules? A political entity won't maintain such rules unless there is no other action that the entity's officers would prefer to pursue.

The theory of free markets envisions societies as operating through the handshakes of trade. There is a coherent economic theory that explains how orderly economic processes can operate within an institutionally governed process based on property and contract. But how can those rules be maintained without resorting to magical thinking? There seems to be a significant difference in the degree of reflexivity as between individuals and the collections of individuals we denote as societies. Individuals certainly have reflexive capacity. They can act as the theory of choice illustrates, but they can also stand apart from those choices and impose limits or constraints on their choices. It is as if the reflexive side of human nature enables us to impose constraints on our choices and actions. A Robinson Crusoe can choose his actions during the day, but he also has the ability to appraise the properties of different patterns of action and impose constraints on his actions to secure more desirable future states. Societies, however, are not sentient creatures. Reflexivity is not a societal property, as against being an amalgamation of similar sentiments across people. Should the reflexivity of most people point in the same direction, something like reflexivity might characterize a society. Short of that, however, all that exists are different people seeking exchanges to promote their advantage. Whether the rules of just conduct are maintained or whether they erode in some fashion depends on the vagaries of political competition.

FRIENDS, ENEMIES, AND CARL SCHMITT'S AUTONOMY OF THE POLITICAL

This book has approached macroeconomics from the perspective of a theory of systems with creative agents. Such systems are modeled as networks of interacting agents, and with those interactions entailing both cooperation and conflict. Traditionally, economics has emphasized cooperation and the exploitation of gains from trade. Yet, conflict is never far away, as Jack Hirshleifer (2001) explains. Indeed, cooperation occurs within the shadow of conflict. Competition can occur peacefully and be guided by an ethic of sportsmanship, but it can also turn violent. Both possibilities reside within human nature, and so are always latent within any historical moment.

Consider the economic theory of a common property resource, as sketched by Scott Gordon (1954). The basic model is familiar. A fishing ground is held in common, meaning no one can exclude anyone else from fishing there. People who fish there choose between fishing there and doing something else. They will choose to fish so long as they can earn more by fishing than the alternative activity offers them. Equilibrium in the number of people fishing the common ground will result when the amount people earn per unit of effort equals what they can earn in the alternative activity. Each person receives the average product from fishing. As the number of people fishing increases, part of the yield they capture comes about through reductions in the yield others receive. The marginal product of an additional person might well be negative, and the common property will be over-exploited relative to what it would have been under private ownership.

This standard and familiar theory of a common property resource is presented under the equilibrium framework of comparative statics, which is an analytical position from outside the situation. The theorist stands outside the environment of action and explains that the openness of the commons attracts an excessive number of people because the marginal yield of additional fishing effort is less than the average yield—and it is the average yield that people receive under common ownership. In their examination of the work of Elinor and Vincent Ostrom, Aligica and Boettke (2009) report that the Ostroms sought to theorize from a position inside the object about which they were theorizing.

Suppose you were to theorize about common property from inside the object. As people started to fish the commons, everyone would earn more than they could earn in alternative employments. They would earn rents, only those rents would not be capitalized into ownership values. Instead, those rents would be eroded as more people started to fish the commons. The comparative statics of the equilibrium analysis has expansion in the people fishing the commons continuing until the average return to fishing the commons equals the marginal product earned in the alternative employment. We may doubt, however, that this peaceful resolution would come about when the alternative is an oceanic equivalent of a range war over closing the oceanic range. How might property rights get established over a commons, or an open range for that matter?

Property rights are often described as equivalent to lines in sand, or as boundaries between mine and thine. But boundaries weren't there prior to people and their activities. Rather boundaries arise in conjunction with human activity. It's possible to imagine boundaries being established peacefully, but they can also be established through conflict and its settlement. Why is a boundary located in one position rather than in another position? It's always possible to describe this selection of position as a product of agreement perhaps augmented by a sense of fairness or justice, though there is surely no good reason to think this is the way of the world. More likely is selection as settlement of a dispute, where each party wanted more but couldn't get more because of the intensity of opposition. Hence, property rights acquire their configurations because this is the best the parties to the conflict can attain. Whether those boundaries are maintained through time depends on the strengths and desires of the parties as time elapses and conditions change.

Carl Schmitt (1932 [1996]) theorized that political action had autonomy within society. This autonomy turned on the inability for any complete specification to limit executive authority, and also rotated on the friend–enemy distinction. Just now, 49 of the 50 American states have constitutional requirements to operate with balanced budgets. Yet few of them operate this way. There are many ways an energetic politician can operate with budget deficits while affirming allegiance to the balanced budget principle. One could always cite exogenous shocks that created conditions calling for extraordinary action. Alternatively, one might distinguish between current and capital budgeting, and declare that balance pertains only to the current budget. Suppose at some later time, balance in the current budget prevents a governor from approving wage increases for teachers whose support he covets in a forthcoming election. That increase could be granted all the same and packaged as a teacher refurbishment program, thereby allowing the program to be incorporated into a capital budget and thereby subject to deficit financing.

In other words, a politician in executive authority who wants to do something badly enough will typically be able to do so and will be able to bend some constitutional authority to enable that outcome. Schmitt's position within liberalism is controversial. In this respect, Wagner (2018) distinguishes between muscular and sentimental liberalism and with Schmitt illustrating the muscular branch. The difference between muscular and sentimental liberalism turns on the place of authority in

maintaining liberal practices. A great deal of liberal thought seeks to eliminate the political from society through some combination of law, ethics,
and economics. Schmitt held that any such effort will be incomplete, and
in this point of incompleteness resides the autonomy of the political.

Schmitt, along with Walter Eucken (1952) asserted that the disintegration of the Weimar Republic was due to the weakness of the state. In
their estimations, the Weimar regime was too weak to resist predation by
interest groups. Indeed, both Schmitt and Eucken claimed that a "strong
state" was necessary to support and maintain a free economy. This notion
of a strong state reflected muscular liberalism, as if anyone knows how
to bring this about independently of the desires of significant numbers of
people to act in this manner. To maintain liberalism against predation in
the face of interest groups requires an ability and willingness to say no
to pleadings that tug upon human sympathies, when succumbing to such
sympathies increases the likelihood that similar episodes will transpire in
the future. Humanitarian sentiments are latent within liberalism; however, giving vent to those sentiments can undermine liberal governance.
It takes some muscularity to resist the call of humanitarianism.

With respect to friends and enemies, Schmitt thought of this distinction mostly in terms of international politics. His view of international
politics was one of regimes trying to expand their domains until they
encountered resistance from other regimes. We can think of Earth as har-
boring many societies of varying sizes and degrees of vigor. If each society
is conceptualized as a network, there will be competition among networks
for space and influence. For Schmitt, the friend–enemy distinction was
largely articulated inside this international arena.

The friend–enemy distinction is also in play inside domestic arenas once
you move away from presumptions of value homogeneity within a society.
At the time of the American Constitutional founding, for instance, many
Americans would rather have remained British, but that wasn't an option
though some did move to Canada. Of the remainder, many of them did
not want to form the national government the Constitution established,
preferring instead to remain within the Articles of Confederation. The
franchise, moreover, was limited to white males who owned property, and
with blacks excluded from everything except for counting as three-fifths
of a person in counting the population at census time.

In other words, friends and enemies characterize domestic politics as
well as international politics, even though we don't typically articulate
these matters in this manner. In two papers, Vincent Ostrom (1984,

1996) described government as entailing a Faustian bargain where political power was deployed to accomplish good ends, recognizing full well that evil ends would be pursued as well. As for evil ends, few things were regarded as so evil as the equalization of property, as Madison explained in Federalist 10. By contrast, these days equalization of property is a central tenet of welfare economics. If one compares the essays of the Federalist in support of the Constitution and the essays of the anti-federalist writers in opposition, one is left with the unmistakable sense that the authors did not disagree so much about the political theory of the matter as they disagreed about the empirical consequences that would attend to the different choices.

In his analysis, Schmitt mostly treated societies as homogeneous, though it was also clear that he knew better as a substantive matter. His focus, however, was on international competition. In this setting, he thought that nations always had to be prepared to fight for their space. A nation where its people became unwilling to fight for their place was a nation on its way to being submerged within another, more aggressive nation. Schmitt's orientation is equally applicable to domestic politics. In this respect, Carolyn Webber and Aaron Wildavsky (1986), in their history of budgeting in the western world, treat budgeting fundamentally as a struggle among people within a nation over how they are to conduct their lives within close geographical proximity to one another. More broadly, Jorge Martinez-Vazquez and Stanley Winer (2014) offer a collection of essays that explore some parameters of coercion and public finance, Sure, budgetary controversies often pertain to such mundane matters as how much to appropriate for a department of parks and recreation versus how much to appropriate for police cars. Beyond these mundane topics, however, budgeting also entails controversies among people over the qualitative aspects of their living together. Behind a controversy over spending on police cars might lie controversy over whether police should be quicker to arrest people or whether they should exercise caution in doing that, opting instead in many cases to look for some therapeutic resolution within the offices of civil society. Behind a controversy over parks and recreation might reside controversy over whether political officers should assume primary responsibility for the care of children after school and on weekends or whether parents should assume such responsibility.

To the extent political controversy revolves around such matters that reflect deep-level heterogeneity among the inhabitants of some territory, the resolution of those conflicts will represent truces in what is really a continuing type of civil warfare, recognizing that such civil warfare is mostly of a simmering and not a boiling intensity. But it is warfare all the same because it reflects temporary resolution of some zero-sum conflict and permanent capture of mutual gains from trade. Should the constitutional framework inside of which governance occurs promote consensual action, political outcomes are likely to reflect mutual gains from trade. In contrast, should those constitutional arrangements facilitate redistributions of power and authority, political outcomes are likely to entail ongoing changes in the political balance of power within a society. Whether political outcomes are congruent with some existing constitutional arrangement or whether they represent de facto amendments to that arrangement is not an easy question to answer, and any attempted answer is likely to be contentious. Contentiousness aside, political outcomes often entail subtle constitutional changes, as Runst and Wagner (2011) explain in their treatment of the idea of a living constitution.

Consider the irony that every person elected President of the United States takes an oath of office where the President pledges to uphold the Constitution and to protect it against all enemies, both foreign and domestic. But what is the Constitution a President pledges to uphold? Compare Grover Cleveland and Woodrow Wilson some 20 years apart, or Wilson and Calvin Coolidge soon after. For someone who is rumored to have asserted that "the business of America is business," it seems clear that the Constitution that Coolidge sought to uphold resembled the original American Constitution, and the same can be said for Cleveland. In contrast, Woodrow Wilson was contemptuous of the original Constitution precisely because of the consensual qualities that were built into the structure of fragmented and divided governmental powers. In his 1885 book *Congressional Government*, Wilson set forth his vision of why the original constitutional arrangement should be replaced by a streamlined arrangement that concentrated political power in the hands of some well-intentioned governing elite. Yet Wilson took the same oath of office to protect the constitution as did Cleveland and Coolidge.

Constitutions, moreover, are not the origin of regimes because that origin resides inside some distribution of moral imaginations within a society along the lines that Gertrude Himmelfarb (1992) illuminates brilliantly. A framework of governance for a set of people who overwhelmingly believe that the establishment of a government is a Faustian bargain will construct a different pattern of government than will a set of people who equally overwhelmingly believe that active governmental engagement throughout society is necessary to withstand impending forces of chaos. While the moral sentiments conveyed by the Faustian presumption is still alive within the American population, it seems likely that the dominant moral sentiment these days holds that government is predominately a source for good. To be sure, this portrayal of the intensity of Faustian beliefs reduces politically relevant beliefs to a spectrum, where those beliefs almost surely would more appropriately be portrayed as residing on some form of manifold. In any case, the central point of this discussion is to emphasize that the impact of any set of constitutional arrangements will depend on the moral sentiments and intuitions alive within the population. This recognition suggests the value of inquiring into the origins and sources of moral sentiments, examination of which would take this book too far afield, but about which Budziszewski (2003) offers acute observation.

REGARDING THE SOCIAL PHILOSOPHY TOWARD WHICH THIS BOOK POINTS

One invariant though purely formal principle of economic theory is that people act to replace situations they value less highly with those they value more highly. This principle says nothing about the objects toward which people act. Our status as biological organisms provide insight into some of those objects, but it is in our status as creatures who recognize our need for one another while also experiencing antagonism that is the source of the truly social part of social science. As social creatures we desire companionship and recognition. Status and standing are among the human wants, which can lead to envy as well as approbation. Where some people admire commercial success, others envy it.

The Keynesian episode in economic theory represents an elaboration of the progressivist vision of a new form of feudalism within a democratic formalism where experts govern amateurs. Between microeconomic theories of externalities and market failures and macroeconomic theories of aggregate demand failures, the ancient mainline of economic theory centered on a constitution of liberty morphed into a mainstream centered on a constitution of control (Lerner 1944; Boettke 2012) where economists provided technical advice on managing the affairs of an exceedingly busy lord of the manor. This progressivist vision reflects mythical and magical thinking and, moreover, misconstrues the operating features of a market economy by attributing properties to private ordering that are really

consequences of public ordering. Progressivism plays on fear and portrays sources of fear coming from all directions within a privately ordered
world. If one accepts the progressivist portraits at face value, the flourishing of the eighteenth and nineteenth centuries could never have happened.

By exposing the incoherent presumptions of the economic theory and
political economy of the progressivist vision wherein most people are
regarded as incapable of living well without political guidance, this book
explains that the only plausible object of domestic fear is political ordering
of human activity. In this respect, it should be noted that the social world
of myriad civic associations is distinct from the political world; where the
social world operates through dyadic transactions, the political world features triadic transactions. In this respect, those who are animated by envy
must have objects of their envy. At one point in Handel's *Messiah*, the
Chorus sings: "Lift up thy voices with strength. Be not afraid." Private
ordering is nothing to be fearful of. To be sure, private ordering requires
participation, and participation requires cooperation with others. Someone might like to carouse into the wee hours but have employment that
requires being at work by eight in the morning. The carouser must change
that pattern of conduct to succeed inside the precincts of private ordering.

Public law establishes the category of victimhood, which is not recognizable within private law. Someone whose desires and talents leads to
a choice between a desire to carouse and a need to go to work to support that carousing can be transformed into a victim through ideological construction followed by collective action. This transformation creates
political space for programs of "social justice." Those programs in turn
embrace the ideological claim that market transactions within the existing social system convert people into vassals through the illusion of free
transactions. This ideology provides societal space for political programs
to be enshrouded within the ideology of social justice, disguising recognition that public ordering invariably provides gains to some people while
imposing disabilities on others. In contrast to progressivism and its economics of control, liberalism and its economics of liberty frees people to
deploy their talents as they choose in generating tomorrow's flourishing
societies, though we should always recognize that living inside a civilization imposes some strain in adapting to the expectations and beliefs that
characterize effective participation within that civilization (Dekker 2016).

At this point we butt up once again against matters of human nature
and human capabilities. Are all humans equally capable of living freely and

being responsible for themselves through generating supporting institutional arrangements along the lines that David Beito (2000) examines in showing how people generated various forms of mutual aid prior to the incursion of political action into those activities. In her insightful treatment of entanglement and inequality, Mikayla Novak (2018) recognizes that inequality can pose concerns for liberal and not just progressivist orientations. Those concerns connect with recognition that the talents and capacities people have as adults emerge through the particular civilizing process through which they grew from infants to adults. A sentimental version of liberalism might hold that people should be responsible for the human capital they acquire. A muscular version (Novak 2018; Wagner 2020) would recognize that the types and qualities of human capital that people acquire will unavoidably influence the qualities of life people experience within relevant geographical areas.

Human nature encompasses an interest in one another that leads understandably to the generation of institutional arrangements and practices that give full recognition that no person need be alone in society without impairing the ability of people individually to form their aspirations and pursue their dreams. The progressivist vision of individual aloneness or solidarity within the precincts of state is utterly wrong. All the same, economic theory since late in the nineteenth century has mostly pursued the image of isolated and rational individuals who step into the market to supply services and buy things, and otherwise live their solipsistic existences. This is a wrong-headed construal of economics as being the study of rational individual action and not the study of civilizations and their processes and institutions. There is a strain to living freely within a civilization that cannot be escaped even while living inside a prison as David Skarbeck (2014) explains. Tocqueville's image of velvet-gloved jailers is surely a fable which Skarbeck exposes, and this exposure would surely suggest that living freely is superior to residing within a progressivist prison with its cadre of velvet-gloved jailers.

We all reside inside civilizational systems that are not of our direct making. They are artifacts that we generate as we move forward in life. Like the tools we create, they shape our environments and influence our experiences of life. Societies cannot be formed or reformed at will, and yet we can increase our understanding of the hidden order through which civilizations acquire their shapes and how those shapes influence the options for living together in the close proximity that people experience. This book has set forth some thoughts about what would be entailed in constructing a theory of the entirety of a social system of interacting agents grounded on the reasonable notion that human nature entails our recognition that we own our dreams while at the same time we both need to and desire to live in close proximity to other people who likewise have their dreams, while further recognizing that sometimes those dreams mesh but sometimes they don't, and yet the need to live in close proximity continues without end.

REFERENCES

Aligica, P.D., and P.J. Boettke. 2009. *Challenging Institutional Analysis and Development*. London: Routledge.

Beito, D. 2000. *From Mutual Aid to the Welfare State*. Chapel Hill: University of North Carolina Press.

Boettke, P.J. 2012. *Living Economics*. Oakland, CA: Independent Institute.

Buchanan, J.M. 1949. The Pure Theory of Government Finance: A Suggested Approach. *Journal of Political Economy* 57: 496–505.

Buchanan, J.M. 2005. Afraid to Be Free. *Public Choice* 124: 19–31.

Budziszewski, J. 2003. *What We Can't Not Know*. Dallas: Spence.

Clinton, H.R. 1996. *It Takes a Village*. New York: Simon & Schuster.

DeCanio, S. 2013. *Limits of Economic and Social Knowledge*. London: Palgrave Macmillan.

Dekker, E. 2016. *The Viennese Students of Civilization*. Cambridge: Cambridge University Press.

Emmett, R.N. 2006. De Gustibus est Disputandum: Frank H. Knight's Response to George Stigler and Gary Becker's 'De Gustibus non est Disputandum'. *Journal of Economic Methodology* 13: 97–111.

Epstein, R.A. 1985. *Takings: Private Property and the Power of Eminent Domain*. Cambridge, MA: Harvard University Press.

Eucken, W. 1952. *Grundsätze der Wirtschaftspolitik*. Tübingen: Mohr Siebeck.

Gordon, H.S. 1954. The Economic Theory of a Common Property Resource: The Fishery. *Journal of Political Economy* 62: 124–42.

Greve, M. 2012. *The Upside-Down Constitution*. Cambridge, MA: Harvard University Press.

Himmelfarb, G. 1992. *Poverty and Compassion: The Moral Imagination of the Late Victorians*. New York: Vintage.

Hirshleifer, J. 2001. *The Dark Side of the Force: Economic Foundations of Conflict Theory*. Cambridge: Cambridge University Press.

Hughes, J.R.T. 1977. *The Governmental Habit*. New York: Basic Books.

Huizinga, J. 1938. *Homo Ludens: A Study of the Play Element in Culture*. Boston: Beacon Press.

Knight, F.H. 1960. *Intelligence and Democratic Action*. Cambridge, MA: Harvard University Press.

Koppl, R. (2018). *Expert Failure*. Cambridge: Cambridge University Press.

Lachmann, L. 1970. *The Legacy of Max Weber*. Berkeley, CA: Glendessary Press.

Lerner, A.P. 1944. *The Economics of Control*. New York: Macmillan.

Martinez-Vazquez, J., and S.L. Winer. 2014. *Coercion and Social Welfare in Public Finance*. Cambridge: Cambridge University Press.

Michels, R. 1912 [1962]. *Political Parties: A Sociological Study of the Oligarchical Tendencies of Modern Democracy*. New York: Collier Books.

Novak, M. 2018. *Inequality: An Entangled Political Economy Perspective*. London: Palgrave Macmillan.

Ostrom, V. 1971 [2007]. *The Political Theory of a Compound Republic*. Lanham, MD: Lexington.

Ostrom, V. 1974. *The Intellectual Crisis in American Public Administration*. Tuscaloosa: University of Alabama Press.

Ostrom, V. 1984. Why Governments Fail: An Inquiry into the Use of Instruments of Evil to Do Good. In *Theory of Public Choice II*, ed. J.M. Buchanan and R.D. Tollison, 422–35. Ann Arbor: University of Michigan Press.

Ostrom, V. 1996. Faustian Bargains. *Constitutional Political Economy* 7: 303–8.

Ostrom, V. 1997. *The Meaning of Democracy and the Vulnerability of Democracies*. Ann Arbor: University of Michigan Press.

Persson, T., and G. Tabellini. 2000. *Political Economics: Explaining Economic Policy*. Cambridge, MA: MIT Press.

Polanyi, M. 1958. *Personal Knowledge*. Chicago: University of Chicago Press.

Rajagopalan, S., and R.E. Wagner. 2013. Constitutional Craftsmanship and the Rule of Law. *Constitutional Political Economy* 24: 295–309.

Roberts, P.C. 1971. *Alienability and the Soviet Economy*. Albuquerque: University of New Mexico Press.

Rousseau, J.J. 1762 [1978]. *On the Social Contract*. New York: St. Martin's Press.

Runst, P., and R.E. Wagner. 2011. Choice, Emergence, and Constitutional Process: A Framework for Positive Analysis. *Journal of Institutional Economics* 7: 131–45.

Schmitt, C. 1932 [1996]. *The Concept of the Political*. Chicago: University of Chicago Press.

Skarbeck, D. 2014. *The Social Order of the Underworld: How Prison Gangs Govern the American Penal System*. Oxford: Oxford University Press.

Suits, B. 1967. Is Life a Game We Are Playing? *Ethics* 77: 209–13.

Wagner, R.E. 2007. *Fiscal Sociology and the Theory of Public Finance*. Cheltenham, UK: Edward Elgar.

Wagner, R.E. 2016. *Politics as a Peculiar Business: Insights from a Theory of Entangled Political Economy.* Cheltenham, UK: Edward Elgar.

Wagner, R.E. 2017. *James M. Buchanan and Liberal Political Economy: A Rational Reconstruction.* Lanham, MD: Lexington Books.

Wagner, R.E. 2018. James Buchanan's Liberal Theory of Political Economy: A Valiant but Failed Effort to Square the Circle. In *Buchanan's Tensions: Reexamining the Political Economy and Social Philosophy of James M. Buchanan,* ed. P.J. Boettke and S. Stein, 9–33. Arlington, VA: Mercatus Center.

Wagner, R.E. 2020. Economic Theory and "The Social Question": Some Dialectics regarding the Work-Dependency Relationship. *Journal of Contextual Economics* 139: forthcoming.

Warren, C.O. 1932. *Congress as Santa Claus.* Charlottesville, VA: Michie.

Webber, C., and A. Wildavsky. 1986. *A History of Taxation and Public Expenditure in the Western World.* New York: Simon & Schuster.

Wilson, W. 1885. *Congressional Government: A Study in American Politics.* Boston: Houghton Mifflin.

Yandle, B. 1983. Bootleggers and Baptists: The Education of a Regulatory Economist. *Regulation* 7 (May–June): 12–16.

AUTHOR INDEX

Potts, J., 4, 14, 35, 177
Prescott, E., 49
Prigogine, I., 164
Pryor, F., 7, 16, 37, 267
Puviani, A., 231, 257, 258

R

Rajagopalan, S., 194, 226, 280
Rauschenbusch, W., 193
Rause, V., 97, 164
Read, L., 99, 117
Resnick, M., 14, 39, 182, 190, 202
Rizzo, M., 12
Robbins, L., 16
Roberts, P.C., 26, 87, 285
Robinson, J., 216
Roubini, N., 174
Rousseau, J.J., 55, 286
Rowe, N., 227
Runst, P., 242, 297

S

Samuelson, P.A., 82
Savage, L., 19, 53
Scheiner, S.M., 99
Schelling, T., 3, 141
Schmitt, C., 45, 107, 202, 266, 292, 294–296
Schmölders, G., 257, 258
Schoeck, H., 154
Schumpeter, J.A., 2, 9, 16, 31, 54, 66, 70, 72, 142, 143, 238–240, 256, 271
Seater, J., 183
Selgin, G., 233
Shackle, G.L.S., 18, 19, 27, 40, 65, 68, 119, 122, 129, 130, 142
Simmel, G., 16, 192, 227, 228, 230–232
Skarbeck, D., 300
Skyrums, B., 55

Smith, V.L., 22, 54, 208
Solow, R., 151
Steedman, I., 70
Sterpan, I., 102
Stigler, G.J., 8, 80, 164
Stiglitz, J., 29
Storr, V., 212
Stringham, E., 88
Sugden, R., 231
Suits, B., 291

T

Tabellini, G., 178, 216, 288
Thaler, R., 54
Tinbergen, J., 128, 190
Tollison, R.D., 191, 193
Trudeau, R., 4
Tullock, G., 206, 258

V

Veetil, V., 1
Vickers, D., 70
Von Neumann, J., 57
Vriend, N., 143

W

Wagner, R.E., 1, 7, 10, 12, 22, 24, 28, 45, 47, 53, 54, 58, 65, 66, 69, 77, 86, 89, 92, 102, 104, 105, 113, 115, 136, 139, 140, 143, 149–151, 158, 165, 170, 171, 177, 178, 184, 192–194, 201, 206, 207, 209–212, 226, 227, 232, 235, 239–242, 246, 256, 260, 279, 280, 283, 294, 297, 300
Walras, L., 7–9, 45, 66, 67, 80, 129, 195, 261
Warren, C., 222, 242, 243, 286
Weaver, W., 40, 189

Subject Index